THE NEW COMPLETE JOY OF HOME BREWING

Other Avon Books by
Charlie Papazian

THE HOMEBREWER'S COMPANION

THE NEW COMPLETE JOY OF HOME BREWING

CHARLIE PAPAZIAN

AVON BOOKS  NEW YORK

THE NEW COMPLETE JOY OF HOME BREWING is an original publication of Avon Books.

Quotation by e.e. cummings copyright 1983 by E.E. Cummings, renewed 1966 by Marion Morehouse Cummings. Reprinted from COMPLETE POEMS 1913–1962 by E.E. Cummings by permission of Harcourt Brace Jovanovich, Inc.

Quotation by Thomas Edison used by permission of Devin-Adair Publishers, Greenwich, Connecticut.

Quotation by Albert Schweitzer, from MY LIFE & THOUGHT. Used by permission of George Allen & Unwin, Hemel Hempstead, Herts., England HP2 4TE.

Transcript material, 1983 Conference Proceedings, American Homebrewers Association.

AVON BOOKS
A division of
The Hearst Corporation
1350 Avenue of the Americas
New York, New York 10019

Copyright © 1984, 1991 by Charles N. Papazian
Published by arrangement with the author
Library of Congress Catalog Card Number: 91-24632
ISBN: 0-380-76366-4

Library of Congress Cataloging in Publication Data:

Papazian, Charlie.
   The new complete joy of home brewing / Charles Papazian.
       p.   cm.
   Rev. ed. of: The complete joy of home brewing. c1984.
   Includes bibliographical references and index.

   1. Brewing—Amateurs' manuals.   I. Papazian, Charlie. Complete
joy of home brewing.   II. Title.
   TP570.P29   1991   91-24632
   641.2′3—dc20   CIP

First Avon Books Trade Printing, Second Edition: October 1991
First Avon Books Trade Printing: September 1984

Printed in the U.S.A.

OPM 30 29 28 27 26 25 24 23 22 21

"Whatever suits you, tickles me plum to death."
W. Jensen

"You never know 'til you check it out." C.L. Matzen

"A beer with balls!" J.A. "Espo" Esposito

"Oh, my soul's on fire." J.A. Stoner

"You never know." L. Prince

"Are you kidding me?" J. Telischak

"Charlie's here." G. Connor

"Where's Charlie?" J. Markel

"Relax. Don't worry. Have a homebrew." Anon.

"What's this?" C.A. Carlson

"Just right, but getting better." M.L. Allmon

"The best beer you've ever made." A. Avila

"P.F.G." T.G. Teague

"Zymurgy?" M.F. Monahan

The New Complete Joy of Home Brewing is dedicated to all of my students, both young and old. You have taught me much more than I have taught you. I thank you for the inspiration given to me.

I especially thank the following people whose special and continued support through the years has made this book possible: Daniel Bradford, Lois and John Canaday, Kathy McClurg and Grosvenor Merle-Smith.

Table of Contents

Contents

Bock & Doppelbock • Munich Helles & Dunkel • Schwarzbier • Dortmunder • Rauchbier • OTHER STYLES OF LAGER BEERS: Australian lagers • American lagers

A compendium of recipes

Mash-extract transition brews • A short course on theory • Mash-extract procedure • MORE RECIPES!

What have you gotten yourself into? • What special equipment will you need?

ENYZMES AND MYSTICISM: Proteins and enzymes • Starch and enzymes • Alpha-amylase • Beta-amylase • Temperature • Time • pH • Thickness • Minerals • INGREDIENTS: Varieties of barley (2-row, 6-row) • Malting and modification • The use of adjuncts: Preparation of adjuncts • Adjuncts commonly used (barley, corn, oats, potato, rice, rye, sorghum, tapioca, triticale, wheat, quinoa, tef, buckwheat, dinkel, amaranth)

Hop Utilization Chart • Calculating International Bitterness Units

What is hard water? What is soft water? • What is measured to determine total hardness? • What is temporary hardness? How does it affect the brewing process? • What is permanent hardness? How does it affect the brewing process? • What is pH? • What minerals influence the brewing process? • How can pH of the mash be adjusted? • How can I find out about my water? • Famous brewing waters • Adjusting your water

Preface

by Michael Jackson*

Everyone knows there are people who spend their lives sampling wines and writing books and newspaper articles about them. The notion that anyone should do the same for beer is apparently harder to accept.

That is what I do for a living: I roam the world tasting distinguished beers and writing about them (pause for incredulity, laughter and/or admiration).

Which beers have I enjoyed the most? A bewildering question, that, because there is such a choice—not just of brands but, much more significantly, of styles. Just as one grape provides a quite different wine from another, and the regions of production have techniques as distinct as those of, say, the Rhine and Champagne, Burgundy and Oporto, so it is with beer, albeit the styles are scandalously less well known outside their countries of origin.

A growing band of devotees is beginning to appreciate this. They know, for example, that to quench the thirst in summer there is nothing as efficacious as a Berlin wheat beer: dry, pleasantly acidic, and described as "the Champagne of the North" by Napoleon's troops. Should it, though, be laced with raspberry syrup or essence of woodruff? Or is the call for a fruitier wheat beer of the Bavarian style; or the yet sharper, cidery Belgian type, perhaps with the raspberries or cherries macerated in the cask?

All of those beers are imported to the United States, but they are easier to find in the cosmopolitan cities than in some smaller or more workaday places. Suppose you can't find them;

*Michael Jackson is the award-winning author of *The World Guide to Beer* (Running Press, Philadelphia), *The Pocket Guide to Beer* (Simon & Schuster, New York) and other books and essays on drink, food and travel. His writing has appeared in *Food & Wine* and *Les Amis du Vin* magazines and *The Times* of London. He lives in London and travels extensively in Europe and the United States.

what do you do then? We'll come to that in a moment . . . first, you must have the thirst, and the sense of which beer you want.

In the earliest, fresh, still-breezy days of spring, Bavarians venture outdoors to their beer-gardens to sample the new season's double bock, an emboldening, extra-strong brew first produced by monks of St. Paul to bless their saint's day. By the first day of May, a less hesitant celebration of spring, a single bock will do, because the weather is warmer. At the other end of the year, in the fall, a malty, amber October beer is appropriate.

Unless you are in England, of course. There, the pub drinker puts aside his bitter ale, with its powerful apéritif qualities, and in October or November seeks a luscious ''barley wine'' (in Scotland, a ''wee heavy''). Save the stouts for other times: a dry Irish one with oysters on the half shell; a rich, rare Russian style with Christmas pudding; a sweet English one after dinner instead of Madeira. Beer and food have been soulmates since the days when the wife brewed ale and the husband baked bread. (The original ale-wife was not a fish.)

Such ruminations may seem esoteric, but they are not. Most of these beer styles were produced in the United States before Prohibition, and some still are. Sad to say, though, Prohibition stamped the color out of the American brewing scene. Today, as though Chablis were the only wine that existed, America finds it difficult to recognize as beer anything other than the sparkling golden product derived from the style of Plzeň, Czechoslovakia. It is a noble enough style but when the overwhelming majority of beers produced in the United States (and the dominant imports) are all, broadly speaking, pilseners, what happened to variety? Isn't choice supposed to be the greatest benefit of capitalism and competition?

What has happened to variety is that it has been taken up by homebrewers. Whatever other highly honorable motives they may have—to save money or to enjoy themselves, for example—the greatest motivation for homebrewers is the opportunity to experiment and to produce beer in all the glorious varieties in which it manifests itself.

The joy of this challenge is that you can learn to walk before you run. The homebrewer can start with a ready-made kit that is easy to use, in which much of the work has already been done, and progress one step at a time until, like a renowned practitioner in California, he has the brewing equivalent of Château Latour in his garage.

This is a frivolous comparison but not an idle one. Prohibition gave beer a bum rap in more than one way: It left its shadow not only on America's selection of beers and drinking places but also on the art of the conscientious homebrewer. The sense of backyard buccaneering is fun but it shouldn't obscure the shining truth that in stylistic variety and interest, the homebrewer can easily surpass the commercial giants. He or she can on occasion also produce a beer of better quality.

How is this possible? In the matter of style, the homebrewer has no jargon-brained market researcher telling him that a beer so strong, or full-bodied, or characterful, was recently rejected by nine out of ten middle income, upwardly mobile white males between ages 25 and 40 living in Minneapolis. Nor, if he wants to make his beer from 100 percent malt, does he have a cost accountant insisting that the product could be priced more competitively if 35 percent corn was used.

In the matter of technical capability, the homebrewer has his limitations, but they can be overestimated. While some of the equipment of the commercial brewer is there to improve his product, much of his arsenal is aimed at ensuring consistency and at saving money and energy. Consistency matters if you are selling a trademark—today's glass of Bud shouldn't taste quite different from yesterday's—but it is less important to the homebrewer. Indeed, part of the fun lies in deciding whether you enjoy this month's brew as much as the one you made for Labor Day. Cost saving and energy efficiency are important if they affect profit margins over millions of barrels, but an extravagant brew in your kitchen is not going to put you irreversibly in debt to the public utilities.

There is a difference, too, between hiding in the hollow, brewing from sugar, while the bootleggers' truck waits impatiently, and using the equipment and knowledge that is today available to the homebrewer, not least in books like this.

The author of this book is academically qualified as a nuclear engineer, but earned his living for several years by teaching children. That combination of skills, for a start, makes him a formidable candidate to teach homebrewing at the highest level to the most unschooled pupils. Because he is a resourceful and adventurous man in the archetypal American tradition, he became first a homebrewer and then an evangelist of this particular faith. When he says, "Relax, don't worry, have a homebrew," he is preaching the credo by which he lives in his hideout in the Rockies. Because he says it, and does it, in such a clear, palpably entertaining way, he has won followers all over North America for the American Homebrewers' Association and its magazine, *Zymurgy.*

Wherever my travels take me in the United States, and whichever commercial beers I am asked to taste, whether by a magazine, a scientific institute or a brewer, I always seem to finish up in someone's garden at the weekend, enjoying their own home-produced vintage. My hosts almost always turn out to be members of the American Homebrewers' Association. It happened again the other day, in Washington, D.C. My hosts were a physicist and his schoolteacher wife. They had friends present, an executive in a government agency and a couple of journalists from a famous newspaper. We enjoyed that same pleasure usually experienced in cooking together, except that we were brewing. While we went about it, we sampled the recently matured product of their last brew. "Let's drink a toast," suggested our hosts. "Let's drink to Charlie Papazian." We did, and so will you.

Introduction to the Second Edition

Seven years have passed between the writing of the first and second editions of *The Complete Joy of Home Brewing*. There's been and still is a whole lot of brewing going on. I'm also happy to report, based on my beer travels, that the intensity of relaxing and pledges to not worry seem to be making an impact on American homebrewing. I know, because I have personally tasted thousands of homebrews brewed by thousands of homebrewers. Please rest assured that the quality of homebrewed beer continues to improve with every batch brewed. I look forward to the day I have the privilege of trying your beer.

But I momentarily digress between sips of my own fresh mug of A Barrel of Monkeys Wheat Stout. What I really intend to say in this introduction to the second edition is that the principles of great homebrewing remain unchanged. If you used the first edition there is nothing I would suggest you change now in order to make great beer.

Included in this new second edition are product and recipe updates, new data, a directory of classic world beer styles and expansion of ideas and techniques that weren't even fermentable seven years ago. They are presented to offer you the opportunity and inspiration to continue developing your skills as a brewer. And to feel relaxed that your beer is great no matter how sophisticated you choose to make your homebrewery.

I encourage all of you to never forget that homebrewing is fun and rewarding and that worrying still can spoil your beer more than anything else. Relax. Don't worry. Have a homebrew. If the mood ever inspires you, drop me a line. I enjoy hearing about your beer experiences and thoughts on the state of our fantastic hobby. I can be reached through the offices of the

American Homebrewers' Association in Boulder, Colorado, whose address appears at the end of this book.

Finally, I wish to express appreciation to Avon Books for giving me an opportunity to present new material in this second edition and to finally include a much-awaited index.

Introduction
The Homebrewer and the Joy of Brewing

This book is written for the "will-be" homebrewer: who will be a homebrewer who will be able to relax and consistently make good beer time after time. It is for you who want to jump right in and brew a batch of beer today! And why not? Stouts, ales, lagers, porters, bitters, milds, Oktoberfests, pilseners, specialty beers and meads . . . they are all easy to make. Many of these styles are even ready to enjoy within three weeks! This book is for you, the will-be homebrewer who wants to enjoy the creative process of doing and learning what beer is all about. Relax.

The four sections of this book are written with the homebrewer in mind: the beginner, the intermediate, the advanced and the inspired. Each section is complete. The beginner need not be anxious about the more advanced recipes in this book, because superb beer can be made just by following the fundamental principles of brewing outlined in the beginner's section. The advanced brewer, however, will find this book valuable from any point of view.

Making quality beer is EASY! Don't let anyone tell you any differently. At the same time, making bad beer is easy, too. The difference between making good beer and bad beer is simply knowing those little things that make a big difference and ensure success every time. Above all, the homebrewer should remember not to worry, because worrying can spoil the taste of beer faster than anything else. Relax. Don't worry.

So now you've decided to brew your own beer. In essence, you've given yourself the opportunity to make the kind of beer that *you* like. Reading this book and learning the fundamentals will give you a foundation to express yourself unendingly in what you brew. Remember, the best beer in the world is the one you brewed.

IS IT LEGAL?

Yes! The majority of the states have statutorily recognized homebrewing or winemaking. Of course, common sense dictates that homebrew prohibition should be repealed in restrictive states as well.

In November 1978, a bill passed by Congress repealed federal restrictions on the homebrewing of beer. In February 1979, President Carter signed the bill into law.

What is the law, and why was it ever illegal in the first place? It all dates back to that "Noble Experiment"—Prohibition. In 1920, it became illegal to make beer, period! In those dark ages the only kind of beer that was available was clandestine homebrew. Millions of Americans got into the act of making homebrewed *alcohol*. Quality was not important; it didn't seem to matter how good homebrew tasted as long as what Grandpa made had a kick to it and the bottles didn't explode under the bed (there were a lot of wet beds in those days—from the bottoms up). Prohibition finally ended and the commercial production of beer was legalized. The homebrewing of wine and/or beer should have been legalized as well. Homemade wine was legalized, but unfortunately through a stenographer's omission the words "and/or beer" never made it into the Federal Register.

Now it is legal and, as far as the federal government is concerned, an adult twenty-one years or older is permitted to brew "not more than one hundred gallons of beer in a year." If there is more than one adult in a household, then two hundred gallons of beer can be brewed in one year. That's a lot of beer!

The beer you brew is intended for your personal use. It is very illegal to sell your homebrew: so don't! The law in most states does provide for removal of homebrew from the "brewery" for organized tastings. No registration forms are required nor are there any permit fees. The point to remember is that your homebrew is meant for your own personal enjoyment. Don't sell it and no one will bother you except friends and neighbors who want to drink your beer.

WHY IS TODAY'S HOMEBREW BETTER?

Before the legalization of homebrewing in the United States, good information and quality ingredients were very difficult to find. Times have changed. Now, the best is available to anyone who seeks it. The technology of homebrewing ingredients, kits and malt extracts has progressed to an advanced state-of-the-art. Credit must be given where credit is due: to the British. Homebrewing was legalized in Great Britain in 1963. As popularity grew over the years manufacturers took more interest. There was money to be made and money to be spent on developing more perfect homebrew products. In the United States we have seen the importation of the best of British technology.

The best, though, is yet to come—not only from across the sea but from the United States. The brewing industry in the United States is only beginning to discover that, as homebrewers, we like good beer. To the brewing industry's initial surprise some of us (comparatively, very few indeed) have started small commercial "microbreweries" (breweries that commercially brew beer in quantities of less than fifteen thousand barrels per year).

WHY BREW YOUR OWN?
You Deserve It!

There are many reasons to brew your own beer. The first thought that comes to most people's minds is economy. Certainly, it can be less expensive to brew your own and that's why many begin. But if you embark on the road to homebrewing because you like beer ("Go yeast, young man!"), you soon discover that *quality*, *variety* and *independence* are the reasons you continue to brew. The taste of fresh beer can't be beat, and the opportunity to brew any style of beer in the world makes this "hobby" indispensable.

As a homebrewer, you will find that your interest in beer will increase. You will begin to understand what beer is all about. You will find yourself appreciating all kinds of beer, both your own and commercially available beer.

Discovering the real joy of brewing is something you deserve, especially if you like beer.

Pass it on.

Relax. Don't worry. Have a homebrew!

Beer, History, America and Homebrew

American beer has as its roots the total brewing tradition of the "Old World." Although American beer is a quality-brewed product, most of the original variety and style has been dramatically altered. Nevertheless, the factors that have influenced the taste of American beer and that of beer throughout the world haven't changed for over 4,500 years!

In the beginning of "beer history," the household was the primary source of beer, followed by the small-town brewery. Eventually today's large breweries evolved. Much has been gained—much has been lost.

A renewed interest in homebrewing is occurring in America, to rediscover, perhaps, the lost truths about beer.

Let's take a closer look at some of the things that have been lost and why beer tastes the way it does.

A LONG, LONG TIME AGO

It all began at home.

Historians have surmised that long, long ago in the early days of the Mesopotamian and Egyptian cultures the first beer was brewed. It was homebrew!

Barley was one of the staple grains of the various Mediterranean cultures. It grew well in that climate and was used as the main ingredient in various breads and cakes. People soon discovered that if barley was wetted, allowed to germinate and subsequently dried, the resulting grain would taste sweeter and be less perishable. This was probably discovered quite by accident when some inattentive member of a household left a basket of grain in the rain and then tried to salvage the mess by drying it. Inadvertently what was made was malted barley. It wasn't

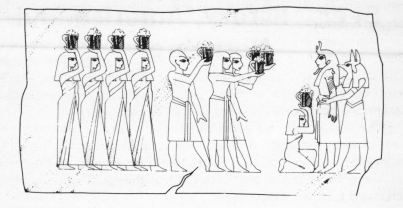

such a mistake after all. As a matter of fact, it made for more pleasant breads and porridges.

It was inevitable that someone would leave their porridge, malted barley flour or bread in the rain. The dissolved sugars and starches were fair game for yeasts in the air. Soon, the yeasts began to ferment the "malt soup." When the mysteriously bubbly concoction was consumed, it was with pleasant surprise that the household felt a mysterious inner peace with their surroundings. However crude the process may have been, the first "beer" had been brewed.

This mildly alcoholic beverage soon became a significant part of the culture of the Egyptians and Mesopotamians, while other native societies simultaneously discovered the joy of naturally fermented drink. Alcohol was not understood. Neither was yeast. But magically these beverages bubbled and made one feel, perhaps, godlike. It is not surprising, then, that religious significance became attached to these gifts of visions. One can easily imagine the ceremonial significance that fermented beverages played in such cultures as the Egyptian, Aztecan and Incan. Rice beers, millet beers, barley beers, honey beers, corn beers . . . even the Eskimos had a mildly alcoholic fermented reindeer's milk.

It all began at home, and in many countries most households brewed their own for thousands of years. This was especially the case in Europe and early America. But as towns and cities developed homebrewing activity began to diminish in Western cultures.

As towns developed, good drinking water became scarcer. Beer, with its mild alcoholic content, was one of the few liquids safe to drink and thus in great demand. At the same time small-town brewers began to relieve the household of the essential task of making beer.

"VARIETY AND STYLE"

Because of the development of the small-town brewery, distinctive beers became indigenous to a region, rather than to every household. Slowly, the variability of climate, agriculture and human activity began to express itself more profoundly. During this transition from household to small brewery modern-day beer came into historic perspective. The centralization of brewing served to consolidate regional trends.

Let's take a look at some of the factors that influence the taste of beer. To a great extent, indigenous ingredients and climate give beers throughout the world much of their distinctive regional character. Different strains of barley and the availability of other grains influence the character of each region's beer. Yeast strains indigenous to an area greatly affect the product brewed. The availability of herbs or hops also characterizes regional beers. For example, beers brewed in those areas with an abundance of hops have a more pronounced hop character. The delicate style of the original Pilsener Urquell from Czechoslovakia may be attributed to the character of the water as well as to the native ingredients. There are literally hundreds of styles of Belgian beer, and for many "it's *not* the water" but a variety of yeasts that are allowed to naturally introduce fermentation to each brewery's beer. The result? Distinctive flavors that cannot be duplicated anywhere else in the world. Agricultural and climatic conditions surely must have influenced a style of beer called wheat beer, brewed in Germany and formerly in the United States.

Human activity has a significant influence on beer styles. For example, bock beer is a strong beer that originated in the German town of Einbeck. It was a beer that gained favor with royalty and was transported great distances for their pleasure. Its high alcohol content prevented the beer from spoiling. It was very different from the low-alcohol beverages often brewed for local consumption. Likewise, India Pale Ale was a style of strong ale brewed in Great Britain for the purpose of providing the British troops with good ale while they occupied India. It was and still is a beer that is high in alcohol and hop content, both contributing preservative qualities to beer. Consequently, human activity warranted the brewing of stronger beers, in order to help preserve it during long transports.

Throughout history, other human activities, such as economic factors and shortages of ingredients, have influenced styles of beer. When wartime priorities were given to feeding troops, a shortage of grain resulted in a shortage of beer and/or a more diluted product. Especially evident today in various parts of the world is the effect of high taxation on brewing styles. Of course, beer contains alcohol and in most countries alcohol is taxed. So, naturally the more alcohol in the beer the more it is taxed, and the more it costs not only the brewery but the beer drinker himself. This situation can be seen most clearly in Ireland, where the world-famous Guinness Stout is brewed. Without a doubt, the locally available stuff is delicious, but upon investigation one discovers that the alcoholic content does not exceed 3 percent. Over 60 percent of the price of a pint of Guinness in Ireland is tax! The Guinness Stout that is made for export is taxed at a lower rate; therefore, it is higher in alcohol and a very, very different product.

AMERICAN BEER

What is American beer? Today's typical American beer is a light-colored, light-bodied pilsener-lager beer, a style very different from the American beer of yesteryear. Through the years, it has been very much influenced by agricultural, climatic, economic, political and cultural factors.

Before Prohibition, literally thousands of breweries existed, each supplying their respective regions with distinctive styles. There were, as well, millions of people homebrewing quality beer. The healthy diversity of beer styles must have been wonderful to experience. One imagines that there was a genuine sharing of kinship among brewers, whether they were home-brewers or professionals. It must have been that important feeling that went into the beer that made all the difference.

Between January 1920 and December 1933, the United States suffered through Prohibition and the dark ages of beer. When it was over, only the larger breweries had survived by

making malt products for the food industry. Low-budget operations combined with equipment left idle and in disrepair for
over a decade eventually led to the demise of the smaller, local
breweries.

What was reborn was an industry of larger breweries. They
were still somewhat anxious about the prevailing attitude toward
alcohol. As incredible as this may seem, many of the richer styles
of American beer were not brewed, in an attempt by the breweries to market beer that would appeal to women.

Mass marketing began to rear its foaming head in search
of the perfect beer that would appeal to the most people. Never
mind diversity. Never mind variety. Never mind the traditional
ideals that American brewers had developed for more than 150
years. Never mind choice.

Then came World War II. A shortage of war material ne-
cessitated the scrapping of steel, some of which was idle brewery
equipment. A shortage of food diminished beer production. The
beer that was made had less malt in it. Many men were out
fighting a war, and the beer drinkers back home were mainly
women.

A lighter style of beer was thus beginning to gain popularity in the United States—and justifiably so. With the warm climate that we in the States enjoy for half a year, a lighter beer can be a refreshing experience. With the agricultural abundance of corn and rice here, these ingredients have found their way more and more into American beer, lightening the taste and body. If it's well brewed and you enjoy it, there is absolutely nothing wrong with this kind of beer. But it is only one type of beer brewed in the world among perhaps 20,000 other different types of beer.

What we are missing now, sadly enough, is choice. The economics of mass marketing have indeed influenced what is offered.

AS A HOMEBREWER

As a homebrewer you give yourself and the people who you know a *choice*: not only to brew the kind of beer that *you* like, but also the opportunity to feel and understand what beer is all about. Personal feeling is exactly what's lacking in a lot of beer brewed these days.

American homebrewers are roofers, museum curators, mental health directors, truck drivers, geneticists, Air Force pilots, film directors, farmers, mortgage bankers, doctors, longshoremen, engineers, dentists, tax collectors, beauticians, secretaries, housewives. . . . There is no one type of American homebrewer. There is no one type of beer.

In all of our diversity, we homebrewers can choose to brew for our own reasons. The tradition of homebrewing is nothing new, but these days it has special significance. At least for now, it is only the homebrewer who can really understand why beer tastes the way it does and perhaps rediscover that "special feeling" of beer that has been lost.

Especially for the Beginner

GETTING STARTED

Brewing your own beer is as easy as opening a can of ingredients and boiling water.

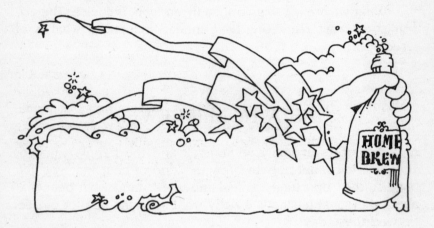

INTRODUCTION

In recent years there has been a deluge of homebrew supplies made available to the homebrewer. It's nice to be able to walk into a homebrew supply store and know that there are potentially more than one hundred different malt extracts and beer kits from which to choose. A conscientious homebrew supplier will only stock quality products, so most of the time you can be assured that the products on the shelf are going to make good beer.

But for you, the beginner, a choice of a hundred different types of products may be a bit staggering. Where to start?

The place to start is with good advice, good ingredients and a simple, absolutely foolproof first batch of beer that can be enjoyed within three weeks.

This Beginner's Section is written especially for you, the

beginner who has never brewed beer before. Maybe you're a bit anxious and wonder whether it is possible to be able to make good beer. You may not even know what good beer is.

This section is written to assure you that brewing fantastic beer is easy and can be done simply, without compromising quality. Many of you may even find yourselves lingering as a "beginner" for quite some time, being very pleased with the results.

So RELAX . . . DON'T WORRY . . . AND BEGIN!

THE BASICS

Ingredients

Beer is made from four essential ingredients: water, fermentable sugars (traditionally malted barley), hops and yeast. These ingredients are processed and combined according to a recipe. Given the right conditions, the yeast will convert (ferment) the fermentable sugars to alcohol, carbon dioxide and the taste we know as beer. The beer is then bottled and aged anywhere from a week to three months (depending upon the style one chooses to brew).

Malted barley is a naturally processed form of barley. Barley is a grain that is similar to wheat in appearance. In order to malt the barley, a "maltster" will steep the barley in water under carefully controlled conditions until it begins to sprout, after which the germinated barley is dried. After drying, the barley is said to have been malted. This process develops sugars, soluble starches and other characteristics in the barley desirable for brewing beer.

The malted barley is mostly converted to sugars through a

process called mashing, whereby the malted barley is immersed in water at controlled temperatures that allow enzymes in the barley to convert starches to sugars. It is these sugars that are converted through fermentation to alcohol, carbon dioxide and the flavor of beer.

Many breweries often will substitute corn, rice, wheat, rye or other grains for a portion of the malted barley. The breweries will process these starches into fermentable sugars. The sugars will ferment as the malt sugars do but will impart their distinctive fermented character to the beer. Most often these other forms of fermentable sugars are used for ''lightening'' the flavor of the beer.

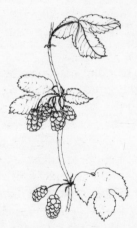

Hops are green conelike flowers that grow on vines and have been used in beermaking for about 200 years. Hops impart a degree of bitterness to beer that provides a balance when combined with the sweetness of the malt. The addition of hops to beer also inhibits spoilage and enhances head retention.

Over 90 percent of beer is *water*. The water you use will lend its character to the beer. Most drinking water supplies in the United States are fine for making quality homebrew. If your water supply is known to have a significant amount of dissolved sulfur, iron or bicarbonates, then it would be to your advantage to use bottled water for your brewing water. If the water tastes good, then brew with it.

Yeasts are responsible for converting the bittersweet "tea" of fermentable sugars and hops to the bubbly, alcoholic beverage we call beer. They are living micro-organisms that use sugar as food for their life cycle. Thousands of different kinds of yeasts can be found everywhere in our lives. As a brewer, it is a bit disconcerting to discover that most of them are wild yeasts. The introduction of these wild yeasts will result in some pretty wild brews, usually not to one's liking. The kind of yeast used for beermaking can, for now, be generically classified as BEER YEAST, that is, specially cultured for the purpose of brewing beer. (Bread yeast is cultured for making bread. Wine yeast is cultured for making wine.)

Generally, there are two types of beer yeast: lager yeast and ale yeast. They are used to brew different styles of beer. Their differences will be discussed later.

The Fermentation Process

A brewery's job is to combine ingredients and pursue fermentation. This fermentation will last from ten days to several months (again depending on the style of beer being brewed). During this period, yeasts reproduce and disperse themselves throughout the fermenting beer, converting sugars to alcohols, carbon dioxide and a variety of flavors. After the initial five to fourteen days, the yeast will have exhausted most of its sugar supply and will begin to settle to the bottom of the fermentation vessel. At this point breweries often will transfer the clearing beer to a second tank in order to isolate the beer from the sediment that forms on the bottom of the first fermenter. When fermentation activity has been completed, the brewery will package the beer in bottles, cans or kegs. Most U.S. breweries will take the beer from aging tanks, filter it, artificially carbonate it and then pasteurize it before bottling. This last bit of processing is done by many breweries for economic reasons and as a means of preserving beer.

As *a homebrewer*, you have the option of starting from scratch and brewing exactly as commercial breweries do: using only raw ingredients.

But unlike the breweries you have the choice of simplicity. You don't have to go through the ritual of malting your own

Can you do the can can? A sampler display of the more than one hundred varieties of malt extracts and beer kits from which a homebrewer may choose.

barley, nor do you have to get involved in mashing your own grains. All that has been done for the homebrewer and takes the form of malt extract.

Malt extract is simply malted barley that has been processed into a sweet "tea." Much of the water is carefully evaporated, leaving for the homebrewer a concentrated syrup (or in the case of dry malt extract where all of the water is evaporated, a dry powder).

Furthermore, even simpler for the homebrewer are the many malt extracts and homebrew kits that are hop flavored. In other words, the hops have already been added. All you need to do is add water and yeast (often supplied with the kit).

The only difference between the potential quality of home-brewed beer and commercially brewed beer is the vast amounts of money spent on consistency and quality control. Big breweries want their beer to turn out exactly the same every time. As a homebrewer, you will come to know your beer intimately and understand the variables that are involved in beermaking. You will make superb beer but it will vary slightly from batch to batch. That is the nature of beermaking and it makes your new endeavor more rewarding.

GETTING YOUR HOMEBREWERY TOGETHER

EQUIPMENT

The following list of special brewing equipment will be adequate for making 4–5 gallons of beer at a time.

1 3–4-gallon-size pot (an enameled canning pot or stainless is best)
1 5-gallon-size glass carboy OR one 6½-gallon-size glass carboy (these are large jugs that are used for bottled water or chemicals)
1 5–10-gallon-size new plastic bucket or trash pail
1 6-foot length of ⅜-inch inside diameter clear plastic hose
1 fermentation lock
1 rubber stopper with hole to fit fermentation lock
1 2½-foot length of ⅜-inch outside diameter (⁵⁄₁₆-inch inside diameter) clear plastic hose OR 3-foot length of 1¼-inch outside diameter (1-inch inside diameter) clear plastic hose
1 large plastic funnel
1 thermometer
1 beer hydrometer
1 bottle washer (optional but recommended)

*Quite a spread; the homebrewery from brewpot to mug!
From left to right: funnel, siphon hose, brewpot,
hydrometer (and flask), charismatic spoon, lever-type
bottlecapper, plastic closed fermenter (with fermentation*

lots of bottlecaps, new and unused

1 bottlecapper

60 returnable 12-oz. beer bottles (anything other than screw-top bottles will do)

OR

25 champagne bottles (most champagne bottles are capable)

You also will need a bottle of household bleach in order to sanitize your equipment.

You can find all of this equipment at your local homebrew supply store. Look in the Yellow Pages under "Winemaking Supplies" or "Beermaking Supplies." Beer bottles can be found at recycling centers and bars. Champagne bottles are found at restaurants and hotels that serve champagne brunches or have just hosted a wedding reception.

*lock), one liter of stout, strainers, glass (carboy) fermenter
with plastic hose, fermentation lock (foreground), glass jar
(to collect overflow during fermentation), bottles,
bottlecaps and bench-type bottlecapper.*

INGREDIENTS FOR YOUR FIRST BATCH OF BEER— 5 GALLONS

5–6 lbs. hop-flavored malt extract or "beer kit"*

OR

3–4 lbs. hop-flavored malt extract or beer kit* plus 1–2 lbs. plain unhopped light dried malt extract (or corn sugar may be substituted; see chart on page 23)

5 gal. water

1 pkg. ale yeast

¾ c. corn sugar OR 1¼ c. plain dried malt extract (for bottling)

*NOTE: Malt extracts and beer kits come in a variety of "flavors." The major distinction is their color: extra pale, pale, light, amber, brown and dark cover the range of choice for the homebrewer. If you desire a lighter beer for your first batch, naturally choose a lighter malt extract. For your darker bock beers and stouts, choose, likewise, a darker malt. Only with experience and experimenting will you begin to discern the various characteristics of the brands of malts available. For now, don't worry about the perfect malt extract for your palate. You will be more than adequately pleased with your initial efforts. RELAX.

WHAT YOU ARE GOING TO DO

Going for Greatness!

1) Combine and dissolve your malt extracts (and sugar if used) in 1½ gallons of water and bring to a boil for 15 minutes.
2) Sanitize your fermenter with a weak household (chlorine) bleach and water solution.
3) Add 3 gallons of clean cold water to your clean and rinsed fermenter.
4) Add your hot malts and water to the fermenter.
5) When temperature is ideally below 78 degrees F, measure the specific gravity with your beer hydrometer and then add yeast.
6) Attach fermentation hose, and after initial fermentation has subsided attach fermentation lock.
7) Ferment for 8 to 14 days.
8) Bottle and cap.
9) Age for 10 days.
10) DRINK THE BEER!

Sound simple? It is. But let's go over each point step by step in order to further clarify the recipe, procedures and equipment.

NOTE: All references to temperature will be in degrees Fahrenheit with degrees Celsius in parentheses.

1. Combine and dissolve your malt extracts (and sugar if used) in 1½ gallons of water and bring to a boil for 15 minutes.

The list of ingredients gives you some flexibility. The chart on page 23 will help you choose the kind of beer that you would like to brew.

Have a homebrew! Making good beer is as easy as having a homebrew and adding a can of malt extract to water in a brewpot.

Beer kits and hop-flavored malt extracts come in a variety of sizes. One of the most common sizes is a 3½-lb. can of malt extract syrup. For your first batch of beer use one can of syrup with only one pound of plain light dried malt extract. If you desire a richer flavor in your beer, use two cans of syrup (no matter what the size, as long as it is 3½ lbs. or less). Sugar is not recommended.

Most beer kits come with instructions. Many of them will recommend the use of sugar equal to the amount of malt extract. But remember: You will always make a far superior beer by eliminating and substituting or minimizing the amount of any refined sugar.

Many beer kits do not instruct the homebrewer to boil their ingredients, although omitting this procedure will make reasonably good beer. Your beer will always be *much* better if your ingredients are boiled for 15 to 30 minutes.

So open your can of malt extract (it helps to immerse the can in hot water prior to opening in order to make the thick syrup more manageable) and add it to a pot of 1½ gallons of water. If you are using dried malt extract or corn sugar, add these ingredients as well. Stir to dissolve all of the ingredients and bring to a boil for 15 minutes.

2. Sanitize your fermenter with a weak household (chlorine) bleach and water solution.

SANITIZING YOUR EQUIPMENT IS ONE OF THE EASIEST AND MOST FUNDAMENTALLY IMPORTANT THINGS THAT YOU WILL DO. If you do not take care to clean your equipment, the best recipe in the world will result in disappointment.

The thing to remember is to relax and not worry . . . do what must be done. It is easy. It is no big deal.

Anything that will come in contact with the fermenting beer should be sanitized. This can be easily achieved by making up a solution of 1–2 ounces of household bleach to every 5 gallons of cold water. Rinse, fill or soak your fermenter (you will use your 5-gallon-size glass carboy as your fermenter) in this solution, then rinse all traces of chlorine odor with hot water.

Caution: Do not mix any other cleaning agent with chlorine bleach.

3. Add 3 gallons of clean cold water to your clean and rinsed fermenter.

Remembering that anything that comes in contact with your beer should be sanitized, measure out approximately 3 gallons of cold water and add it to your carboy. Your sanitized funnel will aid you.

4. Add your hot malt extracts and water to the fermenter.

Carefully pour your hot water and ingredients through the funnel and into the glass carboy. The carboy will not break from

BEGINNER'S CHART

The Flavor Characteristics of Homebrewed Beer With and Without Using Corn Sugar

FOR 5 GALLONS

lbs. of malt extract	50% malt extract 50% corn sugar	75–90% malt extract 10–25% corn sugar	No sugar added. i.e., 100% malt extract*
2½ to 3½	(3 lbs. sugar) thin, light body. dry. 3–4% alcohol content	(¼–1 lb. sugar) good real beer flavor, light body, low alcohol (2½–3%)	excellent real beer flavor, yet very light in flavor, body, and alcohol (2–2½%); a good lower calorie beer
4	(4 lbs. sugar) dry light body. very alcoholic	(½–1 lb. sugar) good real beer flavor, light body, up to 3% alcohol	excellent real beer, medium—full flavor, low alcohol. light body
5	NOT RECOMMENDED	(½–1¼ lbs. sugar) good real beer flavor, high in alcohol (4–5%)	excellent real beer, full flavor, low—medium alcohol (3–3½%). medium body
6	NOT RECOMMENDED	(½–1½ lbs. sugar) good real beer full flavor, very high in alcohol, robust, full body; longer fermentation time required. not recommended for beginners	excellent real beer, full flavor, medium alcohol content. medium—full body
7	NOT RECOMMENDED	(¾–1¾ lbs. sugar) same as above	excellent real beer, full flavor, high alcohol. full bodied, sweeter palate

*¾ cup corn sugar or 1¼ cup dry malt extract should be used at bottling time.

Relax! When using hop-flavored malt extracts and kits, the boiled ingredients can be poured directly into the cold water in the fermenter. When cool, simply add yeast and let ferment for five to ten days.

the shock of the hot water because you have previously added cold water to absorb the thermal shock.

Screw the cap onto the carboy at this point. If there is no cap, use a sanitized rubber cork. Turn the carboy on its side and agitate the contents in order to evenly mix the cold water with the warm ingredients. Then, if there is any remaining space in the carboy add enough cold water to fill the carboy to within 3 or 4 inches of the top or to the 5-gallon level if using a 6½-gallon carboy. Shake the contents once again to mix the cold water evenly. *Warning: When using any kind of hops, strain hot wort before adding to fermenter.*

5. When temperature is ideally below 78 degrees F (26 C), measure the specific gravity with your beer hydrometer and then add yeast.

Take a temperature reading of your beer with your sanitized thermometer. If the temperature is between 68 and 78 degrees F (20–26 C), you are ready to add the yeast—but first measure and record the specific gravity (density) of your "soon-to-be-beer." This is as easy as reading a thermometer, but instead of using your thermometer you will use your beer hydrometer. Your hydrometer will give you an indication of the alcoholic content of your beer and will also tell you when to bottle.

> **What's a hydrometer?** A hydrometer is an instrument that measures the density (thickness) of liquids relative to the density of water. This measure of density is known as the specific gravity. Once upon a time someone proclaimed that the specific gravity (density) of water at a certain temperature would be exactly the number 1.000. So, if we add dissolvable solids such as sugar to water, the solution begins to get denser and the specific gravity rises from 1.000 on up.

> The combination of 4½–5 gallons of water with 5 lbs. of malt extract and/or corn sugar will result in a specific gravity of about 1.035–1.042. As the yeast ferments the dissolved sugars into alcohol and carbon dioxide the density of the liquid drops due to the lack of sugar in the solution and because alcohol is less dense than water.

> Take a good look at your hydrometer instructions and note the temperature at which your hydrometer measures accurately. Most hydrometers read accurately at 60 degrees F (16 C). Therefore, if you are measuring the specific gravity at, let's say, 80 or 90 degrees F (27 or 32 C), you will get an inaccurate reading. Why? Well, let's look at it this way: If you take something like honey and heat it, it becomes

thinner and less dense. Therefore, its specific gravity is less. The same thing happens with your brew but more subtly. For every 10 degrees F, your measurements will be off by .002–.003. So, if at 80 degrees F (27 C) your brew measures 1.038, you've got to add .004–.006 points to know that the real specific gravity is about 1.043 OR wait until your brew cools and take a specific gravity reading OR take a small sample and read it at 60 degrees F (16 C).

Regardless of anything . . . don't worry.

To take a hydrometer reading of the contents of your fermenter, carefully pour and fill your hydrometer flask (the container with which your hydrometer came). Place your hydrometer in the flask and read the specific gravity scale. Record this number, as well as the temperature in a recipe journal. DO NOT RETURN THE UNFERMENTED BEER TO THE FERMENTER! Discard it. It is a small price to pay to make sure that your unfermented beer remains clean.

Once the temperature is below 78 degrees F (70–75 degrees is ideal) [26 C (21–24 C is ideal)] add the ale yeast.

6. Attach fermentation hose, and after initial fermentation has subsided attach fermentation lock.

The fermentation of your beer will be a "closed fermentation." This term indicates that it will be closed off from the air and the environment. You can be 99 percent assured that your beer will not become contaminated with wild yeasts or other microorganisms that may produce off-flavors. (Note: There are no known pathogens, deadly micro-organisms, that can survive in beer . . . so don't worry about dying.)

First sanitize the rubber cork and 2½-foot length of ⅜-inch outside diameter clear plastic hose. After having strained out all hop and grain ingredients from your brew place the hose into the cork's hole. Place this configuration atop the carboy. (See photo, opposite.) If using a 3-foot length of 1¼-inch outside diameter hose, it may be fitted into the neck of the carboy without a rubber stopper. For the initial 2 or 3 days of fermentation, this configuration will serve as a "pipe" that will direct the overflow of fermenting foam out and into an awaiting container. This method of fermentation has the extra advantage of "blowing off'' excessively bitter hop resins, excess yeast and other things that may contribute to hangovers when consumed.

If you are using a 6½-gallon-size glass carboy to ferment 5 gallons (or a 5-gallon size to ferment 4 gallons) of beer it is not necessary to affix a blow-off hose to the rubber cork. Attaching a fermentation lock is adequate, because fermentation foam will not reach the top of the carboy. This method may be used to further minimize the small risk of clogging the hose, popping off the rubber cork and losing beer to the floor and environs.

You will notice a great deal of activity during the first 2 or 3 days of fermentation. It is quite impressive to observe. After those first 3 days, the activity will diminish and you will want to place a fermentation lock atop the carboy for the remainder of the fermentation.

Your fermentation lock is a simple device that allows fermentation gases to escape from the fermenter but will not allow air to enter the fermenter. Sanitize the fermentation lock in your household bleach and water solution. Then place the fermentation lock atop the carboy. Be sure to fill the lock with about ¾ inch of water. YOU MUST FILL IT WITH WATER. You will soon notice that the gas produced by fermentation bubbles merrily through and out the fermentation lock.

Blowing bubbles! Within 24 hours active fermentation will expel excess yeast, excessively bitter hop resins and a small amount of fermenting beer; a small price to pay for smooth, clean-tasting homebrew. The overflow is collected in a small jug, the contents later discarded.

All quiet on the yeastern front! After 2 to 3 days of vigorous fermentation, activity will subside and the yeast will begin to fall (sediment) to the bottom of the fermenter. The "blow-off" hose can be replaced with a fermentation lock, allowing fermentation gases to escape, yet "locking" the still fermenting beer from the outside air.

7. Ferment for 8 to 14 days.

The style of beer you are brewing is an ale. It is brewed at temperatures generally ranging from 60 to 75 degrees F (15–24 C). At these fermentation temperatures there is no advantage to aging or "lagering" the beer during fermentation. If quality ingredients are used, visible fermentation will subside within 5 to

14 days. At this time, you will notice that the beer will appear to become darker. This is the result of the once-active and circulating yeast becoming inactive and settling to the bottom; the beer begins to clear and appears to become darker starting from the top of the fermenter on down. If you choose to do so, or if necessity dictates, you may store the beer in the carboy with an active fermentation lock for one month without any risk of significant deterioration of flavor. But your beer will be at its best if bottled when visible signs of fermentation are negligible. You

The warehouse! Fermenting beer is content to sleep in the quietest of corners.

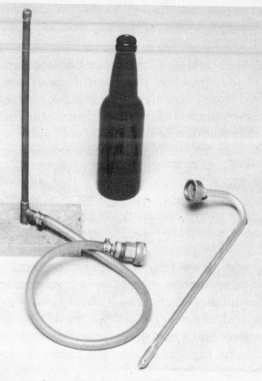

Water wonders—Making life easy! Bottle washers can be made or bought at local homebrew supply shops. They save time, hot water, effort and money; not a bad combination. You'll never regret the small investment.

should assure yourself that it is bottling time by taking hydrometer readings on 2 or 3 consecutive days. If the readings remain unchanged, your brew is certainly ready to bottle. REMEMBER: Pour a small amount (about 1 cup) of beer into your hydrometer flask, take a reading and either drink it or discard it, but do not return it to the fermenter. Note: Your beer may be hazy or even cloudy at the time of bottling. It will clear in the bottle.

8. Bottle and cap.

First of all relax . . . don't worry . . . and have a homebrew (if you haven't had any yet, store-bought beer may do) . . . and get a friend or two to help you. That shouldn't be too difficult.

Once again: Sanitize all of the equipment and apparatus that will come in contact with your beer with a bleach and water solution (2 ounces of household bleach to 5 gallons of cold water). It is easiest to sanitize your beer bottles in a tub or large clean plastic pail. If you have invested in a bottle washer, you will find that the rinsing of not only bottles but carboys and buckets as well will be safer and will conserve on hot water. A bottle washer is a worthwhile investment!

What you will be doing in the bottling process is adding a small amount of "priming" sugar to the now flat, inactive beer. Once in the bottle this small amount of sugar will be fermented by the still living yeast and create the perfect amount of carbonation. It is very important not to exceed the recommended sugar dosage of ¾ cup (or 1¼ cup dried malt extract) per 5 gallons; by no means should you ever exceed 1 cup per 5 gallons. And note that it is a measure of CUPS, not pounds.

Adding an excessive amount of priming sugar will result in overcarbonation and the possibility of exploding bottles. The older method of priming the beer by adding ½–1 teaspoon of sugar to each bottle will result in inconsistent carbonation and bacterial contamination, which may result in excessive foaming. The "Prohibition" method of waiting for the specific gravity to drop to a certain point is undependable because the final gravity of today's quality homebrew will vary with each recipe.

The following steps will help you organize your bottling procedures:

1) Sanitize your bottles.
2) Sanitize your 5–10-gallon-size plastic bucket.
3) Sanitize your 6-foot length of clear plastic (siphoning) hose.
4) Boil your bottle caps for 5 minutes.
5) Boil ¾ cup corn sugar (or 1¼ cup dried malt extract) in 1 pint (16 oz.) water for 5 minutes.

NOW, THEN

6) Place the carboy of beer on top of a table or counter. Remove the fermentation lock.

Giving you more time to have a homebrew, bottle washers make quick work of fermenter and bottle-washing chores. Note empty mug of beer.

7) Position the sanitized plastic pail on the floor (below the carboy) and add the dissolved and boiled corn sugar.

8) Take hold of the sanitized plastic hose and fill it completely full with water (no air bubbles allowed!). Put your clean thumbs over the ends, walk over to the carboy of beer and quickly insert one end into the beer.

9) Your siphon is ready—don't be intimidated by it, it's only beer. Relax. Lower the other end of the hose to the bottom of the plastic bucket (which should be on the floor), let loose and gently transfer the beer into the plastic pail. Be aware of two things: 1) Don't splash the beer or create a lot of bubbles; siphon quietly, and 2) siphon all of the beer out of the carboy EXCEPT the last ½ inch of sediment . . . BUT DON'T WORRY!

10) Take a hydrometer reading to confirm that fermentation is complete and then record the final gravity in your recipe book for future reference. Note: Contrary to what you may have led yourself to believe, your beer is *not* going to have an ending specific gravity equivalent to water: 1.000. There will be some residual, unfermented "sugars" that will give your beer body and a roundness to the flavor. The presence of these "sugars" will result in a final specific gravity of from 1.005 to 1.017 (even higher for your very heavy, all-malt beers). The important thing to remember is that if the hydrometer readings remain unchanged for 2 or 3 consecutive days, your beer is ready to bottle.

11) Place the primed beer on a table or counter and proceed to siphon the beer quietly (again without a lot of splashing) into each bottle. Leave about 1 inch of air space. You will find that you can control the flow of the beer by pinching the hose back on itself and constricting the flow when necessary.

It takes two hands! Anyone can siphon beer in preparation for bottling. The completely fermented beer is transferred to a sanitized plastic brewing pail, leaving the sediment of yeast behind. A measured amount of sugar or malt extract is added and then the beer is bottled.

12) Place the sanitized caps atop the bottles and cap with your bottlecapper.

13) Label or mark your bottle caps to indicate what kind of beer is in the bottle. After all, you *will* be brewing more beer.

14) Store the bottles upright and out of sight in a quiet, dark corner of your home at room temperatures above 55 degrees F (13 C) and preferably below 75 degrees F (24 C).

9. Age for 10 days.

Now comes the hard part. Waiting.

Within 5 or 6 days, your beer will show signs of clearing. The yeast that is in suspension will slowly drop to the bottom of

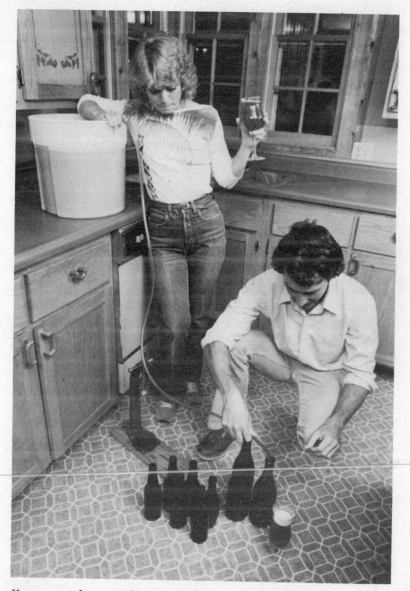

Keep your beer within arm's distance! The flow of
finished beer from the bucket can be restricted by
bending the hose. Careful, don't aerate the beer; put that
hose all the way to the bottom of the bottle and leave
about an inch of air space at the top of the bottle.

Easy does it! Bottling is so easy it seems a blur. Clean bottle caps are gently secured with the aid of a bottlecapper. From this point it is only 7 to 14 days before you'll be enjoying your efforts.

the bottle and form a sediment. At the same time, the yeasts will carbonate the beer over a period of 7 to 14 days—after which your beer will be ready to drink.

10. DRINK THE BEER!

HOT DAMN! It's ready.

But wait a minute: First, you should know that there is an unavoidable sediment of yeast on the bottom of each bottle. It won't filter out and it won't hurt you (it's actually rich with vitamin B), but you probably don't want it in your glass of beer; it will impart a yeasty character to the flavor. So be careful that you don't disturb it by doing something like turning the bottle upside down to see if it was made in Japan.

All you have to do is uncap a lightly chilled bottle of brew and pour all but the last ½ inch (about an ounce) of beer continuously into a glass pitcher (forget the plastic . . . this is *your* beer,

Some people collect butterflies! Ever since bottles were invented there have been hundreds of types of bottlecappers patented. You'll only need one.

so use the best). Now serve in your favorite glass (please no paper or plastic cups).

To drink, slightly part lips as they touch the glass. Let the beer flow into quonchologus and swallow. And be sure to smile when you drink your beer.

APPENDIX TO
BEGINNER'S SECTION

There are various schools of thought in homebrewing technique. All of them have a justified place when taken in proper perspective.

The issues that confront advanced homebrewers as well as beginners are:

Aging (lagering)

versus

Quick beer (as previously outlined)

Single-stage fermentation (as previously outlined)
versus
Double- or two-stage fermentation

Open fermentation
versus
Closed fermentation (as previously outlined)

Open fermentation and brewing in plastic

AGING (LAGERING) VERSUS QUICKLY MATURING BEERS

The temperature of fermentation and quality of yeast determine when a beer will taste its best. Ale yeast and fermentation at temperatures above 65 degrees F (18 C) will result in a beer that will be ready to bottle within 2 weeks. Only with the use of very high quality lager yeast and fermentation temperatures below 45 degrees F (7 C) is there any justification or advantage for lagering and aging beer. It is certainly true that excessive aging after bottling will not be advantageous unless temperatures are below 40 degrees F (4 C) (and often as low as 33 degrees F [1 C]) and a quality yeast is used. Ultimately, the determining factor is: Drink it when you like it, as you like it and when you *feel* it's the right time.

SINGLE-STAGE VERSUS TWO-STAGE FERMENTATION

Two-stage fermentation is a method of fermenting your beer in two different containers. Using this method, the brewer or homebrewer observes the initial fermentation closely during the first days. After the initial activity has subsided, the beer is siphoned into another fermenter and a fermentation lock attached. A sediment of spent yeast cells is left behind in the first fermenter.

The purpose of a two-stage fermentation should be to isolate the beer from prolonged contact with an inordinate amount of inactive yeast cells. For the homebrewer, this is a matter of concern *only* if you plan to ferment your beer over 2 or 3 weeks, because after this period of time the spent yeast will begin to break down and impart a degree of off-flavors to your beer. But remember: There is really no advantage in keeping your beer sitting around for over 3 weeks unless you are brewing at cold temperatures and with quality lager yeast.

Homebrewers may brew with lager yeasts at room temperatures and "lager" in a second fermenter with good results when care is taken in sanitation. But you don't have to wait if you don't want to, because the beer will be freshest and taste its best within 3 or 4 weeks from starting. A second fermenter is convenient for brewers, such as myself, who never know when they are going to have time to bottle. Quite honestly, for one reason or another, I often don't get around to bottling for 4–6 weeks. So it is important for me to use closed fermentation and a second fermenter. I am quite pleased with my results.

OPEN VERSUS
CLOSED FERMENTATION

Open fermentation is a method of fermenting your beer in a loosely covered, cleaned and sanitized plastic container.

When considering that the number-one concern with making clean, fresh-tasting homebrew is sanitation, open fermentation should only be considered in the brewing of fast-maturing and quickly bottled ales (and room temperature "lagers"). Open fermentation can be followed by secondary fermentation in a closed container (locked away from the air with a fermentation lock) for a brief period of 1 or 2 weeks maximum. If the beer is "clean" and free of contaminants, the beer will survive for extended periods of time—BUT with initial open fermentation you add an element of risk. This risk is minimized with sanitation.

When your interest in homebrewing leads you to cold-brew, lager-type beers, you will ensure a much greater degree of success with closed fermentation because the longer it takes you to bottle your beer the cleaner your beer must be.

One advantage of open fermentation is its apparent simplicity for the beginner; also, the equipment (plastic fermenters) may be more accessible. There should be no problem in brewing this way as long as sanitation is emphasized.

Having a strained relationship? Then why not have a homebrew? When hops or grains are added to the brewpot they should be separated from the wort before entering the fermenter. Here, the hot boiling wort is poured into cold water that has already been added to the fermenter. NOTE: If a plastic fermenter is used, it is essential that it be fitted with a lid.

OPEN FERMENTATION AND BREWING IN PLASTIC

If you have purchased a beer kit that comes complete with a 5–10-gallon plastic bucket or brewing pail (often a food-grade trash pail) you can brew beer that is every bit as good as beer brewed in a closed fermenter. However, there are a few points to consider:

- Care should be taken to sanitize the container and everything that comes in contact with the beer.
- Do not use scratched or stained plastic containers. This type of surface is extremely difficult to sanitize because contaminating micro-organisms can hide and resist even household bleach.
- Brew only room temperature ales and "lagers" that will be ready to bottle within 2 or 3 weeks.
- Do not leave the fermenting beer in an open fermenter more than 7 days; either bottle if ready (stable hydrometer readings over a period of 2 or 3 days indicate that fermentation is complete) or carefully transfer by siphoning into a second fermenter and lock it away from the air with a fermentation lock.

ALL OTHER BREWING PROCEDURES ARE THE SAME FOR BREWING YOUR INITIAL BATCHES OF BEER.

Remember: Don't be intimidated. Brewing good beer is EASY. Relax. Don't worry. Have a homebrew.

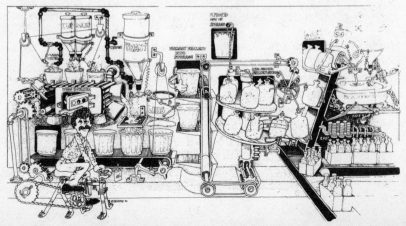

Betterbrew—
Intermediate Brewing
Brewing Our Best from Malt Extracts

INTRODUCTION

Now that you've successfully brewed your initial batches of homebrew you just might be more intrigued about the world . . . and brewing beer. An indeterminable amount of experience awaits you—beyond what you have accomplished so far, beyond the pages of this book. Don't ever believe for even one instant that you know all that you will ever want to know.

This Intermediate Section will increase your awareness of the process of brewing beer and introduce you to the unlimited versatility of brewing with malt extracts. You will learn how to combine malt extracts with traditional ingredients such as grains, hops, water and yeast, as well as unusual ingredients such as honey, fruit and various herbs and spices.

Brewing with "kit" beers and hop-flavored malt extracts is

often so rewarding that many homebrewers continue with their convenience, quality and incomparable character. But for many the intrigue of formulating and using recipes beckons.

Learning about and understanding the varieties of ingredients that go into beer will give versatility in achieving very specific character and flavor in homebrewed beer—perhaps even those perfect flavors that are unavailable to the beer drinker any other way. You will be giving yourself more choice.

This section will introduce you to additional procedures, concepts and the language of the brewer (a complete glossary precedes the appendices). The information provided in this section, as well as in any other part of this book, is for you to grow from and create your own experience. No one can tell you exactly how your beer is going to taste; only you can determine that.

Following recipes will not necessarily improve upon what you do and are able to accomplish . . . but understanding the process and what it is you are dealing with, will. Listening, seeing, learning, doing and FEELING is what brewing better beer is all about.

With this in mind and homebrew in hand you are ready to "Go for Greaterness."

EQUIPMENT

The equipment that you will use as an intermediate homebrewer is identical to that listed in the Beginner's Section with the exception that you may need additional glass carboys and fermentation locks for brewing more than one batch of beer at a time. For those larger batches you may need a larger pot.

When you do decide to enhance your brewing horizons you will need the following, in addition to the equipment listed in the Beginner's Section:

1 small kitchen strainer (approximately 6 inches across)
1 large strainer (at least 10 inches across)
1 extra refrigerator—only if you decide to brew cold fermented lager beers

1 bottle washer: This piece of equipment is listed in the Beginner's Section as "optional." While it is optional here also, it is a highly recommended piece of brewery equipment. Available at most homebrew supply shops, it is a simple device that not only conserves on hot water but is a convenience and a time-saver. Once you have one, you will never figure out why you were ever without it.

Thermometers

You will want a thermometer that reads temperatures from freezing to boiling. In degrees Fahrenheit this range is expressed as 32 degrees F (freezing) to 212 degrees F (boiling, 212 degrees F at sea level and about 200 degrees F at 5,000 feet elevation). In degrees Celsius (the centigrade scale) this range is expressed as 0 degrees C (freezing) to 100 degrees C (boiling at sea level).

A conversion formula is available in Appendix 13.

A good thermometer for homebrewing is one that will read degrees Fahrenheit from freezing to boiling and that will be sensitive enough to accurately indicate temperatures within 10 seconds. A good thermometer will cost between eight to fifteen dollars and is well worth the investment, particularly if you plan on trying your hand at some advanced brewing techniques.

Most references to temperature in this book will be in degrees Fahrenheit with degrees Celsius in parentheses.

Hydrometers

Your hydrometer is a useful tool in determining the status of fermentation activity. It can also indicate the amount of ingredients and alcohol percentage in your brew.

As previously explained, hydrometers are simple devices that measure the density of liquids. You immerse it in liquid, allowing it to float. Note how deeply it sinks into the liquid. When floating, the hydrometer displaces its own weight of the liquid and will therefore sink down deeper in a light liquid than in a heavier liquid (a liquid that may have dissolved sugars, such as unfermented beer).

Your hydrometer will have a specific gravity scale calibrated to read accurately at 60 degrees F (16 C). It is likely to have two other scales useful to the homebrewer. These hydrometers are called "triple-scale hydrometers." In addition to the specific gravity scale (explained in the Beginner's Section), there is a scale for determining the potential alcohol content of your beer and a scale called a "balling scale," read in degrees Plato. All of these scales coincide and are used to determine different types of information from the density of your brew.

The Balling Scale—This is the scale most commonly used by professional brewers in the United States and Continental Europe. It is also directly proportional to the specific gravity scale popularly used by homebrewers and the British brewing industry. The numbers that represent this measurement and expressed in degrees Plato are equal to one-fourth the value of the last three numbers that indicate specific gravity (e.g., 1.040 is equal to 10 degrees Plato; one fourth of 40 is equal to 10).

A density that measures one degree Plato means that 1 percent of the weight of the measured liquid is dissolved sugar. In other words, a density of 10 degrees Plato indicates that there would be 10 pounds of dissolved sugars in enough water to make 100 pounds of solution.

The Potential Alcohol Scale—This is a very easy scale for homebrewers to use. In order to determine the alcohol content of your beer, simply record the initial reading that you get from this scale before you add your yeast. From this number subtract the reading that you take at bottling time. For example, if your original reading was 6 percent and your final reading indicates 2 percent, your approximate alcohol content is 6 − 2 = 4 percent by volume.

The alcohol content of your beer can also be determined in a similar manner by using the specific gravity scale or balling scale.

Multiplying the difference between initial balling and final balling by the number .42 will give you an approximate measure of the alcohol content of your beer by percent weight. For example, if your initial balling was 15 and your final balling was 7, the difference would be 8, and 8 × .42 = 3.36 percent by weight.

To determine alcohol content by means of the specific gravity scale, likewise subtract the final specific gravity from the original specific gravity and multiply by 105 in order to get percent alcohol by weight. For example: $1.040 - 1.010 = 0.030$; thus, $0.030 \times 105 = 3.15$ percent.

Because alcohol is lighter than water, a measured volume of water is not equal by weight to an equal volume of alcohol. To convert percent alcohol by weight to percent alcohol by volume multiply by 1.25. Likewise, to convert percent alcohol by volume to alcohol by weight multiply by 0.80.

COLOR

As anyone knows who enjoys variety, the colors of beer can seem as wondrous as a rainbow. Instead of a pot of gold imagine there is a pot of hot wort at one end of the rainbow and a frothy mug of brew at the other.

From the very pale straw colors of American light lagers to the midnight mysteriousness of Irish stouts, there are hues of gold, orange, amber, brown, red, copper and yellow that enhance our enjoyment of each style of beer. With such variety of colors and intensity it is difficult to assess the "color" of beer in terms of a common language embodied in one system. A system for all styles of beers has never been worked out because beers may be darkened by brown, black, red or copper-colored malts, by added fruit, carmelization during the boil and other factors, all contributing a unique visual effect that cannot be measured by the degree of light passing through.

But something is better than nothing in this case, so brewing scientists have developed standards that measure the intensity of light and dark on a scale that ranges roughly from pale straw to black. Until recently a measuring system called the Lovibond scale was used to describe the color intensity of beer. Beer was compared to a defined set of colored samples of liquid. A vial of beer would be compared to vials of the color samples and assigned a degree Lovibond. It's worth noting that beer samples cannot be compared to printed colors. Why? Because the intensity of beer color will vary depending on the size and shape glass it is in. A test tube of your favorite stout may look brown, while

it is opaque in your favorite pint mug. That's why liquid samples have to be used in standardized vials.

Modern brewers use a system called the Standard Reference Method (SRM) to measure color intensity. This is a more sophisticated method involving the use of light meter–analyzers to assign a number (degrees SRM) to light intensity. Degrees SRM and degrees Lovibond are approximately the same and certainly can be used interchangeably by homebrewers to approximate the color intensity of their beers.

Certainly sophisticated equipment and worried concern about exacting color are beyond the interest of most homebrewers. However, we can use the SRM system to approximate references to color intensity to learn more about beer and brew different styles more accurately.

Here are a few standards that can serve as a guideline to help you interpret the SRM system.

Color Based on Standard Reference Method (SRM)		
Budweiser	2.0 degrees	
German Pils	3.0 degrees (average)	yellow/straw/gold
Pilsner Urquell	4.2 degrees	
Bass Pale Ale (export)	10 degrees	amber
Michelob Classic Dark	17 degrees	brown
Stout	35 and higher	black

BREWING BETTERBREW

What follows is an outline of a typical recipe for 5 gallons of beer made with a malt extract base.

Ingredients for 5 gallons:

   4–7 lbs. plain malt *extract*: syrup or dried powder

Plus one or any combination of the following specialty malts (grains):

   0–1 lb. crystal malt (or caramel malt)
   0–½ lb. black patent malt (or black malt)
   0–½ lb. chocolate malt
   0–½ lb. roasted barley

Other grains such as dextrine (or cara-pils) malt, Munich malt or malted barley may be used in malt extract brewing, but these require advanced brewing techniques and will be discussed later.

> 0–2 lbs. corn sugar (though not recommended)
> 1–2 oz. boiling hops (whole hops or pellets)
> ¼–½ oz. finishing hops
> 1–2 pkgs. beer yeast

The procedure for preparing 5 gallons of "Betterbrew" is almost as easy as brewing kit beers; the only difference is that you add the hops and specialty grains, thus gaining more variety in the beers you make.

From the above ingredients, you will prepare a wort (pronounced: wert). The term *wort* is universally used by all brewers to describe the "concoction" of unfermented beer. To make 5 gallons of beer, a concentrated wort is prepared by combining malt extract with 2 gallons of water, any cracked grains, sugar and hops and boiling for ½–1 hour. Three gallons of cold water are added to the fermenter. The hops and grains are then removed from the concentrated wort by passing the wort through a sanitized strainer and into the fermenter. The concentrated wort is then added to cold water in the fermenter, bringing the total volume to 5 gallons. Once the wort has cooled to below 78 degrees F (26 C) a hydrometer reading is taken and the yeast pitched (*pitching* is the term used to describe the inoculation of the wort with yeast).

From this point a homebrewer with any amount of experience could skip the following sections about ingredients and head straight for the recipes. You'll be able to make some pretty-good-tasting beer. But being able to continually make better beer with each new batch takes more than just using somebody's recipe.

This book is about learning and being able to understand your beer. It is about feeling your beer and letting your beer feel you. This is where the reward of homebrewing comes from.

The following sections describe the ingredients that are available for use by the homebrewer. The information is presented here for you to understand the fundamentals of brewing ingredients and for future reference.

COMPENDIUM OF INGREDIENTS

MALTED BARLEY AND MALT EXTRACT

Malted barley is one of the four essential ingredients of beer. From it is derived the fermentable sugars that contribute to the condition (carbonation), alcohol content and the fermented flavor of beer.

What Is Malted Barley and How Is It Made?

Essentially, barley is germinated to a certain degree, at which point it is then dried. This delicate process of germination and drying develops sugars, soluble starch and starch-to-sugar-converting enzymes (called *diastase*), all of which are valuable to the subsequent brewing process.

The malting process begins by choosing the appropriate variety of barley. Some varieties of barley are more suitable for the production of malt whiskey or food sweeteners. Others are more appropriate for making beer. When the choice of barley has been made, the kernels are tested for moisture, nitrogen (protein content) and viability (ability to germinate).

After barley is accepted for malting, it is taken from storage and cleaned, sorted and conveyed to steep (water) tanks. The procedure from the steep tank to the finished malt varies depending on the type of malt desired. Generally, the barley spends about 40 hours in tanks of fresh clean water with three intervals (eight hours each) during which the water is allowed to drain. Once moisture content reaches about 40–45 percent, the wet barley is conveyed to the germination room. Here it is allowed to germinate at temperatures carefully stabilized at about 60 degrees F (16 C). Over the approximate five-day germination period, air is blown up through the bed of grain. In addition, the grain is occasionally turned to prevent the rootlets from forming a tangle.

After five days, the wet malt becomes what is referred to as "green malt." Subsequent kilning (drying) of the green malt over a period of perhaps 30–35 hours and a gradual raising of temperatures to 122 degrees F (50 C) (for lager malts) or 221 degrees F (105 C) (for more strongly flavored malts) results in

Forever waves of grain! Temperature, air flow and the mechanical turning of the green malt are carefully controlled in the malt house. A germination and kilning room is shown here.

finished malt—a product of sugars, soluble starches and developed enzymes.

From the germination room, the malt is conveyed to machines that separate the rootlets from the malted barley. From here the malted barley is ready for the brewer.

Malting barley is a natural process that has been utilized by man. Normally, barleycorns are produced by barley plants in order to reproduce themselves. Remember, barley is a seed and is designed by nature to germinate and provide food for itself during its initial growth. The starch in barley is stored food. Upon natural germination a sprouting plant develops enzymes. These enzymes convert the stored food (starch) to usable plant food (plant sugars) for growth. As the growing plant is able to manufacture chlorophyll it will then be self-sufficient; chlorophyll will manufacture food for the plant from the sun's energy.

How Is Malted Barley Used in the Brewing Process?

From malted barley, sweet liquid can be made through a process called *mashing*. To this sweet liquid are added ingredients such as hops to complete the process of making a wort.

The first step in mashing involves the milling or grinding of the malt. The malt is ground so that the husk is removed and the kernel is broken into granular-size pieces. A measured amount of water is mixed with the ground malt to dissolve sugars, starches and enzymes. As the temperature of the "mash" is raised to 150–160 degrees F (66–71 C), the diastatic enzymes that are present in the malt become most active and convert soluble starches to sugars. The liquid mash becomes sweet in a matter of time. At this stage, the "spent" grains are separated from the sweet liquid. The sweet liquid is called "malt extract."

In a brewery (or with advanced homebrewing techniques), the sweet liquid is transferred to the brewing kettle and the brewing process is continued with the addition of hops and the boiling of the wort.

How Is the Malt Extract That Homebrewers Use Made?

The malt extract that homebrewers use comes in the form of syrup or dried powder. It would be very inconvenient and uneconomical for the malt extract manufacturers to package brewery-ready malt extract. They use sophisticated equipment to condense the malt extract by carefully evaporating much of the water.

The evaporation of water from malt extract takes place in a vacuum. Under a vacuum, these special evaporators allow liquid to boil at lower temperatures due to lower air pressure. Similarly, water boils at lower temperatures at higher altitudes (blood will literally boil in outer space, where there is no atmospheric pressure). This procedure is more economical as well as less harmful to the flavor of the malt extract. The temperatures at which malt extract will evaporate are usually around 105–160 degrees F (41–71 C).

If the final product is a syrup, the water content is usually about 20 percent, the other 80 percent being sugar and unfermentable solids that are important to beermakers.

If the final product is a dried powder, the malt extract has undergone a complete evaporation process by means of "spray-drying," thus removing almost all of the water.

When you use a malt extract syrup or powder, you add water again, thus "reconstituting" the original malt extract. With clean brewing techniques and quality ingredients, beers made from malt extracts will be every bit as good as similar styles of all-grain (no malt extract) beers.

Are All Malt Extract Syrups and Powders the Same?
No!

Over a hundred varieties of malt extract syrups and powders are available to the homebrewer. They vary quite a bit. All of the variables of making malted barley and malt extract manifest themselves in the final product. Furthermore, some malt extract products contain additives (which may or may not be desirable) such as corn syrup, sugar, caramel, minerals, preservatives, etc.

The variables of the malting and mashing process determine the final character of the beer being brewed. Those variables are things such as variety of barley, kilning time and temperature of the kiln during the malting process. Variables in the mashing process have a great influence on flavor, head retention, body, sweetness (or dryness), aroma, and fermentability of the wort. Most malt extracts for homebrewing are of excellent quality, but they will vary according to the character of beer that was intended by the individual malt manufacturer. The light malt extract made by one malt manufacturer will make a beer distinctively different from that made by another. Likewise, their amber, dark, pale . . . will all vary.

As a homebrewer, you can begin to realize the tremendous variety that awaits you.

Specialty Malts (Grains) for the Malt Extract Brewer
Specialty malts are used by homebrewers to add special and desirable character to beer. Color, sweetness, body and aroma

Go for greatness! Specialty malts add character to beer.

are a few of the characteristics that can be controlled and emphasized. Some styles of beers such as stout and bock cannot be made without specialty malts.

Specialty grains are prepared by crushing them. A small amount of pressure can be applied to a rolling pin as it passes over the grains. For those brewers who enjoy the use of a flour mill (grinder), the grinding plates may be adjusted to allow a slight crushing of the grain as it passes through. Grinding of any malt to powder is undesirable and should be avoided.

When Are Specialty Malts Added to the Homebrewing Process?

This question has been debated by many homebrewers and many homebrewing books. The fact is that when any whole grain is boiled in a wort, the latter will absorb certain flavors that are extracted from the husks of the grain, such as a certain amount of tannin and other substances. The flavor of tannin can be described as astringent or noticeably dry or grainy. Also, in the case of crystal malt, a very small amount of unconverted starches will be extracted that contribute to a haze (that does not affect the flavor) in the beer when it is chilled.

Many malt extract homebrewers boil specialty grains with

their wort, while others prepare a preliminary extract from these specialty grains, then remove the grains from the "soup" before adding malt extract and hops and commencing the boil.

To boil or not to boil, that is the question. . . .

For simplicity, boiling cannot be beat and satisfactory beer will result. Chill haze will not detract from the flavor, and the astringency of the tannin will mellow somewhat with age, though astringency may be so subtle that you won't even detect it.

You can easily avoid boiling grains by using a simple pre-boiling procedure. If grains are used, add them to your brewpot along with 1½ gallons of cold water. Then bring the water to a boil. When boiling commences, remove the grains with a small strainer. This method will extract the goodness of the specialty grains over the 15–25 minutes it takes to achieve boiling. This procedure also decreases the sharp and potential astringency that grains can contribute if boiled along with the malt extract. Aging time will be significantly reduced.

After you have removed the grains, add the malt extract and carry on. REMEMBER: don't worry! Do the best that you can manage and relax . . . Have a homebrew.

Some like it dark! Roasted barley, black patent and chocolate malts add color and distinctive character to stout, porter, bock and other dark beers.

Specialty Malts

Black Malt (Black Patent)—Black malt is produced from malted barley. Its production involves roasting the malted barley at temperatures so high that they drive off all of the aromatics (malt flavor).

Its use in brewing is chiefly for coloring the beer. Black malt will color the foam on beer but to a lesser degree than roasted barley (see Roasted Barley). In excess, black malt will contribute a dry burnt flavor to the beer that may be perceived as a bitterness different from that derived from hops.

There are no enzymes in black malt.

Chocolate Malt—No, this is not the chocolate malt you may have enjoyed as a kid (or still do as an adult). Chocolate malt is a dark brown malt that has been produced by the roasting of malted barley. It is not roasted quite as long as black malt; consequently, it is lighter in color and retains some of the aromatics and flavor of malt's sweetness.

It will impart a nutty, toasted flavor to the beer.

There are no enzymes in chocolate malt.

Crystal Malt (Caramel Malt)—Crystal malt is made from green malt; that is, malted barley that has not been kiln dried yet and

A body builder! Crystal malt lends a copper color as well as sweetness and full body to beer.

is produced by drying the wet germinated barley at controlled temperatures. It is first gently dried for a short time; then during a period of about 45–60 minutes the malt is "mashed" in the grain as temperatures rise to 212 degrees F (100 C). Most of the starch is quickly converted to sugar and while warm remains in a liquid state. Upon cooling, the sugars set to a hard crystal.

Because of the "mashing" process that the crystal malt has undergone, some of the soluble starches and sweet character will not ferment. Its addition to wort will enhance the sweetness of the beer. Adding crystal malt will also increase the body of the beer as well as aid in head retention. Because of its darker color, it will enrich the color, lending a gold or even reddish glow to the beer. Crystal malts come in light, medium and dark color varieties. Color is designated on the Lovibond scale: Light—20; Medium—40; Dark—90.

There are no enzymes in crystal malt.

Roasted Barley—Roasted barley is not made from malted barley. It is made by roasting unmalted barley at high temperatures. During the process, the temperature is gradually increased in excess of 392 degrees F (200 C) and carefully and frequently sampled in order to avoid charring. Roasted barley is not black in appearance; rather it is a rich dark brown.

Tasted as a grain, it has an assertive, roasted flavor, similar to roasted coffee beans. Especially used in the making of stout, it lends a distinctive roasted flavor as well as a bitterness. Its flavor is very distinct from black malt. It contributes significantly to the color of the beer and creates a brown head on the beer.

There are no enzymes in roasted barley.

Dextrine (Cara-Pils) Mild, Vienna and Munich Malts—These specialty malts are also available to the homebrewer. They can be used with malt extract but need to undergo a mashing process. Mashing will be explained later.

There are no enzymes in dextrine malt. It must be mashed in the presence of enzymes supplied by other malts. Its use will lend a fuller body to the beer and aid in head retention.

Mild malt is a very lightly toasted malt in the British style that contains enzymes. It will contribute an amber color to beer.

Vienna malt is a lightly toasted malt in the German style

that contains enzymes. It will contribute an amber color and some degree of fullness to beer.

Munich malt contains enzymes. It contributes a deep amber color to the beer and a malty sweetness.

HOPS

Hops are the conelike flowers of the hop vine. Their bitterness and bouquet are the primary considerations of the brewer. But their importance to the beer-brewing process goes beyond their contributions to flavor and bouquet. To an important extent they inhibit the growth of certain beer-spoiling bacteria. The use of hops also aids in flavor stability and head retention.

History

Brewers first used hops in making beer over a thousand years ago but only in the past 150 years with any regularity. Hops gained favor with brewers and beer drinkers because of their antiseptic and preserving qualities—no small concern before the age of refrigeration. Spoiled, sour batches of beer occurred all too frequently.

A very special elegance! Whole hop flowers are the ingredients that make beer bitter—not to mention giving it its very special bouquet and flavor—while also serving as a natural preservative.

Other plants and herbs were used to preserve beer. According to Sanborn C. Brown in his book, *Wine and Beers of Old New England: A how-to-do-it history*, spruce, ginger, ground ivy (also called cat's foot, alehoof, alecost, alehove, fieldbalm), sweet mary, tansy, sage, wormwood and sweet gale were often used.

Hops became the most popular preserving agent due to its tenacity, ease of cultivation and flavor. As science advanced it discovered that, in addition to preservation, hops can also help to coagulate and eliminate undesirable malt proteins in the brew kettle, aid clarification, promote good head retention and stabilize beer flavors as well as clean the beer drinker's palate of what traditionally was a more sweet, sticky, cloying brew.

Hops are now a major industry. As the demand increases, new varieties are forcing out older breeds in order to find a hop that is less susceptible to disease, retains freshness, has a high bitterness value per weight and is capable of being processed for shipment throughout the world.

Although hops can grow well in many regions of the world the major commercial hop-producing areas are Germany, the south of England, southern Australia, Tasmania and Washington State (U.S.A.). (See Appendix 7: Growing Your Own Hops.)

Hops that homebrewers obtain come from the same crops that supply major breweries and are available to the homebrewer in four forms: compressed whole hops, pelletized hops, hop extract and hop oil.

Hops and the Homebrewer

The most important thing to remember about hops is that it is a flower. If you will recognize this fact, then all the complexities of the hop and its involvement in the brewing process will be understood much more easily.

Hops can be infused into the brewing process at various stages in much the same way as various teas are made. As in tea, the results vary with preparation. Results will also vary with the ingredient, depending on the year-to-year crop and growing season. It is an ingredient in beer that is temperamentally moody and involves itself with every aspect of the brewing and tasting process.

There are dozens of cultivated varieties of hops, just as there are many varieties of apples. Each variety has its own spectrum of characteristics. Varieties of hops are chosen for the properties of bitterness, flavor or bouquet that they will lend to the beer. Different varieties will possess varying degrees of these characteristics. By choosing to use different varieties of hops, the brewer can decide what character his or her beer will have.

Because hops are of plant origin they are perishable. Some varieties are more perishable than others. Once they are picked from the vine they are gently dried. Then they are physically processed and packaged in a manner that will isolate them from excessive heat and oxygen. Heat and oxygen are the deteriorating factors that will spoil hops. As a homebrewer, understanding why oxygen and heat spoil hops will enhance your ability to recognize quality hops and make better beer.

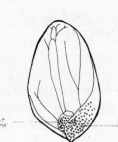

The bittering, flavoring and aroma-enhancing powers of hops come from oils and resins in the hop flowers. The tiny capsules of resin are called lupulin and can easily be identified at the base of the flower petals by what appears to be yellow powder. These resinous glands protect the essential oils but only for a given amount of time. As time, heat and oxygen work their effect on these oils they become rancid, just as any vegetable

Swollen glands! Tiny lupulin oil "glands" coat the base of the hop's flower petals. The lupulin contributes to the bitterness and aromatics of the hop.

oil will. The perishability of vegetable oils is, to a large degree, attributable to the reaction of oxygen with the oil—a process called oxidation. Cold temperatures and the removal of oxygen inhibit oxidation.

Regional styles of beer are influenced to a significant degree by the hops that are used. It is not peculiar for breweries that are situated in hop-growing country to be more highly hopped than in areas where hops must be "imported." For example, beers that are significantly more bitter and more aromatic are quite popular in Washington State and the south of England; both are hop-growing areas. Elsewhere, styles of beer emerge in areas where only certain varieties can be grown; such is the case with the original pilsener beer from Czechoslovakia, called Pilsner Urquell, brewed with the distinctive Saaz hop.

The point is that hops offer quite a bit of variety. Their use will depend on preferences of taste. It is indeed true that everyone perceives preference differently. Some will enjoy very bitter beers while others will prefer milder hop rates. Some disdain the bouquet of hops while others will celebrate the euphoric and aromatic attributes of hops. Brewers who like a lot of hops are often called ''hopheads.'' Whether or not you are a hophead, you have the opportunity to choose the right hop for your type of beer. There is no one right hop for everyone. As a home-brewer, you will be able to experiment to a degree that is not practical by the bigger commercial breweries. You will have more opportunity for choice and experimenting. Enjoy this opportunity.

What Makes Hops Bitter? Where Does the Hop Flavor and Bouquet Come From?

The biochemistry of hops and its interaction with the beermaking process can become quite involved. Yet in all of its wonderful complexity, the basics can be easily understood and effectively utilized as a foundation for the homebrewing of all beers.

As mentioned previously, hops produce lupulin glands containing resins and oils that are the major contribution to beer-making. They appear as bright yellow-gold, powdery balls located at the base of the flower petals (bracteoles). In reality, these yellow balls are not powdery at all but are tiny natural packages of oils and resins. When rubbed between the fingers, the packages will burst, releasing aromatic oils (which you can smell) as well as sticky resins. If these lupulin glands are orange, do not feel sticky or smell aromatic, they have been oxidized and are not suitable for brewing.

There are many other components of hops, but home-brewers are most concerned with the aromatic hop oils and two types of resins. The hop oils contribute to the hop flavor and bouquet in the finished beer. The resins contribute only to the bittering quality of the beer.

Bitterness—The two types of hop resins that are significant in contributing to beer's bitterness are called *alpha* and *beta*. Their presence is expressed in terms of alpha acid or beta acid and is measured by their weight relative to the weight of the hop flower. In other words, 6 percent alpha acids would indicate that 6 percent of the weight of the hop flower is alpha acid resins. It is the alpha acid resins that contribute most significantly to the bitterness of beer; consequently, the bittering capability of hops is expressed in terms of alpha acid percentage.

In order to give you some idea as to the amount of hops used in bittering beers, the following table is presented as a guideline.

HOP BITTERING CHARACTER FOR 5 GALLONS OF LIGHT- TO MEDIUM-BODIED PALE BEER

Percent Alpha Acids

ounces of hops	3–5%	6–7%	8–9%	10–12%
½ oz.			mildly bitter	mild– medium bitterness
1 oz.	very mildly bitter	mild– medium bitterness	medium bitterness	very bitter
2 oz.	mildly bitter	medium bitterness	very bitter	extremely bitter!!

NOTE: Lighter beers take less hops to be bitter. Heavier beers can stand to be more highly hopped.

Bittering Your Beer—Utilization of Alpha and Beta Acids—In order to utilize the bittering acids of the hops you *must* boil the hops with the wort. This boiling is done in your brewpot for 30–90 minutes. A rolling boil is necessary in order to physically and actively mix the alpha and beta acids with the sweet wort.

The reason that hops must be boiled in order to extract their bittering qualities is that the hop resins are not very soluble in water; in other words they will not dissolve into solution. The intense heat of boiling water creates a condition that allows a chemical reaction (called isomerization) to occur which makes the alpha acid resins soluble in water. In contrast, beta acids become soluble only when oxidized, the small amount of bitterness the beta acids contribute being the consequence of this oxidation. As a homebrewer you may be able to get some reasonable bitterness from old and oxidized hops, but off-flavors and inconsistency contribute negatively to the quality of the finished beer. Don't fool yourself.

REMEMBER: The alpha (and beta) acid resins contribute *only* to the bitterness of the beer.

How Bitter Is Bitter?—The Hop Bittering Character chart on page 64 will give you a rough idea of the relation of amount of hops used and the perceived bitterness of a light- to medium-bodied beer. But really, how bitter is bitter and how is it measured?

Brewing scientists have developed a method by which they measure what they call International Bitterness Units (IBU for short). One IBU is equal to 1 milligram of iso(merized) alpha acid in 1 liter of wort or beer. More IBUs in a given beer mean more bitterness perceived. But there is an enigma here because 20 IBUs in a rich, full-bodied malty stout will be perceived by the tongue as having far, far less bitterness than 20 IBUs in a light American-style lager beer. Both have the same amount of bittering substance but the perception will be different. *The lesson here is that a given amount of IBUs (i.e., hops used for bitterness) in a beer does not always equal the same amount of bitterness perceived.*

More information about International Bitterness Units is included later in this book in the Advanced Homebrewing and Hops section on page 265.

How Can a Homebrewer Know How Much Hops to Use to Acquire a Desired Bitterness?—By knowing the percentage of alpha acids in the hops you use, you can accurately match the desired bitterness levels in a given style of beer or recipe.

You may use some simple mathematics to predict IBU levels in any beer you brew (see Advanced Section on page 267). Or you may make a few assumptions and simply base your final beer bitterness on Homebrew Bitterness Units—the ounces and alpha acid content of the hops you use.

Homebrew Bitterness Units—Another method with which home-brewers can determine how much hops to use involves the concept of Homebrew Bitterness Units (HBUs).

Homebrew Bitterness Units = % alpha acid of hops
× ounces of hops

This is a very useful concept when a recipe for a given volume of beer calls for, say 2 ounces of 5 percent alpha acid Hallertauer hops, which is equal to 10 HBUs. It is important to note the volume of beer being brewed when using Homebrew Bitterness Units as a measurement of hops.

1) If your Hallertauer hops are only 4 percent alpha acid you will know to use:

10 HBU ÷ 4% = 2.5 oz. of hops

OR

2) If you wish to use another variety of hops, say Chinook hops at 10 percent alpha acid, you know to use:

10 HBU ÷ 10% = 1 oz. of Chinook hops

Hop Flavor and Bouquet—"Finishing" and Finishing Hops—Utilizing the flavor and aromatic constituents of hops can be quite pleasing. If overdone, it can blow you away. Hop flavor and bouquet is not for every beer drinker, but done with consideration it can provide quite an exciting variety to the character of beer. The process of adding hops for flavor and bouquet is called *finishing*; the hops used are called *finishing hops*.

The flavor of the hop and its associated bouquet come from the hop oils within the lupulin gland. These hop oils are not the same as the bittering resins. They are soluble in water and very volatile—that is, their essence will quickly "boil" away with the steam vapors. Remember, hops are flowers. If you desire to impart flavor and bouquet to your beer, the addition and preparation are similar to brewing a pot of well-made tea. Gently

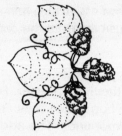

boiling or steeping the freshest hops during the final 1–15 minutes in the brewpot will impart varying degrees of flavor and bouquet (while not contributing much bitterness to the brew).

Dry hopping is a method that some brewers use to impart bouquet and some perception of bitterness (but not Bittering Units) to the finished beer. It is a simple procedure involving the addition of clean, dry hops to the secondary fermenter for 3 to 4 days prior to bottling. One-quarter of an ounce for 5 gallons will assert its character in beer. The dry hops must be removed before bottling. There is some risk involved in that the hops you are using may be contaminated with beer-spoiling micro-organisms. But generally, if hops are packaged well and look clean, the presence of significant amounts of bacteria is minimal. However, in order to reduce the possibility of contamination, I recommend that the dry hopping be done only after the majority of the fermentation is complete. For convenience and minimum of worry and fuss, hop pellets are excellent for dry hopping. The alcohol content and the natural acidity of fermented beer will inhibit bacterial growth. An unfermented wort is the perfect place for bacteria to grow.

I'm a hophead. I don't like to overpower my beers with hop flavor and bouquet, but I do like some recognizable degree of hop character. I have found that the most effective and most sanitary means of introducing hop flavor and/or hop bouquet to the beer is to add a small proportion of my best hops at the end of the boil—no longer than 5–15 minutes for deriving hop flavor and no longer than 1–2 minutes (steeping) at the end of the boil for hop bouquet. You must be ready to transfer and cool your hot wort immediately when using this method. It works, and it works well, without the mess of removing hops from the fermenter.

What Are Hop Oils?

Hop oils recently have become available to the homebrewer. By definition hop oils are the volatile oils in the hop cone. They are a very complex combination of chemical compounds. The addition of hop oils in parts per billion to beer can have a dramatic effect on the hoppy aroma and flavor of beer.

Hop oils should be used sparingly. The instructions provided by the manufacturer should be followed carefully. They can be introduced into beer much the same way that finishing hops are—at the end of the boil, during or after fermentation or just before bottling.

Hop oils are difficult to use properly because they are not soluble in water or beer, therefore the oils must be dissolved in a solventlike medium. Grain (ethyl) alcohol or high-proof vodka are perfect for mixing with a measured amount of hop oil and then adding to the wort or beer. If hop oils are not predissolved you will only get an oil "slick" on your beer and a minimum contribution of flavor and aroma.

Consult the manufacturer's suggestions, but a rule of thumb with which to begin your own experimentation is to use hop oils at a rate of 10 to 50 parts per million (.2 ml to 1 ml) when adding oils to 5 gallons (end volume) of hot wort at the end of the kettle boil. Begin experimenting with adding hop oils at a rate of 1 to 10 parts per million (.02 to .2 ml) when dosing 5 gallons during postfermentation stages.

What Are Hop Pellets?

Hop pellets are nothing more than whole hops mechanically processed by what is called a hammer-mill. This machine pulverizes the entire hop. The pulverized hop and ruptured lupulin glands are then forced into a pelletizing machine for compressing and extruding the hops into pellets. The pellets are held together naturally by their own oils and resins.

The disadvantage of pelletizing hops is debatable. It has

It's not what you think it is! These hop pellets are the result of a mechanical transformation of whole hops. Whole hops are "milled," then compressed into pellets. They are convenient space savers and resist spoilage.

been argued that the rupturing of the lupulin glands will detract from the subtle flavor and bittering ability of the hop. The most significant disadvantage of hop pellets is that they are not easily removed from the wort. For homebrewers, the removal of hop pellets from the wort can be done using a stainless weave strainer and is essential if the blow-off hose method of fermentation is used. The other significant disadvantage of hop pellets is that a natural "filter bed" (used to create clear worts for fermentation) cannot be created during the straining (sparging) process.

Hop pellets are perishable over a period of time. Oxygen will diffuse into the pellet and heat will enhance the process.

The advantages of pelletizing hops are threefold. First, very little storage space is needed. Second, the freshness of the hops is more easily controlled; oxygen can only easily reach the surface layer of resins and oil, the rest of the hop oils and resins are more protected within. Finally, blends of hops can be processed into one pellet.

What Are Hop Extracts?

Hop extract is the liquid bittering essence of hops and is used for convenience in the brewing industry. Some liquid hop extracts are processed with a wide variety of chemical solvents that dissolve the hop resins into solution and chemically "isomerize" these resins so that they are soluble in beer wort. New methods of extraction involving liquid (supercold) carbon dioxide have been developed to extract both the bittering resins and volatile oils. These hop extracts and oils are available to the homebrewer.

Hop extracts presently available have no flavor or aromatic value. Their use by homebrewers is minimal. If you choose to use hop extract, do so with care and knowledge of how powerfully bitter it is. Also, be sure to always boil the hop extract in the wort or at least a small amount of water unless specifically told that it is unnecessary. Some hop extracts are processed with toxic chemical solvents that are still present in very small amounts. Boiling will volatize (evaporate) them.

Hopped Malt Extract and Hopped Beer Kits

If you purchase malt extract that is hop flavored and you are wondering about the character of the hop flavor in the malt, reading the label will begin to give you some indication of what to expect.

Hop-flavored malt extracts are hopped with whole hops, pellets or hop extract. If hop extract is used, there will be no hop flavor or bouquet, only bitterness. If you desire hop flavor or bouquet, you will have to add it yourself. Some beer kits and malt extracts are hopped with whole or pelletized hops. The boiling of worts made from these malt extracts will dissipate much of the hop flavor and bouquet unless done for a shorter period of time.

How to Recognize Quality Hops

It is very important for you, the homebrewer, to get fresh or well-cared-for hops. You are not doing yourself any favors or saving any money by buying old hops. It isn't too difficult to recognize the difference between good and bad hops.

Take your pick—but go for freshness! One-quarter ounce of whole hops (left) contrasts with three ounces of hop pellets (right).

Look, feel, smell . . . listen to all your senses. Whole hops and pellets should be green in appearance. (Some British-imported hops have been sulfured in order to help preserve freshness. They may be gold in appearance.) Oxidation will turn them a dry brown color. The lupulin glands in whole hops should be a recognizably bright yellow color. Lupulin will turn orange in color when oxidized. When rubbed between the fingers, quality whole hops will feel sticky due to the rupturing of the lupulin glands; also, the aromatic oils can be smelled. A nonsticky, dusty feeling and/or cheesy aroma suggests oxidation.

The packaging of whole hops and hop pellets is extremely important. Oxygen-barrier plastic bags or aluminum foil bags from which oxygen has been removed and replaced with nitro-

gen are the best ways of preserving hops for the homebrewer. Refrigeration prolongs the life of packaged hops even longer and is absolutely essential for hop pellets or whole hops packaged in non-oxygen-barrier plastic bags. If you are able to smell hops through a plastic bag, the bag is not an oxygen-barrier bag.

Well-cared-for hops are important. Homebrewers use many varieties that will deteriorate and lose 50–70 percent of their brewing value within weeks if not packaged and stored appropriately.

What Varieties of Hops Are Available to the Homebrewer?

The chart on page 74 is a compilation of varieties of hops with brief descriptions regarding alpha acid content (bitterness), stability (perishability), origin and miscellaneous comments.

REMEMBER: Hops are flowers that come from plants. Their average alpha acid content as delineated in this chart is a generalization and will vary from year to year, crop to crop and with handling. Your source for hops should be able to obtain accurate information about the hops that are being offered. A rating of 4–5½ percent alpha acid content indicates low bittering values; 5½–8 percent alpha acid indicates an assertive medium range of bitterness; while 8–13 percent alpha acid indicates a very powerful bittering value—with these hops be careful not to overhop!

The stability rating in the chart is an indication to you how much care hops need. Ratings of ''poor'' or ''fair'' indicate the importance of refrigeration or proper packaging; they are capable of losing 50 percent of their brewing value within 2 to 3 weeks at room temperatures. ''Good'' or ''very good'' stability indicates that these hops will last a very long time with proper packaging.

There are no set rules for using hops. Any variety may be used as a bittering hop in both ales and lagers; likewise, any variety of hop may be used for flavor and aroma (finishing hop). The ''no rule'' statement is especially true for homebrewers, though it should be recognized that certain varieties of hops are used to impart distinctive types of bitterness, flavor and aromas to traditional styles of lagers and ales. The chart offers some comments on traditional uses of each variety, but feel free to experiment on your own.

Even though there are many classic styles of beer in the world that lay claim to the use of special hops, hops alone do not make for the duplication of a classic style of beer. It is a combination of all of the other ingredients, brewing style and attitude that truly makes for distinctive and world-classic beers— and your homebrew.

As a homebrewer, your affair with hops should be an enjoyable one. If there is ever any doubt in your mind, remember: RELAX. DON'T WORRY. HAVE A HOMEBREW.

WATER

Beer is 90–95 percent water. The flavor and mineral content of water is important in the brewing of beer. However, the importance of water is relative to all of the other ingredients and processes that are involved with the brewing of quality beer. The best brewing water in the world cannot make good beer without good malt, yeast, sanitation and brewing attitudes.

Water and its properties interact with every process of beermaking; malting, mashing, boiling, fermentation, cleaning and tasting all derive their efficiency and character, in part, from the water that is used. The chemistry of water and its interaction with the brewing process can become quite involved. But as a homebrewer you don't need a degree in organic chemistry to appreciate its value in brewing

If the water you use for brewing is suitable for drinking in the United States, then there is only one thing you as a beginner or intermediate brewer might consider doing to improve it. Some municipal water supplies have chlorine content that is excessive for brewing the absolute best beer. Using a countertop activated-charcoal-type water filter will remove chlorine. Or you might consider boiling your water before brewing to rid the water of free available chlorine, thus minimizing the reactions between chlorine and beer ingredients that can result in a perceptible harshness in flavor and aroma.

HOMEBREWER'S REFERENCE CHART—HOP VARIETIES

Variety	Average Alpha Acid Content (percent)	Stability	Origin	Comments
Aquila	6–7.5	Fair	U.S.	Developed as an aroma hop; early 1990s
Banner	9.5–10.5	Fair	U.S.	Developed as a bittering hop; early 1990s
Bramling Cross	5–6	Poor	U.K.	Crossbred Goldings, traditional ale hop, good for ale finishing
Brewers Gold	8–9	Poor	U.S./U.K.	Traditional ale hop
Bullion	8–9	Poor	U.S./U.K.	All-purpose bittering hop, poor aroma
Cascade	5–6.5	Poor	U.S.	All-purpose bittering and aroma hop, citrusy character
Centennial/ CFJ-90	7–8	Poor	U.S.	"Supercharged" Cascade; fine aroma hop, citrusy, developed in late 1980s
Challenger	7–9	Poor	U.K.	Rare
Chinook	11–13	Very good	U.S.	Very bitter, aroma preferred by some
Cluster	6–8	Excellent	U.S.	Popular bittering hop, minimal oil, poor aroma and flavor
Columbia	9–10	Fair	U.S.	Rare
Comet	8–11	Fair	U.S.	Rare
Eroica	10–12	Fair	U.S.	Very bitter

Variety	Average Alpha Acid Content (percent)	Stability	Origin	Comments
Fuggles	4–5.5	Fair	U.S./U.K.	High seed content. traditional British ale bitter and aroma hop
Galena	12–13	Very good	U.S.	Very popular bittering hop. very bitter
Goldings	4.5–5.5	Fair	U.S./Canada	Traditional British ale bittering and aroma hop
Green Bullet	10–11	Good	New Zealand	Very bitter
Hallertauer	4.5–5.5	Poor	U.S./Germany	Excellent aroma: traditional lager spicy flavor and aroma: U.S. and German varieties differ distinctly
Hallertauer Hersbrucker	4.5–5.5	Poor	Germany	Excellent aroma: traditional lager hop. spicy flavor and aroma
Hallertauer Mittelfrüh	4–6	Poor	Germany	Excellent aroma: traditional lager hop. spicy flavor and aroma: considered finer than that grown in the Hersbrucker region: softer impact on palate
Huller	4–6	Fair	U.S.	Good aroma and bittering hop
Kent Goldings	4.5–5.5	Fair	U.K.	Excellent traditional British ale bittering and aroma hop

HOMEBREWER'S REFERENCE CHART—HOP VARIETIES

Variety	Average Alpha Acid Content (percent)	Stability	Origin	Comments
Mt. Hood	5–6	Fair	U.S.	Very good aroma; bred to resemble Hallertauer character
Northdown	7.5–9.5	Good	U.K.	Good bitter. flavor and aroma
Northern Brewer	7.5–9	Fair	U.S./Germany	Traditional European lager bittering hop
Nugget	11–13	Good	U.S.	Very bitter. good aroma
Olympic	10–13	Fair	U.S.	Rare
Orion	7–9	Fair	–	–
Perle	7–9	Good	U.S.	Good bittering and aroma for lagers; bred to resemble German Northern Brewer
Pride of Ringwood	7–9	Good	Australia/Canada	Bittering hop
Progress	7–8	Good	U.K.	Rare
Record	5–7	Fair	Germany	Poor aroma
Saaz	4–6	Fair	Czechoslovakia	Traditional European (pilsener) lager hop; spicy flavor and aroma excellent
Saxon	6.5–8.5	Very good	U.K.	Rare
Spalt	6–7.5	Poor	Germany	Traditional German bittering and aroma hop

Variety	Average Alpha Acid Content (percent)	Stability	Origin	Comments
Stickelbract	9–11	Good	New Zealand/Australia	Very bitter
Styrian Goldings	5.5–7	Fair	U.S./Yugoslavia	Very good British ale hop: good aroma
Super Styrian	7–9	Good	Austria/Czechoslovakia	Similar to Styrian Goldings and Saaz
Talisman	7–9	Good	U.S.	Similar to Cluster: rare
Target	9–11	Poor	U.K.	Widely available in U.K.
Tettnanger	4–6	Poor	U.S./Germany	Very good lager hop: American variety floral and very distinct from German variety (more spicy)
Viking	6–8.5	Good	U.K.	Rare
Willamette	5–6	Fair	U.S.	Developed as a seedless Fuggles: excellent aroma; ale or lager
Wye Target	9–11	Fair	U.K.	Very bitter
Yeoman	10–11.5	Very good	U.K.	General availability in U.K.
Zenith	8.5–10.5	Good	U.K.	General availability in U.K.

About stability—Very good: 90% of bitterness remains after 4 months of storage at 70 degrees F (21 C); Good: 80–90%; Fair: 60–80%; Poor: less than 60% and some will suffer dramatic loss within a month. Note: Stability is extended when stored at cold temperatures and in an oxygen-free environment.

The addition of minerals to your brewing water for malt extract brewing is a very minor consideration compared to the importance of sanitation and quality brewing ingredients.

What Determines Water Quality?

Water quality is determined by its flavor, its suitability for human consumption and the related organic and mineral content. Potable and good-tasting water is almost always suitable for use in homebrewing of malt extract beers; however, it is the mineral content that determines ideal suitability in many phases of the brewing process.

Chemically, water is measured in terms of its hardness (or softness) and acidity or alkalinity (pH or parts per million [ppm] of certain minerals).

Some of the more common brewing "salts" (minerals) that are added or measured in brewing water are calcium sulfate ($CaSO_4$, commonly known as gypsum) and sodium chloride (common salt: NaCl). When these or any mineral salts are dissolved in water they go through a process called dissociation, that is, the calcium (ion) separates itself from the sulfate (SO_4) ion; likewise, the sodium ion separates itself from the chloride ion. The presence of each of these "ions" or any other ion will not only contribute characteristic flavors to the beer but may have the potential to react with other minerals and ions that are present in the other ingredients in the beer.

How Does Water Quality Influence the Brewing Process?

Let it suffice, here, to say that the most important mineral reactions in the brewing process occur during the mash, when the enzymes convert starches to fermentable sugars. Understanding water chemistry begins to become important in the brewing of all-grain beers. A discussion of all-grain brewing and related water chemistry will come later.

As a malt extract homebrewer, all of the mashing reactions have taken place and the addition of minerals is unnecessary. *In fact the minerals that the malt extract manufacturer may add in their mashing process remain in the malt extract.*

For the malt extract homebrewer the only mineral ions that contribute significantly to the brewing process are the ions of gypsum ($CaSO_4$) and common salt (NaCl). The calcium ion will help the clarification process during fermentation; the yeast will more easily sediment. Also, calcium ions will aid in removing proteins, tannins and husk flavors from the boiling wort; if not removed to some degree, they will lend a haze as well as a harsher flavor to the finished beer. Sulfates (SO_4) will lend a dry, crisp palate to the finished beer. However, if sulfates are added in excess, poor hop utilization will result (bitterness will not easily be extracted). Also, a harsh, salty and laxative nature will characterize the finished beer. The sodium ion (Na) will contribute to the perceived flavor of beer by enhancing other flavors. In excess, it will contribute to a harsh, sour or metallic flavor. Chlorides (Cl) will tend to lend a soft, round, full, sweet flavor to beer.

Any mineral in excess will ruin your beer. As a general rule, all of these minerals are present in malt extracts and to varying degrees in your own water source (information about the contents of your drinking water is available at no cost from your local water department). The addition of these minerals to any great degree is not necessary. As a matter of fact, when brewing with malt extracts, distilled or deionized (mineral-free) water is perfectly suitable for brewing.

If you do choose to add gypsum or salt to your water, do so knowing the original mineral content of your water. For water that has very little mineral content (soft), the addition of 1–4 teaspoons of gypsum per 5 gallons is within reason. The addition of salt should not exceed ½ teaspoon per 5 gallons.

Advanced Water Chemistry and Duplication of World-Classic Brewing Waters

Water chemistry begins to get very complex when minerals begin to react with each other and the other ingredients that are used in the brewing process; consequently, not only are the hardness, acidity and alkalinity actively affected by brewing ingredients but the actual mineral content fluctuates as well. The possible outcomes are characterized by terms such as *permanent* and *temporary hardness*, and *permanent* and *temporary alkalinity*, expressed in terms of parts per million of certain minerals or a measurement of pH, respectively.

Adding your own minerals to achieve a desired effect is complicated and requires an effort on your part to understand the chemistry of water. You are only asking for problems by simply following water recipes without, at least, having a feel for what reactions are taking place. You don't need to be an expert. Learning the fundamentals of brewing chemistry is not an unreasonable challenge if you have the desire. A more involved section on brewing water is presented in the Advanced Section.

YEAST

The type of yeast that you use in brewing is as important as any other ingredient in your beer. Yeast is biologically classified as a fungus. It is a living microbiological organism, metabolizing, reproducing and living off the ingredients that you have concocted in order to make beer. Yeast is the thing that finally determines what the flavor of the beer will be.

There are literally hundreds of varieties and strains of yeasts. They are present everywhere as "wild yeast." Only cultivated strains of beer yeast should be used in the brewing of beer. If other strains or wild yeasts contaminate your beer, the result will often be strange flavors, gushing, overcarbonation, haze formation and all kinds of unexplainable fermentation characteristics.

What Are the Main Types of Beer Yeast?

There are two main varieties of beer yeast that are used by brewers. They are classified as *ale yeast* ("top-fermenting" type, *Saccharomyces cerevisiae*) or *lager yeast* ("bottom-fermenting" type, *Saccharomyces uvarum*, formerly known as *Saccharomyces carlsbergensis*). These two varieties of beer yeast are further broken down into categories of specific strains. In the world of brewing today there are hundreds of strains of both ale and lager yeasts, all of which will offer variety to the finished beer.

Varieties of Yeasts and Concerns of the Homebrewer

You can make absolutely excellent beer at room temperatures from either ale yeast or lager yeast. Understanding some basic principles of yeast behavior will help you answer some of the questions arising when using different yeasts.

Ale yeast is a variety of yeast that is best used at temperature ranges of 55–75 degrees F (13–24 C). Lower temperatures tend to inhibit fermentation; some strains will not actively ferment below 50 degrees F (10 C). Some strains of ale yeast exhibit a tendency to flocculate (gather) at the surface of the fermenting beer during the first few days of fermentation; that is why the term "top-fermenting" is associated with all ale yeasts. Eventually, ale yeast will sediment on the bottom of the fermenter. Fermentation by ale yeasts at these relatively warmer temperatures produces a beer which many regard as having a distinctive ale character. It should be remembered that other ingredients play an equally important role in the flavor of ale.

Lager yeast is a variety of yeast that is best used at temperatures ranging from an initial 55 degrees F (13 C) down to 32 degrees F (0 C). Beer can be fermented by lager yeasts at room temperatures with very good results; however, the desired "smoothness" of lager beers can be better achieved with lagering at temperatures usually below 45 degrees for anywhere from three weeks to many months. The final flavor of the beer will depend a great deal on the strain of lager yeast and the temperatures at which it was fermented. All strains of lager yeast will flocculate and then settle to the bottom of the fermenting vessel; that is why they are called bottom-fermenting yeasts.

Where Can Good Brewing Yeasts Be Found and How Are They Packaged?

Good beer yeasts can be found at any homebrew supply shop.

Most beer yeasts used by homebrewers come in the form of dried yeast in sealed foil packages. The popularity of foil packages of liquid yeast cultures has increased with their availability. Numerous strains of both lager and ale yeasts are available from many different companies and some friendly small breweries.

The advantages of dried beer yeast are that it is simple to use, usually very active and foolproof. One can significantly improve the performance of dried yeasts (and consequently the flavor of your beer) by properly rehydrating it. Do this by boiling 1½ cups of water for 5–10 minutes, pour into a sanitized glass jar (washed and boiled for about 15 minutes), cover with clean foil and let cool to 100–105 degrees F (38–41 C). Do not add any sugars. Add dried yeast and let rehydrate for 15–30 minutes, then bring the temperature of the rehydrated yeast close to that of the wort and pitch.

True cultures of dried lager yeasts are difficult to find due to the difficulty in packaging and maintaining the true lagering characteristics. In order to determine whether or not the dried lager yeast will exhibit fermentability at low temperatures,you must experiment and observe. If you find that fermentation is not active at lower temperatures, then you are doomed to ferment those dried lager yeasts at room temperature or use liquid cultures.

True lager yeasts are best propagated from liquid cultures. Their use and care are more involved than the simplicity of using very active dried beer yeast. More about liquid yeasts and their culture will be discussed later.

Fermentation and the behavior of yeasts is a most interesting part of beer brewing. Remember that yeast is a living micro-organism that may be as temperamental as you are. Understanding what makes yeast do its thing will help make your beer better.

MISCELLANEOUS INGREDIENTS OFTEN USED BY HOMEBREWERS

SUGARS

Sugar is the ingredient in beer that lends sweetness to the finished product or becomes fermented by yeasts into alcohol, carbon dioxide and the flavor of beer. There are many, many different kinds of sugar that can be introduced into the brewer's wort. Some are naturally introduced with malted barley or other grains, while others may be "artificially" introduced by the brewer for economic reasons or to achieve some very distinctive flavor characteristics.

Sugars are scientifically classified by names such as sucrose, glucose, maltose, etc., according to their molecular configuration. The sources of sugar are very numerous; for example, sucrose is naturally present in malt, honey, maple syrup, molasses, corn syrup and more.

In order to help you understand the classifications of sugar and the forms that they take, let's look at the basic molecules of sugar.

Sugars are made from various configurations of carbon, hydrogen and oxygen atoms. The general configuration of these

atoms is called a carbohydrate. The way these carbohydrates are linked determines the type of sugar.

The sugars homebrewers encounter most often are dextrose, fructose, glucose, lactose, maltose and sucrose. These sugars are often derived naturally from malt or other starches. Another kind of carbohydrate, starch, is long chains of sugar molecules linked together by chemical bonds. The chemical bonds of starch can be broken by enzymes and chemical reactions, thus reducing the long carbohydrate chains of starch to shorter chains of sugar.

Are you still with me? It is helpful to know that some sugars are sweeter than others; likewise some sugars are more easily fermented by yeast and others are not fermentable at all. Although there are dozens of types of sugars involved in the brewing process, some are more significant than others. Following are sweet and short descriptions of the main types of sugars most often encountered by homebrewers. Their availability is discussed later.

Classifications of Sugars

Dextrose—See ''Glucose.''

Fructose (or levulose)—Fructose is one of the most rapidly fermentable sugars. It is also the sweetest tasting. Besides occurring naturally in malt and fruit it may be derived from a variety of starches and processed to a syrup form. The term ''high-fructose'' syrup does not mean 100 percent fructose, rather more likely a combination of 40 percent fructose and 60 percent glucose and other sugars. Fructose crystals are derived from cane or beet sugar.

Glucose—Glucose is another very rapidly fermentable sugar. As a purchasable form of sugar it has usually been derived from starch. It can be processed into chips, crystals or syrups. The name ''dextrose'' is an industrial term for glucose. Glucose and dextrose are molecularly one and the same. The distinction is that dextrose is glucose that has been derived from a chemical conversion of starch (usually corn) to sugar. Dextrose is often referred to as ''corn sugar.''

Lactose—Lactose is a sugar that is not fermentable by beer yeast (it is fermentable by certain types of wild yeasts). It is derived from milk and can be bought as crystals. Its flavor is minimally sweet.

Maltose—Maltose is fermentable by beer yeasts but relatively more slowly than are sucrose, glucose and fructose. It occurs naturally in malt, as well as in a wide variety of other natural sweeteners. It consists of two glucose molecules linked together.

Sucrose (and invert)—Sucrose is rapidly fermentable by beer yeasts. It occurs naturally in malt. Commercially it is available in crystalline form, usually as common white table sugar. Invert sugar is a type of sugar that is made from an acid treatment of sucrose. The name "invert" refers to the optical effect that a solution of invert sugar has on light.

Like sucrose, it is a combination of one glucose and one fructose molecule. Pure invert sugar is as fermentable as sucrose; but because of by-products that are produced during the acid treatment, invert sugar may be 5–10 percent less fermentable than sucrose and can contribute unusual flavor characteristics.

Availability and Use of Various Sugars Used in Homebrewing
White Sugars

Cane and beet sugars—These common white table sugars are nearly 100 percent sucrose. There is virtually no difference between pure grades of beet or cane sugars. Impure grades can lend distinctively unpleasant flavors to beer. In homebrewing they may be used for economy, to boost the alcohol content, to lighten the flavor and body of the beer. If cane or beet sugar is used in excess of 30 percent of the fermentable sugar, a characteristic "cidery" flavor may develop. White sugar does not contribute to any real flavor of beer.

Cane or beet sugar may be converted to invert (sucrose) sugar by boiling in water with a small amount of citric acid; however, this process is unlikely to eliminate the flavor associated with the excessive addition of sucrose and is a needless process. If sugar is something you want to add to your beer, use corn sugar (dextrose, glucose). The partial or complete inversion of sucrose may occur while being boiled in the naturally acidic wort of malt extract.

For sanitation purposes all common white table sugars should be boiled in water or in the wort.

Corn sugar—Corn sugar is the most commonly used sugar "adjunct" in homebrewing. Processed from refined corn, it is referred to as dextrose; technically it is more accurately glucose and readily fermentable. Purer grades of corn sugar should be used by the homebrewer. Corn sugar can be easily bought at any homebrew supply store.

The addition of corn sugar to homebrew recipes will lighten the body and flavor of the beer and at the same time contribute to the alcohol content. Its use in excess of 20 percent of the total fermentable sugars will often contribute to the flavor characteristic of the finished beer, lending what most homebrewers will refer to as a dry "cidery" flavor. While this character is desired by some, it does not contribute to a true malt beer character. Its use, although economical, should be carefully considered by the homebrewer who values the time spent brewing and waiting for beer to mature and be fully enjoyed.

The addition of corn sugar as a "priming" sugar at bottling time is the most versatile use of corn sugar. A ratio of ¾ cup of corn sugar dissolved and boiled in 1 pint of water is a standard rate for 5 gallons of beer.

Corn sugar should be boiled with wort or water before its addition to the fermenter or finished beer.

Lactose—Lactose can be added to fermenting or finished beer in order to achieve slight sweetness and additional body. It can be purchased at many homebrew specialty shops or health food stores as white crystals. Because it is not fermentable by beer yeasts, its character will remain unchanged. It is not a very sweet tasting sugar, therefore its contribution to sweetness is minimal. Some commercial British breweries will add it to "sweet stouts" in order to contribute to the body of the beer. In the case of British sweet stouts, sucrose is added for sweetness to a pasteurized and conditioned (carbonated) product at bottling time.

Lactose is not easily dissolved in beer; therefore, it should be boiled with small amounts of water before its addition to the beer.

Brown Sugars and Molasses

Light–dark brown sugars—These American household sugars are nothing more than refined white (sucrose) table sugar with a very small amount of molasses added. Current U.S. regulations require that all cane or beet sugar be refined. The addition of brown sugars is no different from the addition of white table sugar with a small amount of molasses (see "Molasses"). Ten percent or less (of the total amount of fermentable sugar) of these types of sugars can contribute a personal touch to your homebrewed beers.

Brown sugars should be boiled in wort or water before adding to the fermenter.

Molasses—Molasses syrups are the uncrystalized sugars and impurities that are removed during the refinement of sugars. They are fermentable to a variable degree, depending on the type of molasses. Their addition to beer will certainly lend a great deal of color and flavor. Because of the strong flavor associated with the unfermentable portion of molasses, its use should be limited. For example, an amount of 1 cup per 5 gallons will certainly be discernible by most people. Its contribution to homebrew is likened to a rich and "buttery" flavor similar to a British ale called Old Peculier. It can contribute a certain pleasantness to beer, but in excess satiates the palate and detracts from the drinkability.

There are three common grades of molasses: light, medium and blackstrap. All molasses contain a varying degree of aromatics that contribute to flavor. The lighter molasses contain a higher sucrose (with some fructose and glucose) content while the darker blackstrap molasses contains less sugar (about 65 percent sucrose) but more aromatics.

Note: Sorghum molasses is a special kind of molasses (see "Syrups: sorghum").

Molasses should be boiled with the wort or water before introducing it to fermentation. For carbonating purposes 1 cup of molasses may be substituted for ¾ cup of corn sugar (for 5 gallons of beer) at bottling time.

Raw sugar (or turbinado)—In the United States, raw sugar is similar in character to a very light brown sugar. A small amount of molasses contributes to its color. Its character is no different from that of cane or beet sugar.

Date sugar—Derived from date figs, this sugar may be worth experimenting with. It is actually ground-up dried date figs with no further processing. I have never used it, but it should contribute uniqueness to your beer. Be aware that because it is literally ground dates it will not dissolve completely.

Syrups

Corn syrup—There is a wide variety of corn syrups available, ranging from "brewers-grade" to common household corn syrup. Consequently, the sugar content of these syrups will vary tremendously. Some corn syrups will be highly fermentable while others will leave unfermentable residual sweetness and character in the finished beer. Brewing grades of corn syrup are usually a mixture of glucose and maltose. It is difficult for the home-brewer to obtain these syrups except when already added to certain varieties of malt extracts. Household corn syrups are available in most grocery stores; however, care should be taken to read the label in order to discern the addition of flavoring (vanilla, etc.) and yeast-inhibiting preservatives, neither of which are desirable in beer. Dark, household corn syrup is nothing more than the lighter variety with coloring added (usually caramel).

Corn syrups may be used in homebrewing. Depending on the type of corn syrup used, they will contribute to the alcohol content and various degrees of residual sweetness, flavor and body. As with any sugar adjunct, an excess of 20 percent will detract from a real beer character.

Corn syrups should be boiled with the wort or with water before their addition to the fermentation.

Sorghum—Sorghum is a dark, sweet syrup similar in character to molasses and sometimes called sorghum molasses. It is derived from the pressed juices of sweet sorghum grown in warmer temperate climates. Its use should be similar to molasses (see ''Molasses'') and lends a unique flavor to beer.

Maple syrup—Yes, it can be used as a beermaking ingredient. It is mostly sucrose, water and trace minerals. In the first edition of this book I confessed I had never used nor tasted beer made from maple syrup. Now, thanks to many readers who have shared their maple-syrup-flavored beer, I feel very privileged to say, ''Yes, please do.'' I enjoyed the samples when maple syrup was used liberally, and only when the beer was a sweeter, fuller-flavored style that allowed it did the maple flavor shine through. I'd recommend at least 1 gallon (oh, how that hurt$) per 5 gallons of beer.

I also have had the pleasure of tasting beer made from maple sap instead of water. Fantastic—the beer had a subtle woodiness to it, dry and crisp.

I'm still game and would enjoy the pleasure of tasting your maple beer should we ever have the opportunity to share a brew together.

Rice syrup—Rice syrup is a combination of sugars derived from a modified natural malting process. Sugars are developed by malting a portion of rice in order to develop enzymes. This ''malted'' rice is added to cooked white rice with an additional amount of malted barley (necessary for the required amount of starch-converting enzymes) and allowed to undergo a mashing process by which rice starches are converted to a spectrum of sugars including glucose and maltose. The subsequent sweet mash is processed to syrup much the same way as malt extract would be.

Rice syrup is available at many homebrew supply shops and some health food stores. It can be used in brewing lighter-flavored American-style lager beers.

Honey

Honey is in a class of sugar by itself and should not be ignored for use by the homebrewer. Its contribution to the flavor of homebrew is wonderfully unique. Many an award-winning flavorful beer has been made with a combination of malts and honey.

There are dozens of sugars that are found in honey. Glucose and fructose are present in the most significant amounts, with traces of sucrose and maltose attributable for less than 5 percent. The "stuff" of honey is not only sugar but a variety of sugar-ripening enzymes (secreted by the bees), wild yeast spores, pollen, beeswax, water (usually less than 17 percent in order to inhibit fermentation), bees' legs, antennae, stingers, eyebrows and various other body parts.

Honey is derived from the nectar of flowers, processed and ripened by honeybees. Because the source of nectar can vary, so does the honey. There are literally hundreds of varieties of honey. The color and flavor is the most recognizable difference.

For beermaking purposes, lighter honeys such as clover and alfalfa are considered to be the best because of the minimal contribution of unusually strong flavors. Honey has a high degree of fermentability and subtly pleasant fermented flavor. It can contribute to a dry crispness, lighter body and a high alcohol content without the off-flavors associated with refined white sugars. In order to maintain real beer character, it should be used in amounts of less than 30 percent. Amounts greater than this are not unpleasant but do detract from what might be considered a traditional beer flavor.

It should be noted that honey lacks yeast nutrients, yet the addition of nutrients is not necessary if honey is combined with malt extract. Barley malt will provide adequate nutrients for healthy fermentation.

Because of the presence of extraneous matter (beeswax, body parts and wild yeast spores) in raw unfiltered honey, it should always be boiled with the malt extract wort in order to pasteurize it. If filtered honey is used, it is still a reassuring practice to boil the honey with the wort. During boiling, extraneous matter may be skimmed and removed from the surface.

Honey can be fermented (with water) by itself or with various fruits, spices or herbs. These fermentations are called mead. Their character can vary from a sweet winelike beverage to a dry sparkling type of champagne. Recipes for making mead are discussed in Appendix 5.

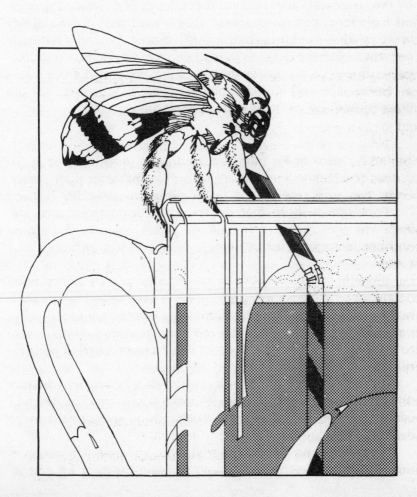

Miscellaneous Sweeteners

Caramel—Caramel is not a sweetener. It is derived from sugar by either a heating process or by chemically treating sugars in order to yield a brown bitterlike substance called caramel. Its use in beer is primarily as a coloring adjunct. It is not generally available for homebrewers but is used in commercial brewing and some malt extracts.

Malto-dextrin—Dextrin cannot be fermented by beer yeast. It is a chain of three glucose molecules that cannot be broken by the fermentation or respiration cycles of beer yeast. The presence of these "unfermentables" in beer lend body, foam stability and a residual sweetness to the finished beer. Dextrin is naturally present in varying degrees in malt extract. Its addition to homebrew recipes as a powder increases the body of the beer. It is a convenience and a means of controlling the character of the finished beer by the malt extract homebrewer.

FRUITS

Any fruit that is fit for human consumption may be used in flavoring beer. Some lend a more favorable character than others. Fruits are very rarely used in flavoring commercially brewed beers, although those that do are quite distinctively pleasant. The most well known fruit-flavored beers come from Belgium and are fermented with cherries, raspberries, peaches or currants.

Whether you use cherries, raspberries, apples, pears, blueberries or whatever, the fruits should be pasteurized before their introduction to the fermentation. This creates somewhat of a paradoxical situation since the most practical and effective way to pasteurize is by heat. But fruits should not be boiled because of their pectin content. If boiled, the pectin will "set" and create some problems with the beer's clarity. Also, boiling may extract or accentuate some of the undesirable flavor characteristics of seeds and pits, not to mention boiling away some of the more desirable delicate flavor of the fruit itself.

In order to pasteurize the fruit, I recommend its addition at the end of the boiling of the wort, turning the heat off and allowing the fruited wort to steep for 15–20 minutes at a temperature of 150–180 degrees F (66–82 C).

If fresh fruit is used (especially berries or cherries), the skin should be broken by crushing. Crushing is not necessary with frozen fruit, as the freezing process has already pierced the skin, allowing juices to flow.

The fruit can be left in the wort and fermented in the primary, but should be removed after initial fermentation. If fruit juice is used, straining is, naturally, unnecessary.

I have made and/or tasted some wonderful cherry, raspberry, apple, blueberry, blackberry, cranberry, peach, pear and cactus fruit beers.

Ahhh, the joys of being a homebrewer.

VEGETABLES

Hot damn. You can let your imagination go wild here, but don't think that you're the first to brew with vegetables.

Chili peppers—Anaheim, Hatch, jalapeño, serrano, cayenne, Szechuan, Thai and many other varieties offer different flavors and different heat sensations. Used in skillful and artful quantities, chili-flavored beer is often a real crowd pleaser. Surprised? So was I the time I sprung my first batch on an unsuspecting crowd. They loved it.

For controlled and best results add to a secondary fermenter measured quantities of roasted (with the skin on if you like the aromatic character of roasted chilis) green chilis, chopped serrano, Thai or jalapeño or dried cayenne or Szechuan. After a few days of steeping in the finished beer, the beer is ready for tasting. Add more chili if the heat is not to your satisfaction. Be careful and start conservatively.

Pumpkin—The Pilgrims may have been the first Americans to brew pumpkin-flavored beer. Use cooked pumpkin and add it to a mash with active enzymes. Do not use canned pumpkin to which preservatives have been added. Feel free to throw in some pumpkin pie spices (ginger, cinnamon, allspice, nutmeg, cloves). Many small commercial brewers brew this as a seasonal treat. It's terrific!

Peas, beans, parsnips, carrots, Jerusalem artichokes, zucchini, potatoes and the "thing" that grew in the neighbor's yard— I've heard tales of all of the above, but can't say I've had the pleasure of sampling many. Maybe I'm setting myself up in the wrong way, but if anyone out there would like to send me a bottle, please do.

GRAINS

The use of whole or processed grains or the starch derived from grains is an option many homebrewers utilize. Wheat, rye, oats, rice, barley, corn, millet, tef (Ethiopian origin), quinoa and triticale (a hybrid grain produced by crossing durum wheat and rye) are a few of the many grains suitable for brewing.

The brewing process that utilizes the starches from these grains is a bit more involved than the methods that have so far been outlined. The main thing to remember is that the starch must undergo processing in order to convert starches to sugars that are fermentable by beer yeast. These grains should not simply be thrown into the boiling pot. The resulting beer may be good, but simply knowing how to properly utilize the goodness of these grains will dramatically improve the results.

What follows is a brief outline of the procedures that should be undertaken by you, the homebrewer, should you choose to experiment with grains; there will be a more complete discussion in the Advanced Brewing section.

The starches that you want to utilize in grains must be converted to sugars. In order to do this, they must be introduced to the starch-to-sugar-converting enzymes present in malted barley. But even before the enzymatic process can be efficiently carried out, the enzymes must have an easier way to "get at" the starches. So, the first step is to coarsely crack or grind the whole grain and then cook it by boiling for at least ½ hour. After boiling is complete, the cooked grain may be introduced to an enzyme-active "mash" of malted barley or diastatic malt extract (an enzyme-active malt extract). Simply speaking, if the "soupy" mash is held at temperatures of 150–160 degrees F (66– 71 C) the enzymes will actively convert starch to sugars. NOTE: "Flaked" grains have been precooked and need not be boiled. Also, modified starch such as household cornstarch need not be cooked.

The use of grains in homebrew will provide for much more variety and an opportunity to experiment with your beermaking. Step-by-step procedures are explained in detail in the Advanced Brewing section for those who want to utilize grains in their brewing.

HERBS AND SPICES

Now here's where you can really make some interesting beers. As a homebrewer, you have the freedom to choose your ingredients . . . anything you so desire, but don't get too cocky about your bright ideas, because a look back into the history and traditions of beermaking will indicate that whatever bright idea you've concocted to add to your beer, well, someone somewhere probably has beat you to it.

In the days before hops were used, many different herbs or spices were employed to add zing to the brew. Two of the more popular flavorings were capsicum and coriander. Capsicum is a botanical name for pepper, usually hot pepper. Capsicum was said to be added for the warm glow it created while indulging. It was also said to "disperse the wind and crudities of indigestion." Wonderful! Just what every beer party needs.

Here are a few spices that homebrewers have found to be a popular addition to beer. If you can imagine enjoyment from these flavors, try them, but be cautious and don't overdo it the first time. Have patience, you can always add a little bit more the next time, but you can't remove anything if you've overdone it.

Cinnamon—Two teaspoons of ground cinnamon or 3 or 4 inches of the whole bark may be added during the final 10–15 minutes of the boil. This can be a very refreshing addition to darker beers. If added in small amounts, its flavor is not quite identifiable, yet its presence is noticed by all.

Coriander seed—This aromatic seed, often used in curries, was a popular beer ingredient in colonial America and eighteenth-century England. It is very assertive, so be sure you enjoy its flavor before adding it to your brew. Boil 1 or 2 teaspoons for a subtle hint in light beers.

Ginger—The grated fresh root of the ginger plant has grown to be a favorite adjunct for many homebrewers. It goes well in both light and dark beers. The refreshing flavor it contributes to beer is appreciated by even those who claim ". . . and I don't usually like beer." It is a winner unless you have an aversion to the flavor of ginger.

It is recommended that only fresh ginger root be used. Dried ginger will work but its flavor is more aggressive. Fresh ginger can be found in the produce section of most supermarkets. Grated on any cheese grater, it is best added during the final 10–15 minutes of the boiling of the wort. One ounce for 5 gallons will add considerable character to any beer. I have used amounts varying from ½ ounce to 4 ounces for 5 gallons of beer, all of which were enjoyed by many.

Many varieties of ginger are grown throughout the world. Galanga is one variety from Thailand that offers a refreshingly unique character to beer. Fresh or dried, add grated or sliced galanga during the last 10–20 minutes of the boil for maximum flavor and aroma.

Licorice—The hard woody root of the licorice plant is often used in beermaking. A 4–6-inch piece of root will contribute some licorice character to the beer and aid in head retention. Licorice is naturally sweet, but the amount present is insignificant to affect fermentation. Homebrew supply shops often carry "brewer's licorice," made from the extract of licorice root. A 2–5-inch piece in 5 gallons will contribute character to the finished beer. Brewer's licorice is easily dissolved in the boiling wort. Licorice root must be shaved or chopped into pieces and added and boiled in the wort for at least 15 minutes. In reasonable amounts licorice can contribute some pleasant qualities to beer, particularly dark beers.

Spruce—The new spring growth from evergreen spruce trees or processed spruce essence is popular among many homebrewers as a flavoring. Spruce was quite popular in colonial America, when hops were not available. Its addition to beer provides a refreshing flavor as well as vitamin C (which helps the stability of finished beer). You may add spruce flavor to your beer by harvesting the tips of new growth on spruce trees, stems and needles. A pint jar loosely filled with spruce twigs will provide adequate character to 5 gallons of brew. I once helped brew a batch of spruce beer in the Queen Charlotte Islands off the west coast of British Columbia, Canada. There, the Sitka spruce provided an abundance of tasty needles. The resulting malt-extract-based brew was astoundingly good. I can describe it very accurately as having a flavor similar to Pepsi-Cola but without the sweetness, and a beer flavor, to boot.

If fresh spruce needles aren't available in your neck of the woods, spruce essence is often available in many homebrew shops. Two to five teaspoons for 5 gallons will be adequate.

Warning: Pine tar is not the same thing as spruce essence. I once heard of a homebrewer who thought otherwise. Incredibly, he poured half a pint of the stuff into his wort. The beer tasted like the road surface of the George Washington Bridge.

Other spices—Cardamon, cloves, allspice, nutmeg, horseradish, horehound, walnut leaves, lime leaves, Szechuan peppercorn, sweet basil, root beer extract flavors (sassafras bark, sarsaparilla shavings, wintergreen, licorice root, vanilla bean, teaberry, deerberry, checkerberry, boxberry, spiceberry and others), anise and juniper berries are a few spices I've tried in beer or that continue to intrigue me.

MISCELLANEOUS INGREDIENTS

There's no doubt that your combined imagination will surpass anything that this book could ever deal with, but here are a few remaining gems deserving recognition.

Chocolate—The addition of bitter baker's chocolate or bittersweet nonmilk chocolate intrigues a growing number of homebrewers. There you are, brewing a batch of dark beer, and perhaps having a few in the process. And there it is just sitting there in the cupboard, staring you in the face . . . a 1–6-ounce chunk of chocolate. "I wonder . . . ," you think. And before you know it, in it goes. Voilà, chocolate beer. And it doesn't turn out badly, in fact you brew one special batch once a year, to celebrate your impulse.

Garlic—"Are you kidding me?" I wish that I was. You've really got to like garlic for this one. The brewers who introduced me to this one (and it was, oh, such a brief introduction) smiled and supportively insisted, "But it goes great with pizza." They had brewed an incredible 5 gallons of the stuff. Frankly, it never got past my nose, but it could have been a great ingredient in a pot of chile or Irish stew.

Smoke—This is not so strange as it seems. There are some traditional beers brewed in Bamberg, Germany, called *Rauchbier*, where they actually kiln-dry and smoke malted barley over open flames. The resulting beer is a delicious, albeit unusual, beer tasting of smoke. As a homebrewer, you may also smoke a portion of your grains in your barbecue pit (apple, mesquite or hickory wood works best) or use "liquid smoke." There are various brands of liquid smoke available in the barbecue section of most supermarkets. Read the label carefully and only use liquid smoke that does not have other flavorings (such as vinegar, salt, spices) or preservatives. Liquid smoke is mighty powerful stuff. Use it sparingly. One teaspoon per 5 gallons will give a well-perceived smoke flavor. Smoke-flavored beers are traditionally brown in color and they are a wonderful treat with smoked foods.

Coffee—Ahhh, what coffee and stout lover wouldn't consider a formulation of Blue Mountain Stout, made from the most exotic of Jamaican coffee beans? Though I haven't tried it myself, I know others who have, and as the word is spread and the stout is shared, more and more homebrewers are trying their hand at formulating coffee-flavored beers, both caffeinated and decaffeinated.

I love good coffee, and in order to preserve the fine flavor and aroma I would use only freshly ground beans and steep (never boil them) during the final 5 minutes before straining and sparging. Another option would be to add freshly ground coffee to the secondary and "cold extract" the coffee essence. How much to use? Give it a shot with half a pound for your first 5 gallons and progress from there. And share a bottle with me if we ever should have the opportunity to enjoy a beer together.

Chicken—I saved this one for last. The recipe for Cock Ale is an authentic one taken from a book by Edward Spencer published in 1899 and entitled *The Flowing Bowl: A treatise on drinks of all kinds and of all periods, interspersed with sundry anecdotes and reminiscences.* Herewith is the recipe:

Cock Ale

In order to make this, the *Complete Housewife* instructs us to take 10 gallons of ale and a large cock, the older the better. Parboil the cock, flea [flay?] him, and stamp him in a stone mortar till his bones are broken (you must craw and gut him when you flea him), then put the cock into 2 quarts of sack [sixteenth-century dry Spanish white wine], and put to it 3 pounds of raisins of the sun stoned, some blades of mace, a few cloves; put all these into a canvas bag, and a little before you find the ale has done working, put the ale and bag together into a vessel; in a week or 9 days bottle it up, fill the bottles but just above the neck, and give it the same time to ripen as other ale. . . .

Holy Moses! What a drink! I have frequently read of the giving of "body" to ale and stout by means of the introduction of horseflesh . . . but to put the rooster into the ale cask smacks somewhat of barbarism.

The addition of a whole chicken to your beer is very unusual, but to find someone who has actually tried it is even more unusual. "It wasn't all that bad," said he. I hope that he held the garlic.

YEAST NUTRIENTS

Beer yeast requires an adequate supply of nutrients and trace minerals for healthy fermentation. These nutrients are naturally present in malted barley or developed by enzymes during the malting or mashing process. The addition of extra prepackaged yeast nutrients to all malt extract beers is unnecessary. The only time that you as a homebrewer need to consider the addition of extra yeast nutrients is if you've used more than 40 percent adjuncts—that is, ingredients other than malt extract.

Yeast nutrients are recommended when brewing honey meads, but more on that later.

There are different types of yeast nutrients and energizers available in homebrew supply shops. If you find the need to use them or think it will make you feel better if you do so, by all means use them, but follow the instructions provided.

CLARIFYING AIDS

During the brewing and fermentation process there will be a lot of different kinds of suspended matter in the brew. If good ingredients are used and attention has been given to sanitation of equipment, then your beer will clear naturally with patience to a sparkling, bright, enjoyable transparency.

If a lot of adjuncts are used in the brew (or if it makes you feel better), clarifying aids are available for use in beermaking. There are two kinds of suspended matter that involve themselves in the brewing process: coagulated proteins developed during the boiling of the wort, and yeast that becomes suspended for a period of time during fermentation.

The ingredients that are added in the brewing process to help clarification are called *finings* (pronounced fine-ings). These ingredients attract suspended matter by the use of their molecular electrical charge, in much the same way as a magnet works. Positive electric charges attract negative ones and vice-versa. Now this wouldn't be so important to know except that the different types of suspended matter in beer have different electrical charges, and different types of finings have likewise different electrical charges.

Irish Moss—The precipitated and coagulated proteins that make for a cloudy wort in the boiling cauldron upon your stove are positively charged. The addition of vegetable-derived finings, such as Irish moss (a seaweed sometimes called carragheen), during the final 10–15 minutes of the boil will aid in settling out the proteins. The negatively charged Irish moss attracts the positively charged proteins; the process takes place in the brewpot. One-quarter to one-half teaspoon of powdered Irish moss added during the final 10–15 minutes of boiling will accomplish what is desired.

Yeast will naturally settle to the bottom after it has completed most of its fermentation. In order for this to happen, proper yeast nutrition is essential. It should be noted that different yeast strains and how they are handled will influence the sedimentation process. Particularly helpful is the addition of positively charged animal-derived finings. Most beer yeasts are negatively charged so the attraction will be active.

Gelatin—Derived from the hooves of horses and cows, gelatin has a positive charge that will aid in attracting and settling suspended yeast. Dissolved and prepared gelatin is added just before packaging the beer. It is best used when kegging homebrew, as there is a longer distance for the yeast to settle through. Prepare the gelatin by adding 1 tablespoon to 1 pint of cold water and gently heat until dissolved. Do not boil the gelatin solution as this will break down the gelatin to uselessness. Add the solution to the beer at the same time you add your priming (bottling) sugar.

Isinglass—Isinglass is a gelatinous substance derived from the internal membranes of fish bladders. Its use is very popular in Great Britain, where their style of beer benefits from the 48-hour clarification induced by the addition of isinglass at kegging time. Isinglass is positively charged but its effectiveness in settling yeast will vary with the strain of yeast being used. Its preparation is time-consuming and involves weak acid solutions that must be done with care over a period of days. Improper preparation will render these finings useless. Its use in American homebrewing is superseded by the more appropriate settling qualities of drinking a glass of homebrew and having patience. But if it is isinglass you wish to use, refer to the instructions that should accompany it.

OTHER CLARIFYING AIDS—CHILL HAZE AND CHILL-PROOFING

Some batches of beer that you will make may be perfectly clear at first but will later develop a haze when chilled in the refrigerator. This "chill haze" is nothing to get anxious about. It is mostly a visual phenomenon and will not greatly affect the flavor.

Chill haze is a result of a combining reaction between proteins and tannins. At room temperature it is soluble and remains invisible. At cooler temperatures it is no longer soluble and will precipitate as a haze.

Chill haze can be minimized by controlling the malting and mashing process more closely, but at the same time this control results in the sacrifice of other aspects that the brewer wishes to achieve. It's often a trade-off.

If the chill haze really annoys you, I could recommend that you drink out of a stone jar or wooden mug, but that would be facetious, so I won't. Following are some additives that can be introduced into your brew to help eliminate chill haze.

Papain—Papain is known as a protelytic enzyme that is extracted from the skin of the papaya. It is used as the active ingredient in meat tenderizer. This enzyme achieves some of the same effect as the ''protein rest'' during the mashing process of malted barley or during the malting process itself. Proper malting or mashing techniques are usually employed by all malt extract manufacturers in order to achieve minimal protein levels, thus minimizing chill haze formation.

If papain is used, it should be used sparingly: ½ gram of papain for 5 gallons will react with the proteins and prevent them from combining with tannin. The enzyme is active at temperatures below 122 degrees F (50 C) and takes several days to complete its reaction. Since it is deactivated with boiling it must be added to a cooled wort. It normally would be added during the latter part of secondary fermentation or maturation.

Papain is difficult to find in an unadulterated state. Some homebrew shops may carry it, but you will more likely find papain at specialty food shops that carry an extensive line of herbs and spices.

PVP (polyvinylpyrdlidone)/Polyclar—Plastic! This substance is an insoluble white plastic powder that, like a statically charged balloon clinging to the ceiling, will electrostatically attract tannin molecules as it drifts to the bottom. This process is called adsorption. It is a physical phenomenon. There is no chemical reaction of the plastic with the beer. After the polyclar has settled, the beer is drawn off, leaving the sediment behind. Because there are no longer any tannins in the beer, its combination with protein is prevented—no chill haze.

Polyclar should be added to the beer after the yeast has sedimented. The addition of 2 grams (2 teaspoons) of polyclar for every 5 gallons of beer should effectively remove tannins within a few hours.

Polyclar is available at many homebrew supply stores.

Activated silica gel—Although not available to homebrewers, this substance is worth mentioning because it is used by many commercial brewers. It does the same thing as polyclar except that it adsorbs protein molecules rather than tannin.

ENZYMES

Enzymes can be described as molecules that are triggered and ready to react with other substances to help create a new substance. They are formed by living things and are activated or deactivated by certain conditions.

The creation and utilization of enzymes in beermaking is essential and occurs naturally during the malting and starch-to-sugar mashing conversion. Diastatic enzymes, as they are called in the brewing process, are adequately developed during the malting stage.

If enzymes are added to malt extract brews or during the mashing process, they will certainly influence the balance of fermentable sugars and unfermentable dextrins that give body and aid in head retention.

Generally speaking, the use of enzymes by a homebrewer is not very controllable; however, if your curiosity leads you to experiment, here are explanations of two enzymes that are sometimes accessible to homebrewers. It is more than likely that your use of them will result in beer that will have less sweetness, less body, less head retention and more alcohol, as you will convert what is normally unfermentable into sugars that are. Your beers will have a flavor characteristic of super-light American beer.

Alpha-amylase—The powder that can sometimes be found in homebrew shops that is labeled "Alpha-amylase" should be of fungal origin (*Aspergillus niger*). Its addition to beer wort, mash or liquefied starch will enzymatically convert starches to the simplest and completely fermentable forms of sugar (glucose) at temperatures less than 140 degrees F (60 C). Temperatures above 140 degrees F will permanently "denature" (deactivate) the enzymes. Fungal alpha-amylase (sometimes called gluco-amylase) is processed at different enzymatic activities; therefore, the amount that should be used will vary with the strength of the powder. Generally, for homebrewing purposes, about 1 teaspoon of enzymes used for 5 gallons of beer should suffice to markedly influence conversion. At temperatures close to 140 degrees F (60 C), conversions should be complete within 3 hours. When used in commercial brewing, alpha-amylase is usually added during secondary cold storage and maturation. In 1 week, reactions will be complete: the conversion of unfermentable dextrin carbohydrates to fermentable sugars that will in turn be fermented by yeast.

Alpha-amylase is often used in the production of barley syrup from unmalted barley. It is sometimes an ingredient in malt syrups that are not 100 percent malt extract.

Bacterially derived beta-amylase is not recommended for use by the homebrewer. It liquefies starches to dextrins, is heat resistant and will survive boiling temperatures. It will result in beer that is unstable and difficult to control.

Koji—The biological name for this enzyme is *Aspergillus oryzae*. Of fungal origin and best known for its use in making Japanese rice wine (sake), koji is actually impregnated rice or barley. Koji concentrate, an enzyme powder, is sometimes available to the homebrewer. Koji seed (tane) is not yet developed into enzymes and is not useful to the brewer. Koji enzymes will convert starches to sugars most efficiently at temperatures between 100–120 degrees F (43–49 C) in about 10–20 minutes. It is deactivated at temperatures above 130 degrees F (54 C). One teaspoon of koji concentrate (enzymes) added to ingredients for 5 gallons should aid in the conversion of liquefied starches (dextrins) to fermentable glucose sugar. *Aspergillus oryzae* enzyme is sometimes used in the commercial brewing of American light beers. It is added during cold secondary storage and allowed at least a week to react with the beer. Time of conversion is very variable and is affected by temperature and strength of the enzyme. As a homebrewer you will need to experiment.

Diastatic malt extract—Manufactured in a way that does not denature the enzyme during the evaporation process, D.M.E. or diastatic malt syrup (D.M.S.) can be used by brewers who wish to convert adjuncts (such as corn, rice, wheat, etc.) but do not have adequate enzyme content in their malted barley.

During homebrewing, this syrup may be added to a mash of cooked starch for proper conversion to sugar at temperature ranges between 150–160 degrees F (66–71 C). Three pounds of diastatic malt extract should be adequate to convert 1 pound of grain or starch.

MISCELLANEOUS BREWING AIDS

Ascorbic acid (vitamin C)—Ascorbic acid, commonly known as vitamin C, is used in many foods as an antioxidant preservative. Oxidation is the process through which oxygen will react and combine with just about anything. When oxygen reacts with finished beer, it will produce off-flavors and instability. The more that a brewer can do to eliminate oxygen from coming in contact with beer once fermentation begins, the better the beer will be.

When added to beer, ascorbic acid provides a way for oxygen to react with it, rather than with the beer. Oxidized vitamin C is less harmful to the stability and flavor of the beer than oxidized beer.

One-half teaspoon of ascorbic acid crystals dissolved in boiled water will help prevent oxidation of 5 gallons of beer. It is not recommended that vitamin C tablets be used, because of other ingredients added to these tablets. Vitamin C crystals are available at all homebrew supply stores.

NOTE: Ascorbic acid is not a necessary ingredient in beer-making. If care is taken not to splash and aerate beer during siphoning and bottles are filled to within 1 inch of the top, oxidation problems will be minimal. Whatever you do, *don't worry*; if adding ascorbic acid will prevent worrying, do it—otherwise, it is an unnecessary option.

Citric acid—I used to think that the addition of citric acid was important in beermaking. Now, because I think I understand beer ingredients and the brewing process more, I can't imagine why one should use it. Its addition increases the acidity of the already acid wort. Malt extracts and all-grain mashes are acid by their very nature. The use of citric acid in malt extract brewing is simply not necessary.

The addition of citric acid in honey meads or wine is justified, however, in order to create a desirable acid flavor.

Brewing salts—Sometimes called Burton water salts, minerals such as noniodized table salt (NaCl), gypsum ($CaSO_4$), and Epsom salt ($MgSO_4$) can be added to beer wort in an attempt to duplicate the brewing water in Burton-on-Trent, famous for its pale ales. It is extremely difficult to duplicate world-famous brewing water without starting with distilled or deionized water. A more complete discussion of water and brewing salts can be found in the Advanced Brewing Section.

Briefly, brewing salts are more important when brewing an all-grain beer. The addition of gypsum to a malt extract wort will be helpful, especially if you know that your water supply is soft. You can ask your city or county water department for a mineral analysis of your water supply. If your water contains less than 50 ppm (parts per million) of calcium, then the addition of 1 to 4 teaspoons of gypsum will aid the fermentation process.

Food-grade gypsum is available at all homebrew supply shops.

Other brewing "salts" such as calcium chloride ($CaCl_2$) and potassium chloride (KCl) may be cautiously considered as brewing ingredients, but not before a more thorough understanding of their effects on brewing chemistry has been established.

Heading liquids—Heading liquids are extracts of odd roots, barks and other things that will have a "detergent effect" on the beer; bubbles will last longer. Their use in homebrewing is not necessary if sanitary procedures are combined with good ingredients. I have been able to get the best heads on the simplest of malt extract beers, as good as the famed Guinness Stout head—really! Don't let anyone tell you otherwise.

If your beer is having problems keeping its head, the problem is more likely the glass you are drinking from. Grease, oils or detergent residues left on glasses will destroy a head. Also, the corn chip and potato chip oils on your lips will also destroy a head, let alone Chap Stick or lipstick.

If you do use heading liquid, follow the instructions on the container.

When you make homebrew you are dealing with a living organism. It is alive—and because it is alive it feels. Every person's brew has its own distinctive characteristics that carry through each batch. The entire process of beer-making depends on one's thoughts and attitude and equally on the lives of millions of tiny organisms called yeasts.

The magic of making homebrew can only come from the magic given it: magic as simple as the space you occupy.

THE SECRETS OF FERMENTATION
How Yeasts Behave

Beer yeast is a single-cell living organism. In its microbial world it is classified as a fungus. The activity during its life cycle offers to the brewer the gift of beer. The "living" part of your beer should never be forgotten or taken for granted. Yeast is not simply some "thing" that is added as an ingredient and quickly forgotten. Sure, left on its own accord it will indeed take it upon itself to make beer. But I can assure you that merely thinking about yeasts as living organisms and involving your own common sense in understanding what they are doing will make your beer better.

The intricacies of the life cycle of yeast are still not fully

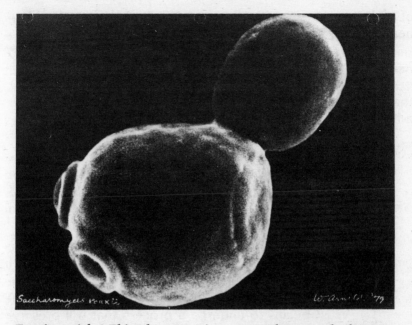

Saccharomyces roux i. W. arnold '79

Turning tricks! This electron microscope photograph shows a typical yeast cell in a budding (reproductive) stage. Scars can be seen lower left and right where other buds have separated. When fermentation is most active, there are 50 million of these cells in 1 milliliter of wort! Beer will appear clear to the naked eye when concentrations of 100,000 cells per milliliter are reached.

understood by microbiologists and never will be. There are simply some secrets that are never unraveled. But quite a bit is known about what yeasts like and how they behave. The purpose of this discussion is to convey to you, the homebrewer, a foundation that will enable you to begin to appreciate and understand yeast and how it makes beer.

It is emphasized that just like any living organism there is a tremendous variety of behavior within a species. The facts and descriptions that follow are accurate but are often generalizations. When dealing with yeast, one must be flexible enough to allow the individualities of yeast to express its own character.

During the brewing cycle, yeast will progress through its entire life cycle. In a matter of days, the population will increase three to five times. While it is tending to the activity of reproduction it is also involved at one time or another with three main activities during its life cycle:

1) *Respiration*: The process through which yeasts gain and store energy for future activities and reproduction.

2) *Fermentation*: The process through which yeast expends energy, converting sugars to alcohol, carbon dioxide and beer flavor. During this period of time, yeast is mostly in suspension, allowing itself dispersal and maximum contact with the liquid beer wort.

3) *Sedimentation*: The process through which yeast flocculates and drifts to the bottom of the fermenter. With fermentation almost completed, the activity of the yeast is "shut down" for lack of food and energy. The yeast begins to undergo a process that will preserve its life as it readies itself for dormancy.

It is important that yeasts do what they do quickly and in good health. There are many other micro-organisms such as bacteria and wild yeasts that can live and propagate themselves in beer wort but they will be inhibited if your brewing yeast can get a good head start in its own life cycle.

In order for brewing yeast to ferment quickly, there are certain nutritional and environmental conditions that are favorable. They involve:

1) Temperature

2) pH (acidity or alkalinity); physical condition of their surroundings

3) Nutrients and food

4) Oxygen

5) Good initial health

In essence, these conditions for life are no different from all other forms of life, including our own.

These conditions are not difficult to understand. When you make the small effort to appreciate the simplicity of these basics, you will be able to answer many questions before you ask them.

Let's take a quick look at the conditions that yeast favor.

1) *Temperature*—Depending on the variety, yeast can have an active life cycle and ferment in the temperature ranges of 33–90 degrees F (1–32 C). Most ale yeast (top-fermenting type, *Saccharomyces cerevisiae*) works best at 60–75 degrees F (16–24 C). Lager yeast (bottom-fermenting type, *Saccharomyces uvarum*) works best and produces the most desirable beer flavors at 35–50 degrees F (2–10 C).

If yeasts are in an environment that is too cold, their activity will be significantly lower or stop altogether.

If the temperature of the beer wort is excessive, the yeast will die (usually at temperatures in excess of 120 degrees F [49 C]) or its activity will be greater. Warmer temperatures increase the risk of bacterial contamination and propagation. Yeast may also produce some very undesirable off-flavors in the beer. These off-flavors can generally be characterized as fruity, butterscotch-like (diacetyl), cidery, grassy (acetaldehyde), solventlike (alcohols other than ethanol); with some yeast strains an aroma of rotten eggs (H_2S, hydrogen sulfide) may occur. None of the above will harm you and may not even occur with the yeast strain that you use, but when they do it usually detracts from your beer.

Just like people, yeasts do not favor sudden changes in temperatures. When culturing or rehydrating yeast, slowly raise or lower temperature of the yeast starter to that of the wort before pitching.

2) *pH and other physical conditions*—Distilled water is neutral; it is neither acid nor alkaline. The measure of neutrality on the pH scale is 7.0. A pH of less than 7.0 is acid, while a pH greater than 7.0 is alkaline (or basic).

Most beer yeasts enjoy an environment that is acidic at a pH of 5.0–5.5. This environment will naturally occur in all beer worts. The homebrewer need not make adjustments.

During the course of fermentation, the by-products of yeast will decrease the pH of the beer to about 4.5.

With regard to other conditions, yeasts can be very sensitive to what is called the "osmotic" pressure of their surroundings. For example, plain water will exert a much different pressure on the cell walls (the "skin") of yeast than a solution of malt sugars and water or beer. As a jet airliner must gradually adjust the pressure of the cabin in order to minimize the strain on its "skin," so would a yeast cell going from one liquid environment to another.

If sudden and drastic osmotic pressure changes are made in a yeast's environment, many yeasts will literally implode or explode (what an ugly sight on a microbial level) and those that do survive such changes reduce their activity while they adjust to the shock.

For optimal yeast health, think like a yeast (sure it does) and make gradual transitions.

3) *Nutrients and Food*—These are the building blocks for all life and occur on the cellular level. In order for any living organism to function properly, life's metabolic activity and healthy cell walls must be maintained. Yeasts require sugars, proteins, fats, and trace minerals (elements).

Sugars are a source of food energy.

Proteins are nutrients that are in the form of (free) amino acids. They are developed in the malting process or during the mashing process. They are required for healthy cell structure.

Fats (oils) are derived from hops and malt. The small amount required is necessary, again, for healthy cell building.

Trace elements are necessary for the overall life processes of yeast cells, the two most important being zinc and calcium. Zinc is derived from malt. Calcium is derived from malt and water. In excess, both elements are toxic to yeast.

Without proper nutrition, many things will result. Generally, a few of these are: sluggish fermentation, mutation of yeasts, poor sedimentation, off-flavors and poor beer stability.

Nutrition requirements will vary with yeast strains. As a malt extract homebrewer, the nutritional requirements are invariably included in the products that you use. Additional nutrients need not be considered.

4) *Oxygen*—Oxygen is an extremely important requirement in the initial stages of the life cycle of yeasts. Essentially, yeast undergoes a process called respiration through which it will store energy derived from sugar and oxygen for the remainder of its life cycle. This process is often described as being aerobic because it utilizes "free oxygen" that is dissolved in the beer wort. There is no disadvantage to having too much oxygen in your initial wort.

Oxygen can be dissolved into the wort by splashing or agitating the wort as it goes into the fermenter. Boiled water or wort does not have very much dissolved oxygen; it is therefore advisable to agitate the cooled wort. Cold tap water that is added to hot concentrated malt extract wort may already have dissolved oxygen. Once the yeast has been added to the wort and fermentation commences, oxygen should never be introduced.

A lack of oxygen in the initial wort may result in stuck, sluggish or incomplete fermentation.

HOMEBREWERS' NOTE: According to research done by the Brewing Industry Research Foundation in Surrey, England, it was found that the "method of yeast culture and propagation will alter response to oxygen" and significantly affect fermentation. The important thing to consider is that oxygen *is* required at some stage. Many of the very active dried beer yeasts that are available to homebrewers are likely cultured under (aerated) conditions that decrease the requirement of oxygen in a homebrewer's wort. If you choose to culture your own yeast, the oxygen requirement is more significant.

5) *Good Initial Health*—Some of the precursors to healthy yeast at the time that it is added to the wort have already been mentioned. In addition, storage or packaging conditions will also affect the health of the yeast. Liquid cultures can be stored in a refrigerated or, with special treatment, frozen state. The dried yeast that is used by homebrewers is warm-air-dried and approximately 70 percent viable. It can be stored at room temperatures but will have a longer "shelf life" if refrigerated.

THE LIFE CYCLE OF BEER YEASTS

Introduction

As a homebrewer, you will observe variability in your fermentation because of the comparatively small scale at which you brew, the variability of conditions and variety of yeast preparations that you use. This need not cause anxiety. (Relax. Don't worry. Have a homebrew.) You, the homebrewer, have the opportunity to observe variations that are not even allowed in many commercial breweries.

The life cycle of yeast is activated from dormancy when it is *pitched* (added) to the wort. During the respiration and fermentation cycle, the population of yeast will multiply three or four times. Yeast cells reproduce by a process called budding approximately every 24 hours until an optimum population of 50 million cells per milliliter of wort is reached. As it reproduces it is also metabolizing food and nutrients.

All yeast activities can be assigned to three main cycles: 1) Respiration, 2) Fermentation and 3) Sedimentation.

Respiration is the initial process that yeast undergoes when pitched into the wort. It is an aerobic process through which oxygen is utilized by the yeast cells. From the available oxygen, the yeast derives energy and other requirements for reproduction, cell construction and fermentation. The energy derived during respiration is almost completely used during fermentation.

Respiration will last about 4–8 hours and varies quite a bit with conditions. During the respiration cycle, the yeast will reproduce and produce carbon dioxide, water and flavor characteristics (there is no alcohol produced during respiration). The flavor characteristics are by-products of yeast metabolism, the most noticeable ones being esters and diacetyl.

The name "ester" is given to the chemicals that are responsible for certain aromas. The ones that are often noticeable in beer are described as strawberry, apple, banana, grapefruit,

pear or raspberry. The type of ester produced will vary with yeast strain, temperature and other conditions. Beer drinkers usually prefer some degree of estery quality in beer.

Diacetyl is the name given to describe a buttery or butterscotch flavor in beer. It can be produced sometimes by bacteria but is always produced to one degree or another by the metabolic activity of yeast. This flavor is later reduced during the fermentation stage while the yeast is in suspension. Sometimes, if the yeast does not stay in suspension long enough it is unable to reduce the butterscotch flavor of diacetyl, which comes out in the final flavor of the beer. Many beer drinkers appreciate this character in certain styles.

The Samuel Smith Brewery in County York, England, produces a beer called Sam Smith's Pale Ale or Bitter. It has a subtle but noticeably butterscotch palate. The fermentation of this brewery's beer takes place in what is called Yorkshire stones—square fermenters made of slate. This method of fermentation and the particular strain of ale yeast used does create some problems in keeping the yeast in suspension long enough during fermentation. They occasionally have to "rouse" (stir) the yeast back into suspension. Because of the yeast's tendency to flocculate (sediment or rise to the surface), it is unable to reduce the diacetyl responsible for the butterscotch character. However, the special character of this beer makes it unique, very enjoyable, and well known.

Fermentation—The fermentation cycle quickly follows the respiration cycle. Fermentation is called an anaerobic process and does not require any free oxygen in solution. As a matter of fact, any remaining oxygen in the wort is "scrubbed" (stripped) out of solution by the carbon dioxide bubbles produced by the yeast.

During the fermentation cycle, the yeast will continue to reproduce until optimum population is reached. Once suspended throughout the wort, it converts sugars to alcohol, carbon dioxide and beer flavors. It is the nature of strains of beer yeast to remain in suspension long enough to quickly convert fermentables. Most beer yeasts that you will use will remain in suspension for anywhere from 3 to 7 days, after which time flocculation and sedimentation will commence.

Occasionally homebrewers will experience a rotten egg aroma in their fermentation. This is not an unusual occurrence of fermentation. It is caused by certain strains of yeast that produce hydrogen sulfide that is, in turn, carried away by carbon dioxide. Changing your yeast or fermentation temperature will often remedy the problem.

A number of things happen during flocculation. At mid-fermentation, the yeast will begin to sense that its energy stores are near depletion. As fermentation moves closer to completion and food is no longer available, the yeast begins to prepare for dormancy by settling to the bottom and creating a sediment.

Sedimentation—During sedimentation, the yeast produces a substance called glycogen. Glycogen is necessary for cell maintenance during dormancy and is used as an energy source for initial activity if the yeast is added to new beer wort. The sediment of yeast produced during the first week of sedimentation is the most viable form of yeast to use if you wish to propagate it.

Very little fermentation occurs after the yeast has sedimented; what little does occurs very slowly. If sedimentation occurs prematurely, it can result in long and slow fermentation. In this case a brewer may contemplate rousing the yeast, but extreme care must be taken not to introduce oxygen or bacterial contamination. As a homebrewer, you need not be concerned with premature sedimentation. If you feel that sedimentation occurred too quickly, you are better off relaxing and not worrying. Three-day complete fermentations are common for homebrewers. Have a homebrew.

If the brewer chooses to mature the beer over a period of many weeks or even months, the beer should be removed from the sediment of yeast. After fermentation is completed, the presence of yeast in great amounts is not necessary. Even though your beer may appear clear, there are still millions of yeasts present in the beer—an adequate amount for final fermentation and carbonation in the bottle.

Flavor changes during maturation are not predominantly yeast-related unless there is a sediment present. Over a period of time, the yeast cells will begin a process of deterioration called autolysis. The by-products of autolysis can contribute a yeasty flavor to the beer.

Almost paradoxically, the small amount of yeast present in bottle-conditioned homebrew actually helps stabilize the flavor of beer. A little live yeast in bottled beer is a significant advantage to flavor stability.

LISTENING TO YOUR YEAST

A summary of tidbits for the homebrewer:

- Behavior will vary with batch size. For example, beer brewed in a gallon jug as opposed to a 5-gallon jug will be more influenced by temperature changes in the room due to the smaller volume and also because relatively there is more surface area (per volume) of the beer in contact with the glass. The yeast will clear more quickly because it has a shorter distance to travel to the bottom. The brew usually ferments to completion in a much shorter period.

- Behavior will vary with ingredients. Different malts, malt extracts and adjuncts will provide variety in the balance of fermentable sugars and nutrients.

- Behavior will vary with temperature. Warmer fermentations increase the rate of activity while colder temperatures inhibit. Cooler temperatures will also aid in sedimentation of the yeast.

- Behavior will vary with contamination. Bizarre behavior is usually the result of contamination by certain other micro-organisms, rather than the yeast or ingredients that you are using. Give more attention to your sanitation procedures.

- If you culture yeast, it is likely that it will change and adapt to your brewery environment. A yeast that has been cultured to be used in a 1,000-barrel fermenter will not behave the same if used to brew the same ingredients in a 5-gallon batch. Remember, yeasts are living organisms that will adapt.

- Pitching rates will influence the behavior of yeast. If you do not add enough yeast to the wort, the yeast will not be able to achieve the optimum population to effect quick and complete fermentation. If too much yeast is added, the yeast will only reproduce until the population reaches the optimum 50 million cells per milliliter (approximate).

There is a subtle flavor called "yeast-bite" associated with overpitching. Scientific explanations have not been found.

- Your at-home brewery may develop what are called "house flavors." Because of the uniqueness of the conditions under which you brew and your attitude, very real "house" character may subtly manifest itself in all your beers. It may be partly attributed to a nonspoiling bacteria or micro-organism that lives at your address.

- Do not add tap water to your beer once fermentation has begun. It contains oxygen, which if added to fermenting or finished beer will contribute to oxidation and bacterial spoilage. If you want to dilute your beer at bottling time or after it goes into the secondary fermenter, use boiled and cooled water.

- Mixing strains of beer yeast can lead to some interesting results. Sometimes the blending of ale yeasts with lager yeasts can produce desired behavior. When this is done by breweries, the yeasts are added separately and at distinctly different phases of fermentation activity. The point is that the yeasts will work and that you can mix them without worrying.

HAIR TOO MUCH YEAST

INTERMEDIATE PART 5 Secrets of Fermentation...

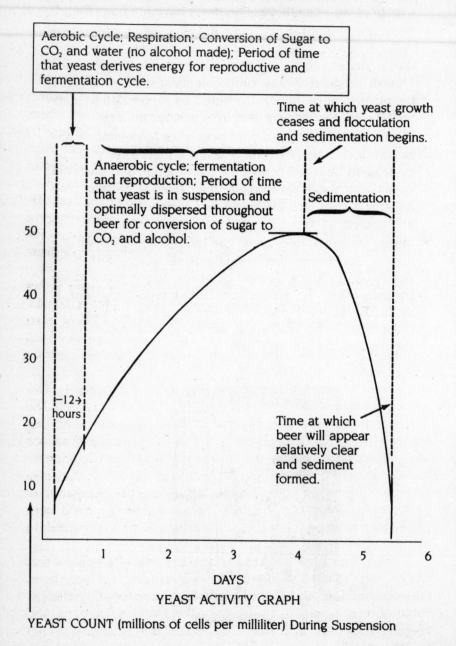

Aerobic Cycle; Respiration; Conversion of Sugar to CO_2 and water (no alcohol made); Period of time that yeast derives energy for reproductive and fermentation cycle.

Time at which yeast growth ceases and flocculation and sedimentation begins.

Anaerobic cycle; fermentation and reproduction; Period of time that yeast is in suspension and optimally dispersed throughout beer for conversion of sugar to CO_2 and alcohol.

Sedimentation

Time at which beer will appear relatively clear and sediment formed.

←12→ hours

DAYS

YEAST ACTIVITY GRAPH

YEAST COUNT (millions of cells per milliliter) During Suspension

CLEANING AND SANITATION IN THE HOMEBREWERY

"Cleanliness is next to goodliness." —Merlin

The single most important factor in being able to make delicious beer is cleanliness. The more that you can minimize the chances of unwanted bacteria and wild yeast contaminating your beer the better your beer will be. The contamination of your beer by uninvited micro-organisms can result in cloudy beer, sour beer, overcarbonation, surface mold, off-flavors and a host of other bizarre occurrences. There are some contaminants that won't drastically affect your beer. Obviously, some are worse than others. You can assure yourself that there are no known pathogens (toxic micro-organisms) that can survive in beer. Your occasional mistake may look weird, taste awful and momentarily depress you, but it won't kill you.

Now don't run away! Keeping your brewery clean is not that difficult. It is simply a question of giving the matter consideration and then doing it. You might still brew good beer even if you don't attend to keeping things clean, but your beer will improve significantly when you do decide to maintain sanitary procedures.

I use the words *clean* and *sanitized* very deliberately. Discouraging unwanted micro-organisms is a two-part process. The word *clean* is used to describe the physical appearance of your equipment. The word *sanitized* describes the equipment that has been disinfected. Sterilization is impractical and nearly impossible. The largest breweries in the world don't sterilize; they sanitize. Sanitization with disinfectants will reduce the population of bacteria and wild yeast to such a degree that the good beer yeast *you* introduce will be in the majority and do its thing before the bad guys have a chance.

Relax, for crying out loud. Don't get any silly notions that you're going to have to play doctor or pressure-cook your beer. Cleaning can be achieved with a little elbow grease and patience. Sanitization is as easy as rinsing or soaking your equipment. And keeping your beer wort free of contamination is as easy as not touching it.

There are a number of cleaners and disinfectants that can be used by homebrewers. The most effective is household bleach. The more specialized cleaners and disinfectants are available at homebrew supply shops.

What follows is a summary of common cleaners and sanitizers used by homebrewers. But before you use any of them, a very serious word of WARNING: NEVER EVER COMBINE OR MIX ANY CLEANERS OR DISINFECTANTS! *The gases that are released by chemical reactions can be seriously toxic.*

CLEANSERS AND SANITIZERS

Household ammonia—Household ammonia and water is most effectively used as a bottle label remover. One cup per 5 gallons of cold water and an overnight soaking of bottles will remove all but metallic labels from bottles. Ammonia is unpleasant to work with. Use in a ventilated area and *never* mix with chlorinated cleaners. A good substitute for household ammonia is plain washing soda.

Chlorine (household bleach)—In certain forms, chlorine is a very powerful cleaner, sanitizer and sterilant. Do not confuse chlorine with chloride. They are two very different chemicals, the latter (chloride) being dissociated from sodium when common salt is dissolved in water. Never mix acids, ammonia or anything else for that matter, with chlorinated cleaners.

Household bleach is the most accessible and effective disinfectant that a homebrewer can use. Most forms of household bleach have only 5 percent available chlorine. The other ingredients are inert and have no disinfecting potential. But don't underestimate the power of household bleach. To give you an idea of just how strong it is, consider the fact that it takes only 0.25 parts per million (ppm) of pure chlorine in distilled water to sanitize it—that is, 1/3 teaspoon of household bleach for every 100 gallons of water.

How does chlorine work? The chlorine in household bleach is available as sodium hypochlorite. The chlorine becomes an effective sanitizer only when it combines with water (of which there is some already in solution) to form hypochlorous acid.

Hypochlorous acid is very unstable in that it breaks down or reacts to form other chemicals that are not useful as a sanitizer but can contribute nasty characters to the water. Hypochlorous acid is reduced by sunlight, heat or by its combination with nitrogen compounds (just about any organic matter, some of which are available from beer wort as protein and yeast nutrients). The combination of chlorine with nitrogen compounds presents a problem because the resulting compounds are very stable compounds such as chlorophenols, chloroform and chloromenes; not only can they contribute off-flavors to beer, but they are toxic when present in significant amounts. These nasty compounds are odorless. The odor of chlorine comes from what is referred to as "free available chlorine" (F.A.C.). It is the F.A.C. that has the ability to disinfect, but is unstable in sunlight or at high temperatures.

How does one safely use household bleach? Not only is chlorine bleach an effective disinfectant but it is also an effective cleaner. It is able to remove some of the most stubborn and inaccessible stains and residues in your glass fermenters and bottles.

Two fluid ounces of bleach in 5 gallons of cold water and an overnight soak will remove the most hardened fermentation residues from the inside surface of your glass fermenter. This strong solution should be thoroughly rinsed with warm or hot water.

For homebrewers, an effective sanitizing solution can be prepared by mixing 1/3–1 1/2 teaspoons of household bleach in 5 gallons of cold water. This mixture will yield chlorine in solution at 5–25 ppm—an effective sanitizer, with a 1/2–1-hour soak, immersion or contact with clean equipment. The necessity of rinsing off this sanitizing solution is debated among homebrewers. Some choose to let the utensils drip dry or don't dry or rinse at all, out of anxiety about the cleanliness of their water supply. If you drink your water from the tap, don't hesitate to rinse all chlorine solutions with hot tap water. Hot water from your water heater is partly sanitized, especially if it has been residing in the tank reservoir for hours. Besides, by that point, you have already minimized the presence of bacteria in your wort to such a degree that any introduction of bacteria from the water would be negligible.

Detergents—Detergents can be an aid to cleaning your homebrew equipment. The nonperfumed varieties are preferable. Applied with a little elbow grease, detergents will remove dirt, grease and oils, making your equipment physically clean. Rinse very well, as residues can alter the character of your beer. NOTE: Do not mix soap with detergents. They are not the same thing, and their combination will render both useless.

Heat—Boiling water or temperatures held above 170 degrees F (71 C) will sanitize equipment.

Iodine—Iodine disinfectants are sometimes available to homebrewers, though not very often. Sold commercially as "iodine detergent germicide," these solutions are very concentrated and have acids such as phosphoric acid added for its cleansing ability. Read the instructions of these concentrates very carefully. A typical dilution ratio of 2 teaspoons added to 5 gallons of cold water will achieve an effective sanitizing solution.

If these disinfectants are available (they are often used in the dairy industry), they offer a practical alternative to the homebrewer. Iodine can be as toxic as chlorine, so care should be taken when handling.

Metabisulfite, sodium or potassium—Sodium or potassium metabisulfite is a bacterial inhibitor. It does not necessarily have the ability to disinfect. It works by releasing sulfur dioxide (SO_2) gas when combined in solution with acids. Metabisulfites added to water alone are not at all effective for sanitizing homebrew equipment.

Metabisulfites should not be used in beermaking. Their use in winemaking is justified, in that their addition to the acidic wine creates sulfur dioxide. Also, wine has a higher alcohol content, which further inhibits bacteria. Metabisulfite is not strong enough for use in beermaking and its addition to beer should be avoided entirely.

Quaternary ammonia—This very powerful and persistent disinfectant is occasionally mentioned by homebrewers and in homebrew literature. A very stable and toxic disinfectant, it is sometimes used in commercial breweries to clean floors and the outside of brewhouse equipment. It should never be used to clean anything that comes in contact with the beer. I do not recommend its use by homebrewers.

Soap—Soap and elbow grease can be used to clean home-brewery equipment. If soap is used, attention should be given to rinse all residues with warm water.

Washing soda (sodium carbonate)—Washing soda is an alkaline cleanser. A solution of ¼–½ cup of washing soda and 5 gallons of water will remove most labels from beer bottles. Washing soda solutions will corrode aluminum and release explosive hydrogen gas. Naturally, don't use an aluminum pot to hold your solution.

CLEANING AND SANITIZING PLASTIC HOMEBREW EQUIPMENT

Siphon hoses and plastic fermenters should appear clean, scratchless and stain-free. Scratches and stains will harbor bacteria and protect them from the most caustic sanitizing solutions. Any of the preceding cleaners and disinfectants can be used. If stains cannot be removed or there are scratches in your plastic and you've been brewing some funky beer, it is time to throw them away. (NOTE: Old siphon hoses are ideal for emergency gasoline—put one in your car.)

All plastic equipment can be immersed or swabbed with disinfectants. Avoid boiling soft plastic such as fermentation locks unless you want some useless pieces of sculpture.

CLEANING AND SANITIZING GLASS CARBOYS AND BOTTLES

Glass should appear stain-free when clean. Any disinfectant can be used to sanitize glass. Five-gallon carboys are awkward to clean. A long-handled bottle brush is useful in order to remove the majority of fermentation stains. Carboys and beer bottles should be attended to as soon as they are empty. A quick rinsing along with agitation will remove most residue. An overnight soak in a solution of 1 to 2 ounces of bleach per 5 gallons of water will remove all residues from the sides of the carboy.

When cleaning beer bottles, make a quick inspection to see if they are stained or have a dried bacterial deposit ringing the inside neck of the bottle. *Inspect them carefully.* If they are stained inside then immerse them for 1 hour in a bucket of bleach cleaning solution (2 ounces of bleach per 5 gallons of cold water). If beer bottles are physically clean, then a quick immersion and a 5-minute wet contact with a sanitizing solution (1 teaspoon of bleach per 5 gallons of cold water) will suffice. Rinse with hot tap water.

CLEANING AND SANITIZING
THE MISCELLANEOUS

Boiling your bottlecaps is a good and easy habit to get into; who knows where they've been?

Wooden spoons are impossible to sanitize. That charismatic wooden spoon is fine and should be used when stirring your boiling wort, but do not immerse the wooden spoon into the wort when it has cooled below 160 degrees F (71 C). "What then do I stir the cooled wort with?" you may ask. Don't, other than to remove some of the wort when measuring its specific gravity or to siphon. There is really no reason to be mucking about in your beer once it is cooled and fermenting.

Avoid putting your hands in the beer when siphoning; if you must, at least wash them thoroughly beforehand.

Avoid using your mouth to start your siphon. If you must, gargle with brandy or 150-proof rum. Your mouth has lots of lactobacillus bacteria; those are the bacteria that love to sour beer. An easy way to start a siphon is to fill it with water before you immerse it in the beer (see Appendix 12).

AND DON'T FORGET. . . .

Don't be intimidated by those invisible critters that want to jump in your beer. You really can't blame them, can you? After you go through your first experience of cleaning and sanitizing, you will develop your own system and the whole procedure will become mindlessly automatic.

Relax. Don't worry. Have a homebrew. Believe me, the quality of the beer that you make will be worth it.

GETTING YOUR WORT TOGETHER

You are about to embark on a journey from which there is no returning, no middle, no end and no bottom. A journey into an area in which there is more meaning—an area called the Twilight Foam.

The Twilight Foam is one step beyond, a simple conjecture, an impulse that leads to the wonderful world of worts. With a little experience comes the realization that there is more choice, variety and quality beer to be brewed by you, the homebrewer, than you had ever imagined.

By this time, you have made the choice and it is simple enough to follow recipes and brew great beer . . . it's that easy. But to understand your beer and why it is you are brewing—now that's what makes the best beer *every single time*! We all know how much satisfaction we get when we serve our beer to our friends and can say "I made that beer," but being able to transmit the depth of feeling brewed into that beer is even more satisfying. You become a brewer who passes on the inspiration to others.

The following section will not only review procedures with which you should already be familiar, but will also detail the whys and what-fors to making better brew. Different combinations of plain malt extracts, hops and grains will allow you an almost overwhelming variety of homebrewed beers. Knowing the reasons for combining ingredients and how these ingredients interact with each other will comfort you and allow you to fearlessly concoct better and better brews. Remember: Relax . . . don't worry . . . have a homebrew!

KEEPING RECORDS

The very first thing that you should do before embarking on brewing a batch of beer is to pop a few bottles of beer into the refrigerator. And get ready to brew.

The second thing that you'll want to consider is your ability to remember what you did to brew that best batch of beer. Because your beer will be worth remembering and you will be using such a variety of ingredients, it is worth your effort to keep a log of recipes and procedures. Keeping a record of your beer-making will enable you to duplicate favorite recipes and improve upon them (not to mention passing them on to friends).

You don't have to record an inordinate amount of detail. Keep it simple. Don't get so involved that keeping records becomes a bother. I assure you that you won't regret it. Here's a simple list of things that you'll want to record in your "Homebrew Recipe Log":

1) Date of brewing
2) Name of beer
3) Volume of beer being brewed (batch size)
4) List of all ingredients and amounts used
5) Time of boil
6) When and how grains and hops are added
7) Temperature of wort when yeast is added (pitched)
8) Beginning specific gravity
9) Dates of when beer is transferred (racked)
10) Date when bottled and amount of priming sugar
11) Ending specific gravity
12) Comments and blow-by-blow descriptions worth saving for posterity

EXAMPLE

February 30, 1984
Grizzly Beer Ale
5 Gallons

5 lbs.	Americana plain light malt extract syrup
1 lb.	crystal malt
2 tsp.	gypsum
1½ oz.	Fuggles hops (for boiling)
½ oz.	Hallertauer hops (finishing hop)
1 pkg.	Pilsener brand ale yeast

Boiled water, malts, gypsum and Fuggles hops for 45 minutes. Added Hallertauer hops during final 5 minutes for finishing.

2/30/84	Pitched yeast. 75 degrees F (24 C). Specific gravity 1.040 (10).
3/4/84	Racked beer to secondary fermenter. Specific gravity 1.017 (4). Still fermenting.
3/6/84	Activity has almost stopped.
3/14/84	Bottled with ¾ cup sugar. Ending specific gravity 1.013. Tastes real good, but a little yeasty.
3/20/84	Tasted first bottle—GREAT—still needs another week for better carbonation.
4/21/84	WOW! Crystal clear. Tastes perfect. Best beer ever. Next time I'll try ½ oz. more Fuggles hops in boil for more bitterness. *Boy, oh boy, am I glad I kept good notes!*

A REVIEW OF THE BREWING PROCESS

1) Have a homebrew. Relax. Don't worry.
2) Preparation of ingredients
3) Boiling the wort
4) Sparging (straining grains and hops from the wort)
5) Fermentation
6) Bottling
7) Have a homebrew. Relax. Don't worry.
8) Preparation of ingredients

1. Have a homebrew

Like sourdough bread, it is a good idea to begin your next batch of beer with a tribute to your last batch.

2. Preparation of ingredients

Your hops and malt extract will not need any preparation other than weighing or proportioning the necessary amount.

When you use specialty grains such as crystal, black patent and chocolate malts or roasted barley, you will need to do some simple preparation. In order to most efficiently utilize these grains, it is recommended that they be gently cracked, which can very easily be accomplished by using a rolling pin or an unopened can of malt extract. Spread a small amount of grain on a flat, hard surface and apply a small amount of pressure as you roll over the grains. (HOT TIP: Put the grains in a Ziploc-type plastic resealable bag and crush the grain in the bag. No muss, no fuss.) The objective is to break the grain into pieces (not to pulverize it into dust) so that the goodness of these grains may be extracted in the hot water or wort to which they will be added. Do not use a blender or food processor as the possibility of making specialty grain "flour" is more likely. If you are fortunate enough to have a flour mill, you may adjust the grinding plates so that their surfaces are far enough apart to crack the grain into four or five pieces rather than grind them into flour.

A crystal gaze! Crystal malt, shown here, has been crushed into granules and is now ready for the brewpot. Crushing allows the gracious goodness of specialty malts to more easily dissolve into the wort.

Overgrinding specialty malts will create difficulty in straining them out of the wort. If an excessive amount of grain powder is allowed to pass on to the fermenter, off-flavors in the beer may result.

The grinding of all your grains should be done in an area away from your fermentation. There is always a small amount of grain dust created when cracking or grinding. This dust carries bacteria that can very easily contaminate your beer.

3. Boiling the wort

During this process, you will boil water, malt extract, grains (or grain extract), hops, minerals, other sugars and adjuncts and finings. Most of these ingredients can be added indiscriminately at the beginning of the boil, but some yield better results when added discriminately.

The most effective way to introduce the goodness of specialty grains in malt extract brewing is to add the cracked grains to the cold water as it is being brought to a boil. Just before the water comes to a boil, simply use a small kitchen strainer and remove as much as possible without undue fuss. You will find that you can easily remove 80–90 percent of the grains. It's that simple! Want something even more simple? Use a grain bag (available from your local homebrew supply shop) and place your grains in it and use like a giant teabag.

After the specialty grains are removed from the water, add your malt extract, minerals, boiling hops and all other sugars. Now, many of you will chuckle when I tell you that your wort will boil over and make a horrendous mess if you don't watch out and watch it. But don't tell me I didn't warn you. It happens to all of us at least once. It's one of those things that we don't learn except by experience.

So, as you continue to heat and bring your wort back to a boil, use your wooden spoon (with charisma) to stir well and dissolve all of the ingredients so they won't stick and scorch on the bottom of the brewpot. You will want to time your boil from when it begins with all of the ingredients. Usually ½–1 hour is an adequate time for boiling your wort.

Hops that are used as flavor or aromatic finishing hops

should be added during the final 1–10 minutes of the boil. Generally, flavor will be extracted and preserved for no longer than 10 minutes of boiling. The aromatics of hops will be dissipated more quickly and should be allowed to steep for only 1–2 minutes if hop bouquet is desired in the finished beer.

Why boil? Boiling extracts the desired bittering qualities of hops. It is necessary to boil hops for at least ½ hour in order to facilitate the desired chemical reactions that allow the bittering resins to dissolve into your wort. The combination of the bittering qualities of the hops along with certain minerals and the physical process of boiling helps coagulate and precipitate undesirable proteins out of the wort. This reaction helps clarify the beer and improves the fermentation and flavor. Called the "hot-break," this reaction can be seen taking place in your brewpot. After a short period of boiling, your wort begins to exhibit a cloudiness and has flakes of coagulated protein floating in it. This coagulation and precipitation can be dramatically demonstrated by removing a small amount of boiling wort into a preheated

glass. You will observe the pea-sized flakes of protein settle to the bottom.

The addition of a small amount (¼ teaspoon for 5 gallons) of Irish moss during the final 5–10 minutes of the boil will aid in settling proteins. It is not necessary to boil wort for any longer than 1 hour.

4. Sparging

Sparging is the process of removing spent grains and/or hops from the wort by straining and then rinsing the spent brewing ingredients with hot water.

Before sparging, a few things must be attended to in order to maintain sanitation. Your fermenter, strainer and ladling device (usually a saucepan) should be sanitized. Procedures for sanitizing your fermenter have already been described. Once the fermenter has been sanitized, partially fill it with cold water. Your strainer may be easily sanitized by immersing it into your boiling wort (if it is a plastic strainer then use a sanitizing solution). Your saucepan may be likewise immersed into the boiling wort or placed in a hot oven to sterilize (only if saucepan is ovenproof). Don't worry—these procedures are simpler than the space it takes to describe them to you—and they work.

If there are no grains, and hop-flavored malt extract has been used, then there is no need to sparge. The hot concentrated wort may be ladled directly into the awaiting cold water.

If grains or whole hops have been used, the hot wort should be passed through a strainer on its way to the fermenter. The spent grains and hops that are caught in your strainer can be rinsed with a small amount of hot water in order to remove all of the goodness to the fermenter.

There is an advantage to sparging out whole hops in that the hops will form a natural filter, filtering out much of the protein coagulated during the hot-break. If the sparging process is bypassed you may notice a significant amount of sediment on the bottom of your fermenter. This sediment is called "trub" (pronounced: troob). Commercial brewers go to great lengths to remove this trub by sparging or whirlpooling the wort as it is drawn from the brewpot. (The whirlpool effect can be evoked

Another strained relationship! Have a homebrew, and remember: Separate the hops or grains in your brewpot from the wort before you put it in the fermenter. Here, boiling wort is poured into a fermenter containing cold water. NOTE: If a plastic fermenter is used, it is essential that it be fitted with a lid.

by stirring a cup of tea—the tea leaves will go to the center of the cup; similarly so will beer trub—the wort is drawn off from the sides of the vessel rather than from the bottom.) The presence of trub in the fermenting wort does affect fermentation and flavor, but for a homebrewer its overall significance is slight compared to all of the other variables that more dynamically affect the outcome of your beer. Relax. Don't worry. Have a homebrew.

It is from this point on that strict attention must be given to sanitation. After sparging, the wort becomes cool and susceptible to contaminating micro-organisms. So relax, don't worry, put your charismatic wooden spoon back in storage and assure yourself that you have sanitized your equipment.

5. Fermentation

Once the cooled wort is in your fermenter, you should muck about in it as little as possible, preferably not at all. If necessary, the wort should be stirred or agitated with a sanitized plastic or long-handled metal spoon. A temperature should be taken and a small amount of wort should be poured or carefully ladled into a hydrometer flask in order that a specific gravity can be read.

Once yeast has been added, put your fermenter in a relatively quiet, out-of-the-way place and away from direct light. Strong light will react with hops and create a skunky or rubbery aroma and flavor. In strong sunlight this reaction can take place in a matter of minutes.

"Primary" (the first stage) fermentation should be maintained at temperatures of 60–70 degrees F (16–21 C) for ales and most dried lager yeasts, but are best started at 70–76 degrees F (21–24 C). True lager yeasts are best begun at wort temperatures between 50–60 degrees F (10–16 C) and maintained at stable temperatures of 35–55 degrees F (2–13 C) once fermentation is achieved.

Once the yeast has been added, signs of fermentation will be noticed within 24 hours, and usually within 36 hours there is a massive amount of activity as the yeast activity churns a rich foamy head (called kraeusen). The kraeusen is topped with a very bitter and brown resinous scum, some of which will adhere to the sides of the fermenter as the kraeusen shortly disappears and falls back into the beer. There is an advantage to the removal of this resin before it falls back into the fermentation: There will be less of a bitter "bite" to your beer. In the process of removing the bitter resins, "fusel" oils are also removed. Fusel oils are a by-product of fermentation and contribute to what are often referred to as "beer headaches." If the removal of hop resins during the kraeusen stage can be done under sanitary conditions then it is advised to do so. The closed fermentation system described in the Beginner's Section ("blow-out" tube and glass carboy) automatically facilitates the removal of the kraeusen during the initial stages of fermentation. If open fermentation is used and there is a risk of contamination, then avoid removing the kraeusen because contamination will affect the flavor of your beer much more than will the minimal effect of the mostly insoluble resins and oils. When in doubt, relax, and don't worry . . . your beer will taste just fine.

After the first 3 to 6 days of fermentation, the kraeusen will fall back into the beer and the yeast will begin to settle. If a one-stage fermentation procedure is undertaken (only one fermenter is used), then the brewer should bottle the beer between the sixth and fourteenth day or when fermentation activity has stopped, whichever comes first.

When fermentation activity stops, the protective layer of foam and/or carbon dioxide is no longer present and the possibility of contamination increases. Fermentation activity can be measured by a hydrometer.

If you are planning to mature the beer in the fermenter over a period longer than 2 weeks, then it is advisable to transfer the beer into a closed fermenter. A closed fermenter can simply be a 5-gallon carboy with a fermentation lock attached. The advantage to "racking" (transferring) the beer under these circumstances is that the beer is locked away from contaminants in the air and is removed from the sediment. After about 2 weeks the sediment will begin to break down and may contribute to off-flavors to the beer.

Racking your beer—Racking is the name used by brewers to describe the transfer of beer from one container to another. The easiest and most effective way for the homebrewer to accomplish this is by siphoning with a clean, sanitized, clear plastic hose.

Your choice of fermenters will have a bearing on the amount of attention you have to give to your beer. A closed fermentation system requires the least amount of attention and has many other advantages. An open fermentation system (the plastic bucket) will produce excellent beer but more attention must be given to the timeliness of transferring and bottling.

Open fermentation—At first, this type of fermentation appears simpler and more economical. In certain ways it is, but it doesn't really allow you the freedom from concern that you deserve. For those of you who choose, or perhaps have no choice, here are a few hints to ensure excellent beer:

1) Keep the fermenter covered at all times, except when taking hydrometer readings.

2) Do not skim the kraeusen foam. Risk of contamination is too great, especially when using a strainer.

3) The disappearance of the kraeusen is a perfect indication that the beer is ready to transfer to a secondary fermenter. You will usually find that by this time your specific gravity has fallen to two thirds of the original specific gravity.

4) Maturing your beer over long periods of time is unnecessary. You should be drinking your beer within four weeks.

Closed fermentation—The closed fermentation system that is described in the Beginner's Section is the most relaxing way to brew beer. It is a system in which the primary stage of fermentation is done in a sanitized container, usually a 5-gallon carboy, atop which an overflow hose is attached. The advantages of this system are many. Maximum sanitation is ensured, and the bitter resins and fusel oils that form on the kraeusen are very efficiently "blown out" the overflow hose—without the brewer so much as worrying a tat. The disadvantage is that you may lose a quart or two of precious brew, but it is an insignificant price to pay for the best beer you've ever brewed.

Racking and siphoning your beer will be necessary if prolonged maturation before bottling is desired (for example, that vacation you wanted to take or those bottles that haven't materialized yet, or the free time you don't have until next week).

Longer and successful maturation of beer is possible with closed fermentation because contamination has been minimized. Thus your beer will be more stable.

6. Bottling

Once fermentation has stopped or you are satisfied that your beer is finished, you should bottle. Bottling procedures for the intermediate brewer are no different than for the beginner. The ¾ cup (NOT POUNDS!) of corn sugar (or 1¼ cups dried malt extract) per 5 gallons of beer is adequate priming sugar for carbonation. It is an amount that will allow you to serve your beer at room temperature without gushing. One cup of corn sugar (or 1⅔ cups dried malt extract) per 5 gallons of beer will safely increase the amount of carbonation, but gushing is likely to occur if the beer is not chilled.

The entire amount of priming sugar should be boiled with a pint or so of water before adding it to the beer. DON'T AERATE OR SPLASH YOUR BEER WHEN BOTTLING. Stick your siphon hose clear down to the bottom of each of the bottles. *Siphon quietly*.

The amount of air space left in the bottle is an area of concern to many homebrewers. Generally speaking, the less air space the better. The oxygen in the air that you leave in the bottle will react, to some degree, with the beer in the bottle. A normal amount of air space to leave is about 1–1½ inches. My own observations have indicated that a bottle that is filled right to the top, with no air space whatsoever, will not develop enough carbonation. An air space of ½ inch will develop the same carbonation as a bottle of beer with 2 inches of air space. A bottle that is half filled with beer may become excessively carbonated and very dangerous if it explodes. My educated explanation is that insufficient or excessive carbonation, due to over- or underfill is related to the fact that yeast activity is inhibited by pressure. A small air space (overfill) will quickly develop high pressure while a large air space (underfill) will not develop enough pressure to inhibit yeast activity.

Kegging your beer—Homebrew can be kegged and served on draft. It is an extremely convenient way to "put up" your brew. See Appendix 2 for complete details on ways to keg your brew and how to reduce your priming sugar so your beer isn't all foam.

7. Have a homebrew—natch.

SOME WORLD CLASSIC STYLES OF BEER

"Beer is beer." Thus these words were uttered a long, long time ago and it was so.

How many different kinds of beer are there in the world? A conservative answer might be in the neighborhood of 20,000— that's 20,000 different kinds of beer. Unlike the United States, there are thousands of commercial breweries in Europe, as well as Asia and Africa. One brewery might make four to six different styles of beer in the course of a year. So that you see, 20,000 is quite a conservative estimate.

What of these styles of beer? What makes one style distinct from another? How does one classify them? The first distinction one might make is whether or not a beer is top-fermented (ale) or bottom-fermented (lager). From these two classes spring the immense variety of top- and bottom-fermented brews.

There are many, many styles of ale being brewed, each

indigenous to its area. Following are some of the more classic styles of top-fermented ales.

Data for each style may be abbreviated as follows:

International Bitterness Units: IBU

Color in degrees SRM: Standard Reference Method

Alcohol expressed in percent alcohol by volume

BRITISH ALE

British ale is a top-fermented beer. When traditionally brewed, it is made of 100 percent malted barley, hops, water and yeast, although these days adjuncts such as sugar, barley, corn, rice or potato starch sometimes find a way into some British ales. It is fermented at temperatures between 60–70 degrees F (16–21 C) for 3 to 5 days, then racked to cellar fermenters to clarify at temperatures closer to 50 degrees F (10 C). From the cellar conditioning, the ale is racked into casks and bunged (with wooden "corks"). The ale is allowed to condition for 2 to 3 days before being served in the British pubs.

If British ale is not filtered or pasteurized, it is often referred to as "real ale." Served at cellar temperatures of 55 degrees F (13 C), it is slightly carbonated and expresses a variety of character depending on the style being brewed.

Some of the traditional varieties of hops used in British ales are Brewers Gold, Bullion, Kent Goldings, Fuggles and Northern Brewer. Small brewers in America emulating this style often use Cascade, Willamette and Centennial, lending a unique character to the ale.

The classic styles of British ale are:

Bitter—A light ale that may be generally available in three strengths. "Ordinary Bitter" is brewed from specific gravities between 1.035–1.038 (9–9.5). "Special Bitter" is brewed from specific gravities between 1.039–1.042 (9.5–10.5) and "Extra Special Bitter" may be brewed from specific gravities between 1.043–1.049 (11–12). While these are generalizations, most bitters fall in these ranges.

Bitter may be highly or lightly hopped (Bitterness: 20–35 IBU), express hop bouquet or none at all. Some styles will have a rich creamy head while others will be served in a less carbonated condition. There are many regional styles of bitter. (Color: 8–14 SRM.)

There are few bottled versions of bitter imported to the United States. One of the few is Fuller's London Pride, but it is not really indicative of a true draft or bottle-conditioned English Bitter. There are numerous commercial microbreweries and pub breweries in both the United States and Canada that brew this style of ale.

English Bitter is one of the easiest, quickest and most satisfying styles of beer that a homebrewer can make.

Mild—Mild is a brown ale of low alcoholic strength. Its tradition evolved from the working-class areas of northern England where great thirsts developed in the steel mills. The consumption of much beer was tempered by the low alcoholic strength. Beer was and still is a very social institution, intended to be enjoyed and savored rather than a vehicle for drunkenness.

Mild is a brown ale that is not particularly robust or hoppy; rather it is thirst-quenching, low alcohol, flavorful and light- to medium-bodied. A small amount of black patent or chocolate malt adds color more than robust flavor.

Other than homebrewed, there are no bottled and very few draft versions of this style of British ale available in the United States. Homebrewed versions of English mild are quick to mature and easy to duplicate authentically.

Original gravities: 1.032–1.036 (8–9). Alcohol: 2.5–3.5 percent. Bitterness: 14–30 IBU. Color: 22–35 SRM.

Pale Ale—Pale ale is a special variety of British ale that tends to be more hoppy and higher in alcohol than its relative, English Bitter.

The *classic style* of English pale ale is brewed with water that is extraordinarily hard and contains a lot of minerals, particularly calcium sulfate and carbonates. The high mineral content lends itself to the use of more hops, the high sulfate content of the water contributes a dry character. Today, pale ales can be found in England on draft or in bottles, often bottle-conditioned and containing a yeast sediment exactly as a bottle of homebrew would.

Many small American breweries brew this style of beer—a classic example is Sierra Nevada Pale Ale. Imports from England representative of this style are Bass Ale, Young's Special London Ale, Whitbread's Pale Ale and Samuel Smith's Pale Ale. Original gravities: 1.045–1.055. Alcohol: 4.5–5.5 percent. Bitterness: 20–30 IBU. Color: 8–10 SRM.

India Pale Ale is a special style of pale ale that has more hop flavor, aroma and bitterness, and a higher alcohol content (5.5–7%); starting gravities can range from 1.055–1.070 (14–17.5). Bitterness: 30–60 IBU. Color: 6–14 SRM. Commercially made, the Anchor Brewing Company's Liberty Ale is one example of the India pale ale style.

Old Ales/Strong Ales are high-alcohol versions of pale ale. With greater strength comes more body and sweetness. Strong ales are often aged longer, consequently the sharpness of hop bitterness softens. Higher original gravities also lend a more fruity character to these old ales. Original gravities: 1.060–1.075 (15–19). Alcohol: 6.5–8.5 percent. Bitterness: 30–50 IBU. Color: 10–16 SRM.

Pale ale is probably one of the more popular styles of homebrew in the United States, due to its clean taste and stability.

Brown Ale—A variety of brown ales are brewed in Great Britain. Generally they are sweeter, fuller bodied and stronger than their relative, mild ales. Some brown ales are light brown and have a sweet nutty character such as Newcastle Brown Ale, while others are more robust and unusual such as Old Peculier. English brown ales are most often brewed from specific gravities of 1.040–1.050 (10–12.5). Alcohol: 4.5–6.5 percent. Bitterness: 15–30 IBU. Color: 15–22 SRM.

A more bitter style of English brown ale emerged among American homebrewers during the 1980s. For lack of a better name, the style was dubbed American Brown Ale, somewhat akin to a dark pale ale with lots of hops. Its bitterness ranges between 25–60 IBU.

Many homebrewers begin their homebrewing endeavors with a quickly maturing, full-bodied and satisfying brown ale. Its full flavor is most impressive, especially for the beginner or someone who has not tasted good homebrew before.

Stout—Stouts are black ales that owe their character to roasted barley and a high hop rate. There are three styles of stout: imperial, sweet and the more popular dry.

Draft versions of *dry stout* are usually surprisingly low in alcohol and often brewed from original specific gravities of 1.033–1.036 (8–9). The classic Guinness Stout, as brewed and served in Dublin, Ireland, is low in alcohol, dry, has a clean bitterness but no hop flavor or bouquet; part of the bitter character is contributed by roasted barley. Its rich foamy head is enhanced by using nitrogen gas when it is dispensed from the cask. The bottled version of Guinness has more of a roasted barley character and offers a subtle sweetness.

With draft Guinness being an exception, most classic dry stouts begin with an original gravity between 1.036–1.055 (9–14). Alcohol: 3–6 percent. Bitterness: 25–40 IBU. Color: 35+ SRM.

The degree of sweetness and dryness will vary in dry stouts, yet they are all top-fermented and have the singularly unique and special character of roasted barley.

Imperial Stout is a robust and sincerely stronger version of dry stout. It is highly hopped for bitterness. In the United States, where the style has been revived by several small breweries and several thousand homebrewers, it is most often dosed with flavor and aroma hops as well. With its high alcohol and high hopping rate, this style of stout can be aged with much grace, meandering through many wonderful changes in flavor complexity. Original gravities are typically 1.075–1.090 (19–22.5). Alcohol: 7–9 percent. Bitterness: 50–90 IBU. Color: 35+ SRM.

Several small American breweries brew this style, the most notable being the Yakima Brewing Company, Yakima, Washington. They brew the award-winning Grant's Imperial Stout, a standard by which many homebrewers gauge their efforts.

Sweet Stout is a rarity among commercially made beers. It lacks most of the hop bitterness and roasted barley character of its dry counterpart. In England the style is often bottled as "farm stout." To achieve the sweet character, sugar or other sweeteners may be added to carbonated beer, which is then pasteurized to stop fermentation activity, a difficult process for the homebrewer. Also, unfermentable lactose sugar may be added, not so much for the minimal sweetness it contributes but for the contribution of body. Original gravities: 1.045–1.056 (11–14). Alcohol: 4.5–6 percent. Bitterness: 15–20 IBU. Color: 35+ SRM.

The world-classic and unique Mackesson Sweet Stout brewed by Whitbread of England is sweetened with sucrose and given more body with lactose sugar just before bottling. It is then pasteurized in order to stop all fermentation. Mackesson Sweet Stout can be described as a very sweet black ale appropriately served as an after-dinner liqueur.

If you like stout, you will no doubt pursue a recipe that will brew this robust and satisfying style of beer. The freshness of brewing it yourself and the satisfaction of making a stout that is every bit as good or better than what you are used to buying is quite an experience. Stout is truly the "espresso" of the beer world.

Barley Wine—Because of their unusual strength, some English ales are often referred to as barley wines. They sometimes can reach an alcoholic strength of 12 percent by volume and are brewed from specific gravities as high as 1.120 (28)! They are indeed alcoholic and full-bodied. Their natural sweetness is usually balanced with a high rate of hop bitterness. The counterpoint is the beer drinker in between, slowly sipping and savoring the often estery, fruity and well-aged character of this specialty, brewed most often to celebrate events. Because of the high hop rate and alcohol content, some barley wines are meant to be aged for over 25 years!

Most barley wines are golden or copper colored. One style that is a deep rich copper brown is Russian Imperial Stout brewed by the Courage Brewery in England. It is a style unto itself, not really a stout in the traditional sense, but historically named for its strength.

Original gravities: 1.090–1.120 (22.5–30). Alcohol: 8.5–12 percent. Bitterness: 50–100 IBU. Color: 14–22 SRM.

Porter—A traditional description of this style would be hard to come by and likely to be controversial. It is a dark ale; unlike stout its character does not come from roasted barley but more from dark malts. Its alcoholic strength (4.5–6%) is not excessive, usually brewed from an original specific gravity of 1.040–1.055 (10–14). Generally, it is medium-bodied with varying degrees of sweetness and hop character. Bitterness: 25–35 IBU. Color: 25–35 SRM.

Historically, it was a style of ale that was the granddaddy of today's stout. Porter was the common man's drink and often homebrewed. Its character was expressed with a wild assortment of adjuncts, herbs and miscellaneous ingredients. It was originally brewed commercially by Arthur Guinness and Sons in Ireland. When the alcoholic strength of porter was boosted, it was described as stout porter. The name stout was soon adopted for this style.

Today, porters are brewed in the United States and England on a relatively small scale. In the United States, Anchor Brewing Company of San Francisco, California, brews a robust black and sharply bittersweet version of porter, while other American small breweries and microbreweries brew a less bitter version. England's Samuel Smith Brewery brews a medium-brown, sweet version of porter.

This rich black style of ale offers the homebrewer an opportunity to brew a rich black ale without the bite of roasted barley, characteristic of stouts.

Scottish Ale—These ales brewed in the northern climates of the United Kingdom are the counterparts of English ale. The significant differences are reflected in their maltier flavor, relatively darker colors and occasional faint smoky character. Scottish Light 60/ (''/'' means shillings), Heavy 70/, Export 80/ are

cousins of English Bitter, and Strong ''Scotch'' Ale is a maltier and darker version of English Old/Strong Ale.

Light 60/—Original gravities: 1.030–1.035 (7.5–9). Alcohol: 3–4 percent. Bitterness: 9–10 IBU. Color: 10–12 SRM.

Heavy 70/—Original gravities: 1.035–1.040 (9–10). Alcohol: 3.5–4 percent. Bitterness: 10–11 IBU. Color: 11–13 SRM.

Export 80/—Original gravities: 1.040–1.050 (10–12.5). Alcohol: 4–5.5 percent. Bitterness: 11–13 IBU. Color: 12–15 SRM.

Strong ''Scotch'' Ale—Original gravities: 1.075–1.085 (19–21). Alcohol: 6–8 percent. Bitterness: 14–16 IBU. Color: 14–17 SRM.

OTHER TOP-FERMENTED STYLES OF BEER

Wheat Beers—Until the mid-1980s beers made with wheat were available only in the countries of their origin: Belgium and

Germany. With the popularization of homebrewing and new small breweries opening in America some traditional styles of wheat beer are enjoying growing popularity worldwide. Of the traditional styles of wheat beer from Germany and Belgium, there are three very distinct styles: Weizenbier or Weissbier from southern Germany, Berliner-style Weisse, and Belgian Lambic.

German Weizenbier (or Weissbier)—These are the wheat beers of southern Germany. Their character is refreshing, light-bodied, lightly hopped, yeasty, highly effervescent, slightly sour and with flavor and aroma suggestive of cloves and banana. Twenty-eight percent of all of the beer consumed in Germany is this style of beer and it is becoming increasingly popular with homebrewers now that wheat extracts and special yeasts have become available to brew this style.

Weizenbiers have at least 50 percent wheat malt. The yeast is a special type that is top-fermenting but produces a clovelike and banana flavor. The wheat itself contributes to the fruitiness of Weizenbier. Traditionally, the special top-fermenting yeast is filtered out before bottling or kegging, at which time a more flocculant (better settling) lager yeast is added for natural bottle conditioning. Southern Germans love their Weizenbier and they love it with the yeast (*mit Hefe*).

Original gravities: 1.045–1.050 (11–12.5). Alcohol: 4.5–5 percent. Bitterness: 8–14 IBU. Color: 3–8 SRM.

Dunkelweizen—The dark version of Weizenbier. It can be a bit stronger. With a chocolatelike maltiness this brew tones down the clove and banana character somewhat, but still maintains the tang and pizazz of the style. Original gravities: 1.045–1.055 (11–14). Alcohol: 4.5–6 percent. Bitterness: 10–15 IBU. Color: 17–22 SRM.

Weizenbock—Everything you'd expect it to be if you know the traditional bock style. Stronger and more robust than Dunkelweizen, but with the telltale traits of the traditional southern style. It can be either light or dark (*helles* or *dunkel*). Original gravities: 1.066–1.080 (16.5–20). Alcohol: 6.5–7.5 percent. Bitterness: 10–15 IBU. Color: 7–30 SRM.

Berliner-style Weisse—Brewed with 60–75 percent malted wheat, this commercially made brand of beer is a most unusual

German beer. It undergoes a combination of yeast and lactic bacterial fermentation, resulting in a mouth-puckering sourness. This north German style is very pale, effervescent, having virtually no bitterness and often is considered a summer drink. Disciples of Berliner Weisse mix in sweet syrups of raspberry, lemon or woodruff (an herb).

Because of the uncontrollable nature and unpredictability of the lactobaccilus bacteria and the unique strains of top-fermenting yeast employed in making this style, homebrewing northern Weisse beer is a risky business. Consult Appendix 6 for more information on how to make a controlled sour beer.

Original gravities: 1.028–1.032 (7–8). Alcohol: 2.5–3.5 percent. Bitterness: 5–12 IBU. Color: 2–4 SRM.

Belgian Lambic—Of all the beers in the world, I personally think this surely rates as one of the most intriguing, mysterious and erotic styles of beer ever made.

Airborne wild yeasts and bacteria unique to a 15-square-mile area southwest of Brussels, Belgium, fall into freshly brewed wort to slowly make a transformation to a uniquely sour wheat beer. Lambic breweries are temples where dirt is evident everywhere and spiders are worshipped. From 30 to 40 percent unmalted wheat is cooked, then combined and mashed with malted barley. Hops that have been aged years at room temperatures are used exclusively and sparingly. Fermentation takes place in age-old wooden vessels.

There are several stylistic variations of lambic, but generally all of them are, at the very least, pungently sour, very low in bitterness, very effervescent, peculiarly aromatic, aged for years and strangely addictive. Original gravities: 1.040–1.050 (10–12.5). Alcohol: 4–6 percent. Bitterness: 3–5 IBU. Color: 4–8 SRM.

Gueuze is a combination of a young (approximately 3 months fermenting) lambic with an old lambic. New fermentation begins in the bottle and is ready after one more year.

Faro is a unique combination of high- and low-alcohol lambic to which sugar and sometimes caramel (for coloring) are added.

Kriek lambic continues in the tradition of strange brews. Cherries are combined with young lambic, inducing a new fer-

mentation lasting 4 to 8 months. The kriek is then filtered, bottled and aged yet another year before ready.

Framboise, peche and cassis lambic styles are similar to kriek lambic with a substitution of a particular fruit such as raspberry, peach or black currant.

American Wheat Beer—After all of the special characters attributable to European-origin wheat beers, the new American

wheat beers may at first lack luster. Furthermore, they defy definition. For the most part what has been referred to as the American wheat style is no more than substituting wheat for a portion
of malted barley. Malted or unmalted wheat is not responsible
for the unique characters of the European styles of wheat beer,
so their impact on recipe formulation is low. Unique yeasts and
bacterial fermentations used in German and Belgian styles of
wheat beer are avoided for the American style. So what makes
it for American wheat? If I'm forced to give a description at this
time I'd have to say American wheat beers are low in bitterness
with a somewhat fruity esteriness from the wheat. Perhaps in
time a truer style definition will emerge.

   German-style Ale—A German ale tradition survives in the
Düsseldorf and Köln (Cologne) areas of Germany. Brewed with
pure cultures of top-fermenting yeast, there are two very distinct
varieties.
   Düsseldorf-style Altbier—Altbier, literally translated, means
"old" beer; the way it used to be made in the old days before
the discovery of lager yeast. Altbier is an ale tradition that survives in the Düsseldorf area of Germany. It is a deep amber to
dark brown ale lacking hop flavor or aroma but often exploding
with bitterness. Fruitiness from top fermentation can be a character, but is often minimized by the unique process of "lagering"
or storing in a secondary fermenter at very cold temperatures,
much colder than your typical English ale. Original gravities:
1.044–1.048 (11–12). Alcohol: 4.5–5 percent. Bitterness: 28–40
IBU. Color: 16–19 SRM.
   Kölsch is light, fruity, slightly acidic, medium-hopped, dry
and a reminiscently winelike top-fermented ale or bottom-fermented lager brewed in the area of Cologne. Kölsch yeast strains
would have to be sought by the homebrewer to come close to
duplicating this style of German ale. Sometimes malted wheat is
used as an ingredient. Original gravities: 1.040–1.045 (10–11).
Alcohol: 4–5 percent. Bitterness: 16–30 IBU. Color: 4–10 SRM.

   American Cream Ale—A style of ale that at one time employed the use of both ale and lager yeasts during fermentation.

Essentially its character is reminiscent of a hoppier, slightly stronger, slightly fruity cousin to a standard American light lager. More often than not it is brewed with adjuncts such as corn or rice. Well carbonated and refreshing on a hot day when you want to remember some bitterness in that cold light American beer. Original gravities: 1.044–1.055 (11–14). Alcohol: 4.5–7 percent. Bitterness: 10–22 IBU. Color: 2–4 SRM.

Belgian Specialty Ales—Belgium is a land of hundreds of unique styles of beers. My time would be better spent going to Belgium and sampling 20 varieties than listing them each here. Belgium is the Disneyland of the beer world.

However, a few styles often available outside the homeland are worth mentioning.

Flanders Brown Ale—Hard to find but a unique blend of slight sourness, richness of brown malts with the fruitiness of a top-fermented ale. Hop flavor and aroma do not make an impression, though the bitterness can be assertive. Original gravities: 1.045–1.055 (11–14). Alcohol: 5–6.5 percent. Bitterness: 35–50 IBU. Color: 16–20 SRM.

Saison—Brewed traditionally in the spring for the summer season. As with most Belgian ales, Saison has a unique Belgian fruitiness and pungent sourness, accented with aroma hops. Light to amber in color, this ale is distinctively bitter but not assertive. A crystal maltiness is sometimes evident. Strength can vary greatly, but most Saisons are brewed in the middle range. Original gravities: 1.052–1.080 (13–20). Alcohol: 5.5–7.5 percent. Bitterness: 25–40 IBU. Color: 4–10 SRM.

Belgian White Beer—From the Disneyland of beer emerges yet another delightfully fun and awesome brew. Brewed with unmalted wheat, malted barley and sometimes oats, the style is enhanced by the addition of coriander seed, curaçao (orange peel may be substituted), Hallertauer or Saaz hops and is traditionally bottle conditioned just like homebrew. A fun, lively and surprisingly delicious brew. Original gravities: 1.044–1.050 (11–12.5). Alcohol: 4.5–5 percent. Bitterness: 20–35 IBU. Color: 2–4 SRM.

Belgian Trappist Ale—Somewhat a style by itself, but more accurately the name given to beers brewed by the six remaining Trappist monasteries in Belgium. The beers are generally strong, amber to copper colored, fruity with a unique Belgian spiciness and slight acidity that sets them apart from all other ale traditions. Often three varieties are made: a house brew, a special (or double malt) and an extra special (or triple malt). In order to duplicate this style, access to the original yeast from these breweries is almost essential and possible because most of the Trappist beers are not pasteurized. Many have been cultured by homebrewers with great success.

House brew—Original gravities: 1.060–1.065 (15–16). Alcohol: 6–6.5 percent. Bitterness: 25–40 IBU. Color: 15–25 SRM.

Double malt —Original gravities: 1.075–1.085 (19–21). Alcohol: 7.5–8 percent. Bitterness: 30–40 IBU. Color: 17–30 SRM.

Triple malt—Original gravities: 1.090–1.100 (22.5–25). Alcohol: 8–10 percent. Bitterness: 35–50 IBU. Color: 20–30 SRM.

GERMAN AND CONTINENTAL LAGERS

German lager brewing is a style of beer that has enjoyed the most popularity throughout the world. German brewmasters have taken their art to the United States, China, Japan, Mexico and most other major brewing nations of the world.

Lager beers are brewed with bottom-fermenting types of yeast at temperatures generally below 50 degrees F (10 C). It was not until the late nineteenth century that lager yeasts were recognized, identified and isolated. The beers that were brewed under cold fermentations were cleaner tasting and more stable, perhaps initially due to the inability of many beer-spoiling bacteria to propagate in cold beer wort. Beers were able to be aged for longer periods of time and with this ability new and enjoyable flavor characteristics were discovered.

The German word *lager* means "to store." Initial or primary fermentation usually takes place for 4 to 6 days at temperatures of 40–50 degrees F (4–10 C). All true lager beers are lagered and matured for usually a minimum of 3 weeks in a secondary fermenter at temperatures below 40 degrees F (4 C). Some styles of lager beer are lagered for over 3 months.

Lager beers may be available to the beer drinker pasteurized or not, filtered or unfiltered, on draft or bottled. There is a tremendous variety of German and Continental styles of lager beer. They are all intended to be served chilled at 45–55 degrees F (7–13 C), are well carbonated and display a rich head.

Some of the traditional types of hops that are used are Hallertauer, Northern Brewer, Perle, Spalt, Saaz and Tettnanger.

Some of the classic styles of German and Continental lagers are:

Pilsener—The original pilsener beer was brewed in Plzen (which means "green meadow"), Czechoslovakia. Upon introduction in 1842, it created quite a stir in the brewing community because of its pale golden color. Prior to this all beers were dark. The golden beer from Plzen gained in popularity as its fame spread and was duplicated in all parts of Europe, America and throughout the world. There are two classic styles that we can truly recognize as pilsener today. Both are pale to golden colored, brewed with very soft water and made with an assertive but varying amount of hops.

Bohemian/Czechoslovakian Pilsener—What remains of the original style is pale, golden and alluring. A creamy dense head tops a well-carbonated brew with an accent on the rich, sweet malt that the beer is made from. Medium-bodied Bohemian-style pilsener really makes its impression with the bitterness, flavor and aromatic character of the indigenous Czech Saaz hop. Clean, crisp, hop-spicy, bitter with malty overtones, pale and simply luscious. Original gravities: 1.044–1.056 (11–14). Alcohol: 4–5.5 percent. Bitterness: 35–45 IBU. Color: 2.5–4.5 SRM.

German Pilsener—"Pils" for short, this style is an offspring of the original from neighboring Czechoslovakia, but with an inclination for more bitterness and a drier, less malty character. The most popular beer style in all of Germany, German Pils is brewed with exactness and a distinctly pungent and refreshing bitterness. To duplicate the definitive German Pils character, German "noble" hops such as Spalt, Northern Brewer, Tettnanger, Hallertauer or Saaz plus very soft water are absolute musts in the brewing process. Original gravities: 1.044–1.050 (11–12.5). Alcohol: 4–5 percent. Bitterness: 35–45 IBU. Color: 2.5–4.5 SRM.

Oktoberfest, Märzen and Vienna Lagers—These similar styles of beer originated in southern Germany and Austria, where beers tend to express themselves with malty sweetness. These three lagers are easily brewed by homebrewers. Their home-brewed freshness often surpasses the imported varieties that have traveled thousands of miles from the brewery under uncertain conditions.

Oktoberfest and Märzen are rich, amber-orange, copper-colored lagers. Their aroma is assertively malty and appropriately balanced with quickly sharp but not lingering hop bitterness. A seasonal style, traditionally brewed in March (Märzen), this rich beer is quite strong in alcohol and served at the fabled German Oktoberfests in liter and half-liter steins. Original gravities: 1.050–1.060 (12.5–15). Alcohol: 4.5–6.5 percent. Bitterness: 20–30 IBU. Color: 8–14 SRM.

Vienna-style Lager is almost commercially extinct. It may no longer be brewed in Austria. It remains true to form only at a very few breweries in Mexico! It was to Mexico that Austrian brewmasters emigrated during the political events that preceded World War II. Even in Mexico there are but a very, very few examples of this style. Negra Modelo is one example (though brewed with corn and barley malt) that is available in the United States on a limited basis. It is an amber-red to copper color, with an overall character reminiscent of German Oktoberfest, but a less robust sweet malt character. Original gravities: 1.046–1.052 (11.5–13). Alcohol: 4.5–5.5 percent. Bitterness: 18–30 IBU. Color: 10–20 SRM.

Bock and Doppelbock—No, bock beer is not made from the bottom of the barrel, and it is only in America that this rumor could have originated. Bock beer is a highly respected all-malt dark lager of considerable alcoholic strength. German law even dictates requirements for what a bock beer is. It is traditionally a well-lagered beer that is sometimes associated with a goat (the reason: *bock* in German means "goat"). Christmas bocks often are brewed to be consumed under the astrological sign of Capricorn. This style of beer also is celebrated in the spring as a tribute to Saint Joseph (March 19) by monasteries in Munich. Bock beers can be brewed simply by any homebrewer. Most brands of malt extract and specialty malts will brew a lusciously strong batch of bock beer. The quality of yeast will aid in brewing a bock of real strength, but a very satisfying result can be brewed at kitchen temperatures with quality beer yeasts.

German Bock beers can be either dark or light (*helles*) in color. Their character is strong in alcohol with a very malty-sweet overall character. Hop bitterness is low and only suggests itself in order to offset the sweetness of malt. The character of the dark malts should not taste roasted or burnt in bock beer. Traditional German bocks do not have hop aroma or flavor of any consequence. Original gravities: 1.066–1.074 (16.5–18.5). Alcohol: 6–7.5 percent. Bitterness: 20–30 IBU. Color: For helles bock: 8–18 SRM; for dark bock: 18–35 SRM.

Doppelbocks are a stronger version of bock beers with an original gravity decreed by German law to not fall below a certain degree. They can be pale or dark, very sweet or balanced with bitterness. But they all pack a wallop. In Germany all doppelbocks can be identified by the suffix "-ator" on the name. Elevator, Alligator, Exterminator, Incubator; whatever you name it, it certainly is a beer to be respected. Original gravities: 1.074–1.100 (18.5–25). Alcohol: 7.5–14 percent. Bitterness: 20–40 IBU. Color: 12–35 SRM.

Munich Helles and Dunkel—The mainstay of Bavarian festive beer drinking. Light (*helles*) Munich-style lager is served everywhere throughout Bavaria. The style offers the homebrewer easy access to the rich brewing tradition of southern Germany. Generally lower in alcohol than many of the other celebratory styles, this is a beer for everyday quaffing. Even I have downed two or three liters of the stuff with only a grin to show for it.

Munich Helles—A mildly hopped, malty, pale-colored beer. A common tendency for homebrewers is to overhop this beer.

Go easy on the hops. Yes, there is a pleasing bitterness, but it does not linger at all. Furthermore, hop aroma and flavor are generally absent in this style. Original gravities: 1.046–1.055 (11.5–14). Alcohol: 4.5–5.5 percent. Bitterness: 16–25 IBU. Color: 2–5 SRM.

Munich Dunkel—The dark counterpart to Munich Helles with a distinctly roasted (not burnt), chocolatelike character complimented with an overall malty sweetness and low hop bitterness. The perception of dunkel is that it is more bitter than helles because of the contribution of bitterness by the roasted malts used in the formulation. Original gravities: 1.050–1.055 (12.5–14). Alcohol: 4.5–6 percent. Bitterness: 18–27 IBU. Color: 10–20 SRM.

Schwarzbier—Literally translated, this is "black beer." A Bavarian tradition, this specialty black lager is colored as its name implies, but with judicious amounts of roasted malts so as to not impart a burnt flavor. Schwarzbier is a relatively low-alcohol brew with the smoothness of a lighter beer. Moderate bitterness and very little hop aroma or flavor round out the character. Original gravities: 1.040–1.046 (10–11.5). Alcohol: 3.5–4.5 percent. Bitterness: 25–35 IBU. Color: 25–40 SRM.

Dortmunder/Export—Generally a strong pale lager that is characterized by more bitterness and less maltiness than Munich Helles but far less bitterness and more malt body than German pilseners. It was originally brewed for export from the city of Dortmund, hence its name. Original gravities: 1.050–1.060 (12.5–15). Alcohol: 5–6 percent. Bitterness: 25–35 IBU. Color: 4–6 SRM.

Rauchbier—Smoke-flavored beers! One of my personal favorites. I was introduced to this style with a taste of Schlenkerla Rauchbier from the Franconian brewing town of Bamberg, Germany. Holy smokes, was I ever impressed. A velvety smooth Oktoberfest style of lager beer laced with a rich smoke flavor. This brew goes exceptionally well with almost any kind of meat dish and is a real treat if you like smoked food. The flavor is imparted by the malts that have been dried over wood flames and smoke. German beechwood is used, but the homebrewer may smoke his or her malts with apple, peach, hickory, cherry, mesquite or other favorite barbecue smoking wood.

Original gravities: 1.050–1.060 (12.5–15). Alcohol: 5–6 percent. Bitterness: 20–30 IBU. Color: 12–17 SRM.

OTHER STYLES OF LAGER BEERS

Some of the other major lager drinking countries of the world are Australia, Canada, China, Japan and the United States—all of which have been influenced by a German brewing tradition. Yet for the most part the lager beers brewed by these countries are lighter; specifically one might refer to the style as a very light-flavored pilsener, very often brewed with such adjuncts as corn or rice.

Australian Lagers—In a country that experiences dry, hot summers, Australian lagers quench the thirst of Australians with almost a macho gusto; it is one of the biggest beer-drinking (per capita) countries in the world. Generally, the alcohol contents of their lagers are similar to those of other light lager beers that are brewed in the United States and Canada. The notion that Australian beers are stronger is probably true, due to the packaging of some of their beers in 1 liter cans! Australians do brew some very distinctive ales and stouts but these are an exception and not at all categorized as Australian lagers.

More than likely, you'll have to go to Australia to enjoy a quality Australian light lager or brew it yourself. Although Australian light lagers are commonly available in the United States, their quality often suffers during the long journey to your favorite beer store.

Authentic Australian lagers are easily made by homebrewers with the use of Australian malt extract and Australian-grown hops—beyond those ingredients you'd have to call it your own.

American Lagers—The most common style of beer produced in Canada and the United States can be referred to as American Standard. With all due respect to the Canadians, the mass-produced beer called Canadian lager or Canadian ale is too similar to a standard light lager to be called anything else. Canadian light lagers may suggest a bit more hop character, but in general the lighter style of American Standard is what most North Americans are drinking.

American Standard—This style of beer is usually brewed with 60–75 percent barley malt, the remainder being exclusively or a combination of rice, corn, sugar syrups and sometimes wheat. The beers are dry, lightly hopped, light-bodied and highly carbonated. Original gravities: 1.035–1.045 (9–11). Alcohol: 3.5–5 percent. Bitterness: 5–17 IBU. Color: 2–4 SRM.

American Premium—An all-malt beer, or one made with very few adjuncts. It is a bigger beer all around, but still is a relative to American Standard light lager. Original gravities: 1.045–1.050 (11–12.5). Alcohol: 4.5–5 percent. Bitterness: 13–22 IBU. Color: 2–8 SRM.

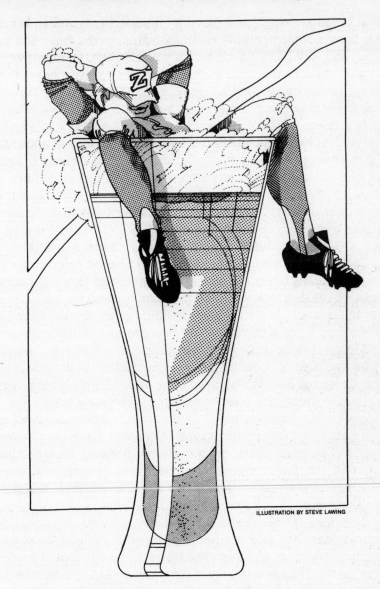

ILLUSTRATION BY STEVE LAWING

Diet/"low-cal" beer—Often referred to as a watered-down version of an American Standard light lager. This is close to the truth in flavor, but often low-cal beers will carry just as much alcohol as some of their American Standard counterparts. Low-calorie beers are often processed with added enzymes to break down tasty nonfermentable carbohydrates so the beer will be thinner and have less flavor and fewer calories. Homebrewers can come close to this style by brewing lower gravity beers that are very fermentable. Original gravities: 1.024–1.040 (6–10). Alcohol: 2.5–4.5 percent. Bitterness: 5–15 IBU. Color: 1–4 SRM.

Dry Beer—Originally invented in Japan in the mid-1980s, this style has been copied in the United States and adapted to the American taste. It is basically an American Standard light lager beer that has been fermented out even more so there is little or no flavor remaining. In fact, that is the objective and the style: a beer that has no aftertaste. Special yeast strains are used to make this beer. Original gravities: 1.040–1.045 (10–11). Alcohol: 4–5 percent. Bitterness: 15–23 IBU. Color: 2–4 SRM.

California Common Beer—This could also be referred to as American Steam Beer, but the only remnant of this style commercially available today is Anchor Steam brewed by the Anchor Brewing Company in San Francisco. The name "Steam Beer" is trademarked by this company. Its fine product, Anchor Steam, is a style that originated a hundred years ago in California before ice was available for cooling lager fermentation. In general, California Common Beer is a style of beer brewed with lager yeasts but at ale fermentation temperatures. Aggressively hopped and having a residual sweetness of caramel or crystal malt, Anchor Steam Beer is but one result of type of process, but is considered a standard because there are no known brewing records that can define the flavor character of this almost forgotten beer style. Original gravities: 1.045–1.055 (11–14). Alcohol: 4–5 percent. Bitterness: 35–45 IBU. Color: 12–17 SRM.

American Dark Beers—Essentially colored versions of American Standard and Premium lagers with minimal, or sometimes no, roasted or chocolatelike characters contributed by the darker malts. They are usually a bit heavier than the lightest of the American Standard lagers. American-style bock beers sometimes come under this category because of their low original gravity and alcohol, compared to their German counterparts. Original gravities: 1.040–1.050 (10–12.5). Alcohol: 4–5.5 percent. Bitterness: 14–20 IBU. Color: 10–20 SRM.

BEER STYLES TABLE

	Original Gravity (balling)	Percent Alcohol by Volume	International Bittering Units	Color (SRM)
Ales				
Barley Wine	1.090–1.120 (22.5–30)	8.4–12	50–100	14–22
Belgium-style Specialty				
a) Flanders Brown	1.045–1.055 (11–14)	5–6.5	35–50	16–20
b) Trappist Ales				
House Brew	1.060–1.100 (15–25)	6–10	25–50	15–30
Double Malt	1.060–1.065 (15–16)	6–6.5	25–40	15–25
Triple Malt	1.075–1.085 (19–21)	7.5–8	30–45	17–30
	1.090–1.100 (22.5–25)	8–10	35–50	20–30
c) Saison	1.052–1.080 (13–20)	5.5–7.5	25–40	4–10
d) Lambic	1.040–1.050 (10–12.5)	4–6	3–7	4–8
Faro	—	4.5–5.5	—	—
Gueuze	—	5.5	—	—
Fruit (Framboise, Kriek, Peche . . .)	—	6	—	—
e) White	1.044–1.050 (11–12.5)	4.5–5	20–35	2–4
Brown Ales				
a) English Brown	1.040–1.050 (10–12.5)	4.5–6.5	15–30	15–22
b) English Mild	1.031–1.037 (8–9)	2.5–3.6	14–37	22–34
c) American Brown	1.040–1.055 (10–14)	4.5–6.5	25–60	15–22

BEER STYLES TABLE

	Original Gravity (balling)	Percent Alcohol by Volume	International Bittering Units	Color (SRM)
Pale Ales				
a) Classic Pale Ale	1.043–1.050 (11–12.5)	4.5–5.5	20–30	8–10
b) India Pale Ale	1.055–1.070 (14–17.5)	5.5–7	30–60	6–14
c) Old Ale/Strong Ale	1.060–1.075 (15–19)	6.5–8.5	30–50	10–16
British Bitters				
a) Ordinary	1.035–1.038 (8.5–9.5)	3–3.5	20–25	8–12
b) Special	1.038–1.042 (9.5–10.5)	3.5–4.5	25–30	12–14
c) Extra Special	1.042–1.050 (10.5–12.5)	4.5–5.5	30–35	12–14
Porter	1.040–1.050 (10–12.5)	4.5–6	25–35	25–35
Scottish Ales				
a) Light	1.030–1.035 (7.5–9)	3–4	9–10	10–12
b) Heavy	1.035–1.040 (9–10)	3.5–4	10–11	11–13
c) Export	1.040–1.050 (10–12.5)	4–4.5	11–13	12–15
d) Strong "Scotch" Ale	1.075–1.085 (19–21)	6–8	14–16	14–17
Stouts				
a) Dry Stout	1.036–1.055 (9–14)	3–6	25–40	35+
b) Sweet Stout	1.045–1.056 (11–14)	4.5–6	15–20	35+
c) Imperial Stout	1.075–1.090 (19–22.5)	7–9	50–80	35+

Lagers

	Original Gravity (balling)	Percent Alcohol by Volume	International Bittering Units	Color (SRM)
Bock				
a) Dark	1.066–1.074 (16.5–18.5)	6–7.5	20–30	18–35
b) Helles	1.066–1.074 (16.5–18.5)	6–7.5	20–30	8–18
c) Doppelbock	1.074–1.100 (18.5–25)	7.5–14	20–40	12–35
Bavarian Dark				
a) Munich Dunkel	1.050–1.055 (12.5–14)	4.5–6	18–27	10–20
b) Schwarzbier	1.040–1.046 (10–11.5)	3.5–4.5	25–35	25–40
American Dark	1.040–1.050 (10–12.5)	4–5.5	14–20	10–20
Dortmunder/Export	1.050–1.060 (12.5–15)	5–6	25–35	4–6
Munich Helles	1.046–1.055 (11.5–14)	4.5–5.5	18–25	2–5
Classic Pilsener				
a) German	1.044–1.050 (11–12.5)	4–5	35–45	2.5–4.5
b) Bohemian	1.044–1.056 (11–14)	4–5.5	35–45	2–5
American Light Lager				
a) Diet/Lite	1.024–1.040 (6–10)	2.5–4.5	5–15	1–4
b) American Standard	1.035–1.045 (9–11)	3.5–5	5–17	2–4

BEER STYLES TABLE

	Original Gravity (balling)	Percent Alcohol by Volume	International Bittering Units	Color (SRM)
c) American Premium	1.045–1.050 (11–12.5)	4.5–5	13–22	2–8
d) Dry	1.040–1.045 (10–11)	4–5	15–23	2–4
Vienna				
a) Vienna	1.046–1.052 (11.5–13)	4.5–5.5	18–30	10–20
b) Märzen/Oktoberfest	1.050–1.060 (12.5–15)	4.5–6.5	20–30	8–14
Hybrid Beers/Lagers, Ales				
Alt				
a) German Altbier	1.040–1.050 (10–12.5)	4.5–5.5	28–40	16–19
b) Kölsch	1.040–1.045 (10–11)	4–5	16–30	4–10
Cream Ale	1.044–1.055 (11–14)	4.5–7	10–22	2–4
Fruit Beer				
a) Fruit Ale	1.030–1.110 (7.5–27.5)	2.5–12	5–70	5–50
b) Fruit Lager	1.030–1.110 (7.5–27.5)	2.5–12	5–70	5–50
Herb Beer				
a) Herb Ale	1.030–1.110 (7.5–27.5)	2.5–12	5–70	5–50
b) Herb Lager	1.030–1.110 (7.5–27.5)	2.5–12	5–70	5–50

	Original Gravity (balling)	Percent Alcohol by Volume	International Bittering Units	Color (SRM)
Specialty Beer				
a) Specialty Ale	1.030–1.110 (7.5–27.5)	2.5–12	0–100	0–100
b) Specialty Lager	1.030–1.110 (7.5–27.5)	2.5–12	0–100	0–100
Smoked				
a) Bamberg Rauchbier	1.050–1.055 (12.5–14)	5–5.5	20–30	12–17
b) Other styles with smoke flavor				
California Common Beer				
a) California Common Beer	1.045–1.055 (11–14)	4–5	35–45	12–17
b) Anchor Stream brand lookalike	1.050 (12.5)	4.6	40–45	15
Wheat Beer				
a) Berliner Weisse	1.028–1.032 (7–8)	2.5–3.5	5–12	2–4
b) Weizen	1.045–1.050 (11–12.5)	4.5–5	8–14	3–8
c) Dunkel	1.045–1.055 (11–12.5)	4.5–6	10–15	17–22
d) Weizenbock	1.066–1.080 (16.5–20)	6.5–7.5	10–15	7–30
e) American Wheat	1.030–1.050 (7.5–12.5)	3.5–5	5–17	2–4

GUIDELINES FOR BREWING

Style	Light Malt Extract (pounds)	Amber Malt Extract (pounds)	Dark Malt Extract (pounds)	Crystal Malt (pounds)	Black Patent Malt (pounds)	Chocolate Malt (pounds)	Roasted Barley (pounds)
English Bitter (a)		5					
English Bitter (b)	5						
Strong Special Red Bitter		6					1/8
India Pale Ale		6–7		1			
Old Ale	9–10			1		1/4	
Scottish Ale/Heavy	5			1			
Strong/Scotch Ale	10–11			1		1/4	
Australian Light Lager	6–7						
Bohemian Pilsener	6–7			0–1/4			
German Pilsener	6–7						
California Common Beer (a)	6–7			1/2			
California Common Beer (b)		6–7		1/4			

5 GALLONS OF TRADITIONAL BEER

Toasted Malt	Boiling Hops (total ounces) Homebrew Bitterness Units (see page 66)	Finishing Hops (total ounces)	Yeast Type	Original Gravity Range (Balling)	Percent Alcohol (by volume)
	1.5-2 Fuggles, Goldings, Cascade or Willamette. 7.5-10 HBU	½ Fuggles, Cascade, Goldings or Willamette	Ale	1.035-1.039 (9-10)	3-3.5
	2 Fuggles, Goldings, Cascade or Willamette. 10 HBU	½ Fuggles, Cascade, Goldings or Willamette	Ale	1.040-1.044 (10-11)	3.5-4.5
½	1-2.5 North. Brewer or 3-4 Fuggles, Cascade or Golding. 10-20 HBU	1 Cascade	Ale	1.055-1.065 (14-16)	5.5-6.5
	1.5 Northern Brewer or 3 Fuggles, Cascade or Golding. 15-18 HBU	½ Cascade or Willamette	Ale	1.060-1.070 (15-17.5)	6.5-7
¼	1.5 Fuggles, Goldings, Cascade or Willamette. 6-8 HBU		Ale	1.035-1.039 (9-10)	3.5-4
¼	2 Fuggles, Goldings, Cascade or Willamette. 8-12 HBU		Ale	1.075-1.080 (19-20)	6-7.5
	1-1.5 Northern Brewer or Pride of Ringwood. 8-11 HBU		Lager	1.045-1.052 (11-13)	4-6
½	2.5 Saaz. 10-12 HBU	¾ Saaz	Lager	1.044-1.050 (11-12.5)	4-5
	3-3.5 Hallertauer, Spalt. Tettnanger or Saaz. 13-15 HBU	½ Hallertauer, Saaz, Spalt or Tettnang	Lager	1.044-1.050 (11-12.5)	4-5
¼	1.5 Northern Brewer or 2.5 Cascade. 12 HBU	½ Cascade	Lager	1.044-1.050 (11-12.5)	4-5

Style	Light Malt Extract (pounds)	Amber Malt Extract (pounds)	Dark Malt Extract (pounds)	Crystal Malt (pounds)	Black Patent Malt (pounds)	Chocolate Malt (pounds)	Roasted Barley (pounds)
American Standard	4–5						
Cream Ale	5–6						
American Diet/Low-cal	3½–4						
Canadian Ales/ Lagers	5–7	OR 5–7		0–½			
German Weizen Wheat	4 Barley Malt +3 Wheat Malt						
German Dunkelweizen	4 Barley Malt +3 Wheat Malt				½	¼	¼
Vienna		6–7		½		¼	
Oktoberfest/ Märzen		6–7		½		⅛	
English Mild	4–5				¼–½		
Brown Ale (a) Brown Ale (b)	5–6	5–6		½	¼ ¼	¼ OR ¼	

5 GALLONS OF TRADITIONAL BEER

Toasted Malt	Boiling Hops (total ounces) Homebrew Bitterness Units (see page 66)	Finishing Hops (total ounces)	Yeast Type	Original Gravity Range (Balling)	Percent Alcohol (by volume)
	1 Cascade or Willamette. 4–6 HBU	0–½ Cascade	Lager	1.032–1.038 (8–9.5)	3–3.5
	.5–1.5 Cascade or Willamette. 3–7 HBU	¼–½ Cascade	Lager	1.042–1.046 (10.5–11.5)	4–4.5
	½–¼ Cascade or Willamette. 3–4 HBU		Lager	1.028–1.032 (7–8)	2–2.5
	1.5–2 Cascade or Willamette. 7–10 HBU	0–½ Cascade or Hallertauer	Lager or Ale	1.038–1.050 (9.5–12.5)	3–5
	1 Hallertauer, Saaz or Tettnanger. 4–6 HBU	0–¼ Saaz, Tettnanger or Hallertauer	Ale (Special Yeast)	1.044–1.050 (11–12.5)	4–5
	1 Hallertauer, Saaz or Tettnanger. 4–6 HBU	0–¼ Saaz, Tettnanger or Hallertauer	Ale (Special Yeast)	1.044–1.050 (11–12.5)	4–5
	1.5–2 Hallertauer, Saaz or Tettnanger. 5–9 HBU	½ Saaz, Tettnanger or Hallertauer	Lager	1.042–1.050 (10.5–12.5)	4–5
½	1.5–2 Hallertauer, Saaz or Tettnanger. 5–9 HBU	½ Saaz, Tettnanger or Hallertauer	Lager	1.044–1.050 (11–12.5)	4.5–5
	1–1.5 Fuggles, Goldings, Cascade or Willamette. 5–8 HBU		Ale	1.032–1.038 (8–9.5)	2.5–3.5
	2 Fuggles, Goldings, Cascade or Willamette. 8–12 HBU	½ Willamette, Cascade or Fuggles	Ale	1.040–1.043 (10–11)	4–4.5

Style	Light Malt Extract (pounds)	Amber Malt Extract (pounds)	Dark Malt Extract (pounds)	Crystal Malt (pounds)	Black Patent Malt (pounds)	Chocolate Malt (pounds)	Roasted Barley (pounds)
American Brown Ale		5–6			$1/4$	$1/4$	
German (dark) Bock			7–8	$1/2$		$1/2$	
German Helles (light) Bock	7–8			$1/4$		$1/8$	
German Doppelbock (dark)		7	3–6	$1/2$		$1/2$	
American Bock		5–6		$1/2$	$1/4$		
Munich Helles	6–7						
Munich Dunkel	7–8	OR 7–8		$1/2$		$1/2$	
Schwarzbier			5–6	$1/2$	$1/8$	$1/4$	
Dortmunder/Export	7–8						
Porter (a) sweeter Porter (b) sharper		7–8 7–8			1	$1/2$	
Dry Stout			6–6$1/2$	$3/4$	$1/3$		$1/3$

5 GALLONS OF TRADITIONAL BEER

Toasted Malt	Boiling Hops (total ounces) Homebrew Bitterness Units (see page 66)	Finishing Hops (total ounces)	Yeast Type	Original Gravity Range (Balling)	Percent Alcohol (by volume)
	2–3.5 Fuggles, Goldings, Cascade or Willamette. 7–17 HBU	½–1 Cascade, Willamette or Fuggles	Ale	1.040–1.043 (10–11)	4–4.5
½	1.5–2.5 Hallertauer, Saaz or Tettnanger. 6–10 HBU		Lager	1.066–1.072 (16.5–18)	6–7
½	1.5–2.5 Hallertauer, Saaz or Tettnanger. 12–15 HBU		Lager	1.066–1.072 (16.5–18)	6–7
½	1.5–3 Hallertauer, Saaz or Tettnanger. 12–20 HBU		Lager	1.074–1.100 (18.5–25)	7.5–11
¼	1–1.5 Hallertauer, Saaz or Tettnanger. 4–6 HBU	½ Tettnanger or Hallertauer	Lager	1.038–1.044 (9.5–11)	3.5–4
	1–1.5 Hallertauer, Saaz or Tettnanger. 5–8 HBU	¼ Tettnanger or Hallertauer	Lager	1.042–1.048 (10.5–12)	4.5–5
	1–1.5 Hallertauer, Saaz or Tettnanger. 5–8 HBU	¼ Tettnanger or Hallertauer	Lager	1.050–1.055 (12.5–14)	4.5–6
	1.5–2 Hallertauer, Saaz or Tettnanger. 7–10 HBU	¼ Tettnanger or Hallertauer	Lager	1.038–1.042 (9.5–10.5)	3.5–4
	1.5–2 Hallertauer, Saaz or Tettnanger. 7–12 HBU	¼ Tettnanger or Hallertauer	Lager	1.050–1.055 (12.5–14)	4.5–6
	2.5 Cascade or Fuggles 3.5 Cascade or 1.5 Northern Brewer. 12–16 HBU	½ Tettnanger	Ale	1.050–1.055 (12.5–14)	4.5–6
	1 Northern Brewer or 2–2.5 Goldings, Fuggles or Willamette. 8–12 HBU		Ale	1.047–1.052 (12–13)	4–5.5

GUIDELINES FOR BREWING

Style	Light Malt Extract (pounds)	Amber Malt Extract (pounds)	Dark Malt Extract (pounds)	Crystal Malt (pounds)	Black Patent Malt (pounds)	Chocolate Malt (pounds)	Roasted Barley (pounds)
Sweet Stout			6–6½	1	¼		¼
Imperial Stout		10–11				½	½
Russian Imperial Stout		10–11		1	¼		¼
Barley Wine	10–12						
Alt		5–6		¾		⅓	

**Relax. Don't worry.
Have a homebrew.
Because worrying
is like paying interest on a debt
you may never have owed.**

5 GALLONS OF TRADITIONAL BEER

Toasted Malt	Boiling Hops (total ounces) Homebrew Bitterness Units (see page 66)	Finishing Hops (total ounces)	Yeast Type	Original Gravity Range (Balling)	Percent Alcohol (by volume)
	½ Northern Brewer or 1.5 Goldings, Fuggles or Willamette. 4–6 HBU		Ale	1.047–1.052 (12–13)	4–5.5
	4–6 Northern Brewer or 3.5–4 Chinook. Eroica or Galena. 40–45 HBU	1.5 Cascade or Willamette	Ale	1.072–1.077 (18–19)	7–8
	4–5 Fuggles or 2–2.5 Chinook. Eroica or Galena. 20–30 HBU	½ Fuggles or Cascade	Ale	1.072–1.077 (18–19)	7–8
	4–4.5 Galena. Eroica or Chinook. 50–60 HBU	1 Cascade + 1 Willamette	Ale	1.072–1.085 (18–21)	7–9
	2–3 Hallertauer or 1–1.5 Northern Brewer. 8–12 HBU		Ale	1.040–1.045 (10–11)	4–4.5

Déjà-Brew
We have all been beer before.

WORTS ILLUSTRATED
Homebrew Recipes

The joy of brewing lies partly in concocting your own recipes, and the preceding sections of this book have provided the foundation for your doing so.

Whatever concoction you put together, the responsibility for success is yours alone. A recipe is only the result of somebody's trial and error and ultimate success. Use your own imagination, flair, courage and common sense. Above all, whatever you do, relax. Don't worry. Have a homebrew.

The recipes presented in this section are for those who would like a bit more direction in their first batches and are looking for something in particular but don't know which malts result in which brews. The recipes are favorites and have enjoyed notoriety for their superlative qualities.

Before you get yourself involved with these recipes, be sure to read the following "Notes, Substitutions and Adjustments."

Notes, Substitutions and Adjustments

- Don't be afraid to substitute other varieties of hops. You may substitute hop pellets for whole hops at any time.
- Don't be afraid to substitute ale yeast for lager yeast and vice-versa.
- All specific gravity readings are made with a hydrometer accurate at 60 degrees F (16 C). Degrees Balling are given in parentheses.
- Always use ¾ *cup* of corn sugar or 1¼ *cup* dried malt extract for each 5 gallons brewed when bottling (except where noted). Do not make the error of misinterpreting this, i.e., do not use ¾ *pound* of corn sugar. If honey is used, use ½ cup honey.
- When brewing you may always substitute malt extract for corn sugar for a brew with more body and character. Substitute approximately pound for pound.
- All recipes may be lightened in body and flavor (while not diminishing alcohol) by substituting corn sugar (approxi-

However, there is still a great deal of satisfaction in knowing that although the moon is smaller than the earth, it is much further away!

—Jackson Wolfe

mately pound for pound) for malt extract. For best results, corn sugar should never be substituted for more than 20 percent of the malt extract.

- To lighten body, flavor and alcohol, the amount of malt extract may be decreased. The amount of hops should be decreased proportionately.

- The addition of grains is best done during the 15–30 minutes it takes to bring the water to a boil. The spent grains can then simply be removed with a kitchen strainer.

- You may end up with a beginning specific gravity other than noted. Relax, don't worry. There may be some variation due to varieties or batches of malt extract, temperature or inadequate mixing of the wort in the fermenter. The important thing is not to worry.

- Manufacturers of malt extract are constantly changing their packaging. What may be available in a 2-pound can at the time of this publication may later only be available in 3½-pound cans. Use your common sense when making adjustments.

- Don't be afraid to use a pound more or a pound less in any given recipe. It will alter the character of the beer, but it certainly will not ruin it.

- lb(s). = pound(s), tbsp. = tablespoon(s), tsp. = teaspoon(s), c. = cup(s), pkg(s). = package(s), oz. = ounce(s) (weight), O.G. = Original Specific Gravity, F.G. = Final Specific Gravity.

- When grains, whole or pellet hops are added to the wort always use a strainer to separate particulates from the wort as it passes into the fermenter. Hops or grains may clog the "blow-out" hose and cause hazardous pressure buildup in the fermenter.

- Whether using whole hops or hop pellets, always pass your hot wort through a sanitized strainer before allowing it to flow into your fermenter.

- Motivate yourself to learn how to use liquid cultured ale and lager yeasts. Some liquid yeast cultures available to homebrewers can dramatically improve the quality of your homebrew, especially your lager beers. Liquid yeasts may be substituted for dried yeast in *all* recipes.

- Five U.S. gallons equals 19 liters. One ounce equals 28.3 grams. One kilogram equals 2.2 pounds. 3.3 pounds equals 1.5 kilograms. One U.S. gallon equals .8 Imperial British or Canadian gallons. One Imperial British or Canadian gallon equals 1.2 U.S. gallons. These are conversions you may find useful when using British, Australian or Canadian products.

- HBUs, or Homebrew Bitterness Units, are a measure of the total amount of bitterness potential in a given volume of beer. They are very easy and useful units to use for beginning and intermediate homebrewers when formulating or converting recipes. Bitterness units are calculated by multiplying the percent of alpha acid in the hops by the number of ounces. For example, if 2 ounces of Northern Brewer hops (9% alpha acid) and 3 ounces of Cascade hops (5% alpha acid) were used in a 10-gallon batch, the total amount of bitterness units would be 33: $(2 \times 9) + (3 \times 5) = 18 + 15 = 33$. Bitterness units per gallon would be 3.3 in a 10-gallon batch or 6.6 in a 5-gallon batch, so it is important to note volumes whenever expressing Homebrew Bitterness Units. HBUs are not related to IBUs (International Bitterness Units) except that they both measure bitterness in beer.

    All boiling hops in recipes quote HBUs as a guide for the homebrewer should he or she desire to substitute other varieties of hops. For example, 2 ounces of 4.5 percent Saaz hops equals 9 HBUs, which is equivalent to 1 ounce of 9 percent Northern Brewer in the boil.

So let's cut the Shuck and Jive and get on with the recipes.

ALL RECIPES ARE FOR 5 U.S. GALLONS UNLESS OTHERWISE NOTED.

ENGLISH BITTERS
Righteous Real Ale

The taste of Righteous Real Ale is excellent and authentic within 14 days of brewing. It is brewed in a style of "ordinary bitter" served in parts of London and in hop country to the south. It is a distinctly hopped ale with a beautiful hop bouquet. Bear in mind that authentic bitter may not be as carbonated as you are used to. If more carbonation is desired, add ¼ cup additional corn sugar at bottling time.

Ingredients for 5 gallons:

> 5 lbs. dried amber English malt extract
> 1½ oz. Cascade hop pellets (boiling): 7–8 HBU
> ½ oz. Goldings or Willamette hop pellets (finishing)
> 2 tsp. gypsum
> 1–2 pkgs. English ale yeast
> ½ c. corn sugar or 1 c. dried malt extract (for bottling)

Original Specific Gravity (O.G.): 1.036 (9)
Final Specific Gravity (F.G.): 1.007–1.010 (2–2.5)

Boil for 45 minutes with 1½ gallons of water the malt extract, Cascade hops and gypsum. During the final 1 minute of boiling add the finishing hops, after which immediately transfer to a waiting 3½ gallons of cold water in the fermenter.

After the tenth day you should be able to bottle with the addition of ½ cup corn sugar or dried extract. Store for 4 days and try it. It will be terrific within 7 days of bottling.

Wise Ass Red Bitter

Wise Ass Red Bitter is a rich-tasting bitter ale that offers a bead of head that stays with the brew and the sides of the glass right to the last luscious swallow. Excellent body and malt aroma coupled with a deep garnet red (contributed by the roasted barley) appearance satisfies the palate's great expectations.

Hopped malt extract is used, giving this ale a sharply bitter bite.

Ingredients for 5 gallons:

> 4.4 lbs. Premier Malt hopped light malt extract
> 1½ lbs. dried light plain malt extract
> ⅛ lb. (or ½ c.) roasted barley
> 2 oz. Cascade hop pellets: 10 HBU
> ½ oz. Hallertauer hop pellets
> 1–2 pkgs. ale yeast
> ¾ c. corn sugar or 1¼ c. dried malt extract (for bottling)

O.G.: 1.038 (9.5)
F.G.: 1.009–1.011 (2–3)

Brewing procedures are identical to those for Righteous Real Ale, except that more priming sugar is used and aging in the bottle for 2–3 weeks may be necessary in order to develop carbonation.

Palace Bitter

Everyone's house can be a castle, but if I had my druthers, I'd go for a palace. And if I had a palace, then naturally my house bitter would become my Palace Bitter. Brewing your own gives a special feeling to your home whatever shape it's in. Brewing Palace Bitter and having it on tap or in bottles will make your home that much more special. I guarantee it.

Brewed in a very traditional style of "ordinary bitter," this light amber English ale has the earthy character of English hops and drinkability of a relatively low-alcohol ale.

Ingredients for 5 gallons:

> 4½ lbs. English light dried malt extract
> 12 oz. crystal malt
> ½ oz. English Fuggles hops (boiling): 2.5 HBU
> ¾ oz. Styrian Goldings hops (boiling): 3.5 HBU
> ¼ oz. English Fuggles hops (flavor)
> ¾ oz. Styrian Goldings hops (flavor)

½ oz. Styrian Goldings hops (aroma)

1–2 pkgs. ale yeast

¾ c. corn sugar or 1¼ c. dried malt extract (for bottling)

O.G.: 1.036–1.040 (9–10)
F.G.: 1.008–1.012 (2–3)

Add crushed crystal malt to 1½ gallons of water and bring to a boil, then remove the grains with a strainer. Add malt extract and bring to a boil. Add boiling hops and boil for 30 minutes. Then add ¼ oz. each of Fuggles and Goldings for flavor and boil for 15 more minutes. Then add another ½ oz. of the Goldings and boil for 15 more minutes for flavor. Add ½ oz. Goldings during the final 2 minutes of boil for aroma. Sparge the wort into your cold water and fermenter. When it cools add ale yeast.

Excellent within 2 weeks, sometimes sooner.

Palilalia India Pale Ale

India Pale Ale is a style of ale noted for its alcoholic strength and bitterness. Palilalia India Pale Ale is not quite as dry as a traditional I.P.A. but has plenty of character contributed by a generous amount of crystal malt and hops. Its palate is bitter-

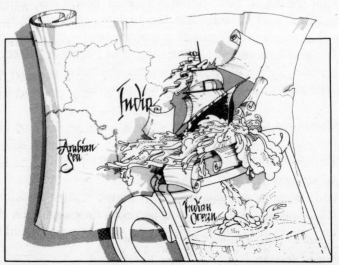

ILLUSTRATION BY STEVE LAWING

sweet and assertive. The toasted malted barley lends a copper color and malty aroma to the brew. Palilalia tends to become drier with age. For additional authenticity you may want to add a generous handful of steamed (sanitized) oak chips during primary or secondary fermentation, for I.P.A. is often aged in oak.

Ingredients for 5 gallons:

> 7 lbs. light or amber plain dried malt extract
> 1 lb. crystal malt
> ½ lb. toasted malted barley
> 2 tsp. gypsum
> 1½ oz. Northern Brewer hops (boiling): 13 HBU
> ¾ oz. Cascade hops (finishing)
> 1–2 pkgs. ale yeast
> ¾ c. corn sugar or 1¼ c. dried malt extract (for bottling)

O.G.: 1.048–1.052 (12–13)
F.G.: 1.014–1.017 (3.5–4)

Toasting malted barley is a simple process. Preheat your oven to 350 degrees F (177 C) and spread ½ lb. of whole malted barley grain on a screen or cookie sheet. Within 10 minutes a wonderful aroma will emanate from your oven and the malted barley will have turned a slight reddish color. Remove the grain at this time. Prolonged toasting will turn the inside of the malted barley a deeper nut brown and will contribute a roasted flavor. The nutty malt aromatics of a 10-minute toast is desired for this recipe.

Add the cracked crystal malt and cracked toasted malted barley to 1½ gallons of cold water and bring to a boil. When this "mash" begins to boil, remove as much of the grains as is conveniently possible with a kitchen strainer.

Add the malt extract, Northern Brewer hops, gypsum and boil for 45–60 minutes. Add the finishing Cascade hops during the final 1 minute of boiling. Sparge the wort into your cold water and fermenter. When it cools add ale yeast.

Because of Palilalia's strength and high hop rate this ale is best aged 3–4 weeks in the bottle before drinking, but that's not saying it won't be good within 2 weeks.

Avogadro's Expeditious Old Ale

Avogadro's Expeditious Old Ale is a bastardization of an already very fine recipe. Old Ale is a uniquely hopped beer kit available in many homebrew supply shops. When brewed to instructions it produces a very strong, traditional, hoppy, copper-colored English ale. The recipe for Avogadro's Expeditious Old Ale has a touch of hop bouquet contributed by the finishing hops. "This is my kind of beer," an English lass once said of this brew. I smiled and poured another as the quenching dryness of the ale succumbed to aromatics.

The use of hop pellets contributes to the ease of brewing this recipe.

Ingredients for 5 gallons:

7 lbs. Munton & Fison's Old Ale Kit
½ oz. Cascade hop pellets (finishing)
1–2 pkgs. ale yeast (supplied with kit)
½ c. corn sugar or ¾ c. dried malt extract (for bottling)

O.G.: 1.048–1.052 (12–13)
F.G.: 1.012–1.018 (3–4.5)

This is a quickie. Boil the Old Ale hopped malt extract with 1½ gallons of water for 15 minutes. Add the Cascade hops during the final 1 minute. Pour immediately and with all due haste into your cold water and fermenter. It will be ready to drink in 2–4 weeks, depending on how expeditious you are.

AMERICAN & CANADIAN BEERS
Freemont Plopper American Light

The malt extract is notably used for this recipe for the dry and clean finish that the beer will have. Freemont Plopper is a lightly hopped, lightly flavored beer similar to the American pilsener.

It is satisfying and a thirst quencher during the midsummer's day heat.

Due to unfermentable dextrins in malt extract it is likely that you'll find more flavor here than in most American pilseners.

Ingredients for 5 gallons:

2½ lbs. Bierhaus Hopped Lager Kit (malt extract syrup)
1–2 pkgs. yeast supplied (ale or lager)
¾ c. corn sugar or 1¼ c. dried malt extract (for bottling)

O.G.: 1.022–1.025 (5.5–6)
F.G.: 1.003–1.006 (1–1.5)

Boil the malt extract with 1 gallon of water for 15–30 minutes. Add directly to cold water in the fermenter. Bottle when fermentation has stopped.

Serve it ice-cold for authenticity.

Canadian Lunar Lager

Brewed with a Canadian malt extract (made from Canadian malt) Lunar Lager has appropriate dryness and adjunct lightness, while not sacrificing the alcohol content. It is typical of many Canadian ales and lagers. It's a surprising pleasure to partake of Lunar Lager, if only for the satisfaction of saying "I brewed it and it comes close to the real thing."

Ingredients for 5 gallons:

4–5 lbs. Brew-pro light or amber hopped malt extract
½ oz. Willamette or Fuggles hops (finishing)
1–2 pkgs. ale or lager yeast
¾ c. corn sugar or 1¼ c. dried malt extract (for bottling)

O.G.: 1.032–1.038 (8–9.5)
F.G.: 1.007–1.011 (2–3)

Boil the malt extract with 1½ gallons of water for 45 minutes. During the final 5 minutes add the finishing hop for flavor

(rather than bouquet). Sparge into your cold water and fermenter. Lunar Lager will be ready by the first full moon or in 3 weeks,
whichever comes later.

"The Sun Has Left Us On Time" Steam Beer

Thomas Edison once wrote in his diary, "The sun has left us on
time, am going to read from the *Encyclopaedia Britannica* to
steady my nerves and go to bed early. I will shut my eyes and
imagine a terraced abyss, each terrace occupied by a beautiful
maiden. To the first I will deliver my mind and they will pass it
down, down to the uttermost depths of silence and oblivion."
One can only imagine that he might have been holding a homebrew as he continued his conjectures with vivid details of a
hundred maidens offering him solace.

"The Sun Has Left Us On Time" Steam Beer is a dry yet
paradoxically full-bodied bitter beer traditionally brewed with
lager yeast at ale-fermenting temperatures. The adding of the
distinctive Northern Brewers hop and finishing with Cascade hop
lends a wonderful bite to this refreshing quencher. If bitter beers
are not your forte then try something else. A bit of crystal malt
is added to sweeten and round out some of the bitterness.

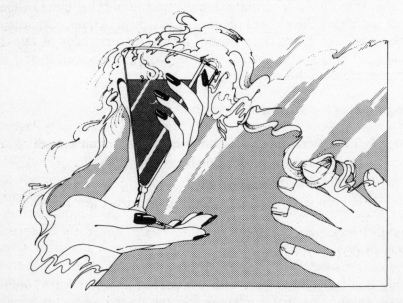

When you reach the bottom of the glass, indeed, you too will see that the sun has left us on time.

Ingredients for 5 gallons:

8 lbs. Alexander's light malt extract
½ lb. crystal malt
1½ oz. Northern Brewers hops (boiling): 14 HBU
½ oz. Cascade hops (finishing)
1–2 pkgs. lager yeast
¾ c. corn sugar or 1¼ c. dried malt extract (for bottling)

O.G.: 1.044–1.048 (11–12)
F.G.: 1.009–1.013 (2–3)

Combine the cracked crystal malt with 1½ gallons of cold water and bring to a boil. Remove the crystal malt with a strainer, then add malt extract and Northern Brewers hops and boil for 45 minutes. During the final 2 minutes of boiling add the Cascade hops. Immediately transfer to the fermenter and cold water. Add yeast when cool. If two-stage fermentation is used then the beer will be improved if matured for 2–3 weeks at temperatures about 50 degrees F (10 C) before bottling. Bottle when fermentation stops or after 2–3 weeks of secondary maturation.

Jeepers Creepers Light Lager

A superlight and economical beer, but with a satisfying flavor. Because the alcohol content is low, you will be able to drink a lot of this beer and continue to appreciate it. There are only 3½ lbs. of malt extract in this 5-gallon recipe, so be careful not to overdo the hops. A wisp of malt character is infused with ¼ lb. of toasted malted barley; a subtle tingle of hop bouquet is suggested with the addition of ¼ oz. finishing hops. It is the balanced and flavorful lightness of this brew that makes it attractive. One typical response you may get from a friend is "Hey, I like this beer and I don't normally like 'lite' beers."

Ingredients for 5 gallons:

> 3½ lbs. Edme D.M.S. plain malt extract
> ¼ lb. toasted malted barley
> ½ oz. Cascade hops (boiling): 3 HBU
> ¼ oz. Tettnanger or Hallertauer (finishing)
> 1–2 pkgs. lager yeast
> ¾ c. corn sugar or 1¼ c. dried malt extract (for bottling)

O.G.: 1.028–1.032 (7–8)
F.G.: 1.004–1.006 (1–1.5)

Toast the malted barley in an oven for 5–10 minutes at 350 degrees F (177 C). Grind or crack the malted barley while it is still warm and add it to 1 gallon of cold water. Bring the water to a boil and remove the grains at the instant boiling commences. Add the malt extract and boiling hops and boil for 45 minutes. Add the finishing hops during the final 2 minutes and sparge immediately into the awaiting fermenter and cold water. Add the yeast when cool and ferment to completion. Bottle within 2 weeks. This beer should be ready to drink in a very short period of time unless very cold lagering temperatures are used; in that case bottling should be done within 4 weeks.

EUROPEAN (CONTINENTAL) LIGHT AND AMBER BEERS

Hordeaceous Dutch Delight

Although the original gravity is peculiarly low and the final gravity is peculiarly high, the light Continental style of beer produced from this malt extract is uniquely delicate with a full-bodied flavor that is not imposing. The hop bouquet, malt-induced flavor and estery quality of this malt extract is worth discovering. It is deliciously drinkable and bound to please drinkers of full-bodied beer.

Ingredients for 5 gallons:

6.6 lbs. Laaglander Dutch Lager kit (2 cans hopped malt extract syrup)
1–2 pkgs. lager yeast
½–¾ c. corn sugar or 1–1¼ c. dried malt extract (for bottling)

O.G.: 1.034–1.036 (8.5–9)
F.G.: 1.016–1.018 (4–4.5)

Boil the hopped malt extract for 15 minutes with 1½ gallons of water. Add to fermenter and cold water. Pitch yeast when cool. Bottle when fermentation is complete.

Winky Dink Märzen

I've always wanted to name a beer after one of my favorite childhood cartoon heroes. Winky's ability to magically transcend spaces by way of crayoned lines drawn on the television screen always seemed to invite him into the house . . . but he never came. Now that there's homebrew, maybe he'll appear, star hat and all.

Winky Dink Märzen is a wonderfully golden German-style lager. The German malt extract that is used produces an authentic, rich, full-bodied and aromatic lager, even when brewed at room temperature. The rich maltiness that is married to the crisp and flavorful hop bitterness enlivens this beer as a real treat for those inclined toward simplicity and German lagers.

It is most flavorful and best served at temperatures between 50–55 degrees F (10–13 C)

Ingredients for 5 gallons:

7 lbs. Bierkeller light plain malt extract syrup
½ lb. crystal malt
½ c. chocolate malt
2 oz. Hallertauer hops (boiling): 10 HBU
½ oz. Hallertauer hops (finishing)
1–2 pkgs. lager yeast
¾ c. corn sugar or 1¼ c. dried malt extract (for bottling)

O.G.: 1.042–1.047 (10.5–12)
F.G.: 1.014–1.018 (3.5–4.5)

Add the crystal and chocolate malts to 1½ gallons of cold water and bring to a boil. Remove the grains with a strainer when boiling commences. Add the malt extract and 2 oz. Hallertauer hops and boil for 45–60 minutes. Add the finishing hops during the final 2–5 minutes of the boil. Sparge and add the wort to the fermenter and cold water. Bottle when fermentation is complete.

If you have the patience and the facilities, this brew can be improved by maturing in a secondary fermenter for 2–3 weeks at temperatures of 45–50 degrees F (7–10 C), but "beer" in mind that Winky Dink Märzen is wonderful stuff brewed at kitchen temperature.

Whoop Moffitt Vienna Lager

Whoop, a late nineteenth-century Scandinavian architect and the father of the game of marbles, died from a steelie striking him between the eyes during a tournament for all of the marbles in Vienna. What a guy. What a beer.

It doesn't get much easier than this to experience the style of beer that is nearly extinct in the commercial world. A smooth, malty flavor that isn't quite as rich in flavor as Oktoberfest. It is thirst quenching and the type of brew that would complement many a meal. Deep amber, a touch of hop finesse, perhaps a bit more than was used traditionally a half century ago (but who's around to point the finger anymore). Not too bitter, it is pleasing to almost any palate.

This recipe is brewed to a volume of 4 gallons in a 5-gallon fermenter with ease to spare.

Ingredients for *4* gallons:

6.6 lbs. B.M.E. Vienna Amber malt extract syrup

1¾ oz. American Tettnanger hops (boiling): 8 HBU

¼ oz. Cascade hops (boiling): 1 HBU

¼ oz. American Tettnanger hops (flavor)

¼ oz. Cascade hops (flavor)

⅓ oz. American Tettnanger hops (aroma)

⅓ oz. Cascade hops (aroma)

1–2 pkgs. lager yeast

½ c. corn sugar or 1 c. dried malt extract (for bottling)

O.G.: 1.048–1.052 (12–13)
F.G.: 1.010–1.014 (2.5–3.5)

Combine the malt extract and boiling hops with 1 gallon of water and bring to a boil. After 40 minutes of vigorous boiling add the flavor hops and continue to boil for 20 more minutes. Add the aroma hops during the final 2 minutes. Sparge the hot wort into the fermenter and add cold water to make 4 gallons total. Add yeast and ferment to completion. Bottle when ready.

Propensity Pilsener Lager

Although one of the ingredients may be unusual, do not dismiss this as an exceptionally realistic Czechoslovakian pilsener. It is one extract beer that has come close to the lusciousness of Pilsner Urquell or the original Czechoslovakian Budweiser.

The use of light honey in this recipe captures the character of a light-bodied pilsener that still celebrates the roundness of malt and the crispness of hops. Simply brewed, Propensity Pilsener Lager is a treat for the connoisseur of true pilseners.

Ingredients for 5 gallons:

        5 lbs. plain light dried malt extract
        1 lb. crystal malt
        2½ lbs. light clover honey
        2½ oz. Saaz hops (boiling): 10 HBU
        ½ oz. Tettnanger hops (flavor)
        ½ oz. Saaz hops (finishing)
        1–2 pkgs. lager yeast
        ¾ c. corn sugar or 1¼ c. dried malt extract (for bottling)

O.G.: 1.048–1.052 (12–13)
F.G.: 1.007–1.010 (2–2.5)

Add the cracked crystal malt to 1½ gallons of cold water and bring to a boil. When boiling has commenced remove the grains with a strainer. Add the malt extract, honey and boiling hops and boil for 45 minutes. Add the Tettnanger hops 10 minutes before the end of the boil. Add the Saaz during the final 1–2 minutes of the boil. Sparge immediately and add the hot wort to the fermenter and cold water. Add yeast when cool and bottle when fermentation is complete. Propensity Pilsener can be matured for 3–4 weeks in the bottle at room temperatures and longer at cool temperatures. Drink and appreciate when you are ready!

Crabalocker German Pils

Who remembers the crabalocker fishwife or the elementary penguins singing Hare Krishna? It was indeed magical and mysterious, but there's nothing mysterious about this serious-tasting German-style pilsener beer. A bit drier and much more hoppy than its Bohemian cousin. With a rich white head of foam, this is a brew you could die and go to heaven for. Serve chilled and dream of Deutschland and the fresh taste of Pils.

Don't let the simplicity fool you. The secret is in the choice of the freshest hops of German origin and how their wondrous character is infused into the wort. The infusion of the flavor hops continues to add bitterness to the wort in various degrees and character.

Ingredients for 5 gallons:

5½ lbs. light or extra-light dried malt extract
¾ oz. Hallertauer Hersbrucker hops (boiling): 3 HBU
½ oz. Saaz hops (boiling): 2 HBU
½ oz. Hallertauer Hersbrucker hops (flavor)
½ oz. Saaz hops (flavor)
1 oz. Hallertauer Hersbrucker hops (aroma)
1–2 pkgs. lager yeast
¾ c. corn sugar or 1¼ c. dried malt extract (for bottling)

O.G.: 1.045–1.050 (11–12.5)
F.G.: 1.009–1.013 (2.5–3.5)

Add the malt extract and boiling hops to 1½ gallons of water and bring to a rolling boil. Boil for 30 minutes, then add ¼ oz. each of Hallertauer and Saaz flavor hops and continue to boil for 15 more minutes. Then again add ¼ oz. each of Hallertauer and Saaz flavor hops and boil for 15 minutes for a total of 1 hour. Add the aroma Hallertauer hops and steep for 2 minutes, then sparge into your fermenter and cold water. Add yeast when wort has cooled and ferment. A quality liquid lager yeast culture and lager fermentation temperatures in the range of 45–55 degrees F (7–13 C) will enhance the quality of this traditional German lager. Bottle when fermentation is complete.

WEIZENBIER/WEISSBIER

Lovebite Weizenbier

Mit hefe (with yeast), this is the real thing, and now homebrewers can make a superdeluxe version of this brew with barley and *wheat* malt extract. Not only does the ease of wheat malt extract make this superpopular beer style part of your beer cellar, but even the unique Bavarian weizenbier yeast is now available to homebrewers. Ask your local homebrew supply shop to special-order it for you if they don't carry it regularly.

Have you ever been to Bavaria and sipped a tall, cloudy weizenbier with a twist of lemon or enjoyed the imports such as Ayinger, Paulaner or Spaten Weizen or Weissbiers? If you enjoyed their spicy, clovelike and bananalike aroma and flavor along with the special and healthful yeastiness, then bud, this beer's for you.

Ingredients for 5 gallons:

> 7 lbs. 50%/50% wheat and barley malt extract syrup
>   OR 4 lbs. Light German malt extract AND
> 3 lbs. 100% wheat malt extract syrup
> 1 oz. Hallertauer hops (boiling): 5 HBU
> Liquid Weizenbier Ale yeast
>   OR 2 pkgs. Red Star Ale yeast
> ¾ c. corn sugar or 1¼ c. dried light malt extract (for bottling)

O.G.: 1.046–1.050 (11.5–12.5)
F.G.: 1.008–1.014 (2–3.5)

Add the wheat and barley malt extract and hops to 1½ gallons of water and boil for 1 hour. Sparge and add the hot wort to the fermenter and cold water. Add yeast when cool. Ferment and bottle. After about 2 weeks serve slightly chilled.

Many Germans roll the bottle on the table before opening it to get the yeast sediment well mixed with the beer. This is an option you might want to try for authenticity. If I liked weizenbier at all I'd prefer it without the yeast. But then it's a style I don't care for. I just and simply don't, but I'm in the minority here, as you will see when you brew and serve this beer to your friends.

BELGIAN LAMBIC

Vicarious Gueuze Lambic

Belgian Lambic beers are unmistakably unique, sour to the bone with a special pungency that wild yeast and bacterial fermentation naturally bring on in Belgium. Trying to duplicate these brews to perfection is improbable for the American homebrewer. But for those who love that special and pungent tartness in their brew, there is hope. A detailed explanation about how you can come close to this style and recipes are in Appendix 6.

GERMAN ALTBIERS

Osmosis Amoebas German Alt

A trip to Düsseldorf, Germany, is a trip to Alt heaven. My advice: Go to the Altstadt (the "old city") and spend your German marks on more than a dozen different Altbiers, half of which are brewed right on the premises of the pubs. And they're all within walking distance of each other.

Osmosis Amoebas replicates this bitter, dark brown style of German ale accurately with a subtle yet satisfying maltiness, simply complemented by assertive bitterness from hops. There are no memorable hop flavors or aromas in this traditional rendition, just a good clean German ale that satisfies until osmosis amoebas.

Ingredients for 5 gallons:

6 lbs. Ireks (German) amber malt extract
1¾ oz. Northern Brewers or Perle hops (boiling): 16 HBU

⅓ lb. chocolate malt

⅛ lb. black patent malt

1–2 pkgs. ale yeast or liquid culture German Altbier yeast

¾ c. corn sugar or 1¼ c. dried malt extract (for bottling)

O.G.: 1.040–1.044 (10–11)
F.G.: 1.007–1.011 (2–3)

Add the crushed chocolate and black malts to 1½ gallons of water and bring to a boil, then immediately remove the grains. Add the malt extract and hops and boil for 1 hour. Sparge into the fermenter and add cold water. Add yeast when cooled. Bottle when fermentation is complete.

AUSTRALIAN LAGER

Australian Spring Snow Golden Lager

Australian Spring Snow Golden Lager is brewed in spite of the reputation that Australian lagers are alcoholically strong. Spring

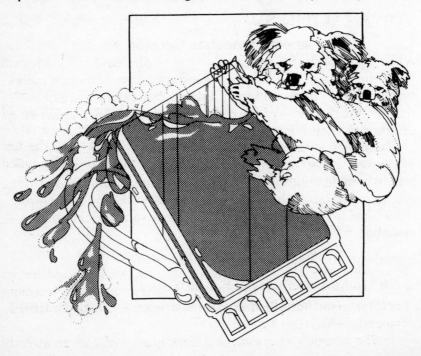

Snow is a medium-bodied pilsener that briefly lingers, then melts upon your palate as a smile of satisfaction springs upon your disposition. Its clean palate refreshes. Its hop bouquet and estery character gently nudges your thoughts of the equinox and anticipation of an all-around sweetly golden summer.

Australian Spring Snow brings you from down under as you gaze upon the last snowfall while you lean over the gently steaming and aromatic brewpot on your stove.

Ah, the equinox.

Ingredients for 5 gallons:

6 lbs. Australian plain light malt extract
1 oz. Willamette or Fuggles hops (boiling): 5 HBU
½ oz. Perle hops (boiling): 4 HBU
½ oz. Cascade hops (finishing)
1–2 pkgs. lager yeast
¾ c. corn sugar or 1¼ c. dried malt extract (for bottling)

O.G.: 1.036–1.040 (9–10)
F.G.: 1.008–0.011 (2–3)

Boil the malt extract and boiling hops with 1½ gallons of water for 60 minutes. Add the finishing hops during the final 1–2 minutes of boiling. Sparge the wort immediately into the fermenter and cold water. Add yeast when cool and bottle when fermentation is complete.

DARK BEERS

English Milds and Brown Ales

Elbro Nerkte Brown Ale

A world-renowned and award-winning recipe, heralded for its quick maturity, this favorite brown ale has long been a first-time brew for many impatient homebrewers, for it can be deliciously enjoyed within 10–14 days!

The addition of crystal and dark grain malts to an already

luscious brown malt extract beautifully enhances the flavorful and mildly sweet richness of this brown ale.

Elbro Nerkte might have been a famous late nineteenth-century Scandinavian marbles player and cousin of Whoop Moffitt, but maybe not.

Ingredients for 5 gallons:

7 lbs. Edme S.F.X. dark plain malt extract syrup
½ lb. crystal malt
¼ lb. black patent malt
2 oz. Fuggles hops (boiling): 10 HBU
½ oz. Fuggles or Cascade hops (finishing)
4 tsp. gypsum (optional)
1–2 pkgs. ale yeast
¾ c. corn sugar or 1¼ c. dried malt extract (for bottling)

O.G.: 1.042–1.046 (10.5–11.5)
F.G.: 1.010–1.014 (2.5–3.5)

Add the cracked crystal and black patent malts to 1½ gallons of cold water and bring to a boil. When boiling commences remove the grains with a strainer. Add the malt extract and boiling hops and boil for 45–60 minutes. During the final 5–10 minutes of the boil add the finishing hops. Sparge the hot wort into the fermenter and cold water. Pitch the yeast when cool and bottle when fermentation is complete. Because of the quickly maturing character of this recipe, Elbro Nerkte lends itself to single-stage fermentation and bottling within 5 to 6 days!

Naked Sunday Brown Ale

No comment on the name of this ale.

You might like to try your hand at brewing a strong rich brown ale similar in character to Newcastle Brown Ale (England). The malt extract used is available in 4-lb. cans and with the addition of 2 lbs. of light dried malt extract it will make a potent 4 gallons of a flavorful, nut-brown, mildly bittered brown ale.

Ingredients for *4* gallons:

  4 lbs. Ironmaster Northern Brown Ale kit hopped malt extract
  2 lbs. light malt extract
  1–2 pkgs. ale yeast
  ½ c. corn sugar or ¾ c. dried malt extract (for bottling)

O.G.: 1.052–1.056 (13–14)
F.G.: 1.006–1.010 (1.5–2.5)

Boil the malt extract with 1 gallon of water for 5 minutes. Pour the hot wort into the fermenter and add 3 gallons of cold water. Add yeast when cool and bottle when fermentation is complete.

Dithyrambic Brown Ale

This unusual brown ale cannot be compared with any commercially available beers that I have ever encountered, domestic or otherwise. Medium-colored, it is riotously flavored with the distinctively dry character of roasted barley, an ingredient that is usually reserved for stouts.

This beer is simple to brew and offers a dry, sharp character without the balancing sweetness of a full-bodied stout. It is a refreshing alternative to the other sweeter varieties of brown ale, perhaps comparable to a good cup of coffee—hold the cream and sugar.

Ingredients for 5 gallons:

  3.3 lbs. Munton & Fison plain, *dark*, malt extract syrup
  3.3 lbs. Munton & Fison plain, *light*, malt extract syrup
  ½ lb. roasted barley (if available, half of the amount of brewer's roasted barley should be substituted with Japanese "Mugi" torrefied [dried or parched by heat, like puffed wheat] and roasted barley)
  ¼ lb. black patent malt

1½ oz. Northern Brewer hops (boiling): 13 HBU

¼ oz. Willamette or Cascade hops (finishing)

1–2 pkgs. ale yeast

¾ c. corn sugar or 1¼ c. dried malt extract (for bottling)

O.G.: 1.042–1.046 (10.5–11.5)
F.G.: 1.012–1.016 (3–4)

Add the crushed roasted barley and black patent malt to 1½ gallons of cold water and bring to a boil. Boil these grains for 3–5 minutes—no longer! Remove with a strainer and add the malt extract and boiling hops. Continue boiling for 45 minutes. Add the finishing hops during the final 5–10 minutes of the boil. Sparge immediately into the fermenter and cold water. Add yeast and bottle when fermentation is complete.

Cheeks to the Wind Mild

For those who have a fondness for a traditional English mild, here's a light-bodied, delicately dark brown traditional beer that you can drink a lot of and continue to enjoy.

Ingredients for 5 gallons:

4 lbs. English dried light plain malt extract

½ lb. black patent malt

1 oz. Fuggles hops (boiling): 5 HBU

1–2 pkgs. ale yeast

¾ c. corn sugar or 1¼ c. dried malt extract (for bottling)

O.G.: 1.032–1.035 (8–9)
F.G.: 1.006–1.010 (1.5–2.5)

Crush the black patent malt and add it to 1½ gallons of cold water. Bring the water to a boil and remove the grain when boiling commences. Add the malt extract and hops and boil for 60 minutes. Sparge and add the hot wort to the fermenter and cold water. Add yeast when cool. Bottle when fermentation is complete.

PORTER

Goat Scrotum Ale (formerly Tumultuous Porter)

This is a fun beer to brew. It offers you the opportunity to use everything but the kitchen sink as ingredients. Despite its free style it brews a deliciously well balanced, slightly sweet style of porter with interesting nuances. Believe it or not, all of the ingredients were traditionally used in the brewing of porter hundreds of years ago.

Enjoy yourself and do not be fearful; the wonderfulness of this porter is a tribute to creativity and the adventurousness that many homebrewers develop. Relax. Don't worry. And this is certainly a session of brewing with friends that calls for having a homebrew.

(Commercial breweries, eat your heart out!)

Ingredients for 5 gallons:

5 lbs. plain dark malt extract
1 lb. crystal malt
¼ lb. black patent
¼ lb. roasted barley
1½ oz. boiling hops (your choice)
¼ oz. finishing hops (your choice)
1 c. brown sugar
1 c. blackstrap molasses
2 tsp. gypsum
1 lb. corn sugar
1–2 pkgs. ale yeast
¾ c. corn sugar or 1¼ c. dried malt extract (for bottling)
And one or all of the following ingredients:
2–4 oz. freshly grated ginger root
1–2 inches brewing licorice or bruised licorice root
2 Tbsp. spruce essence or ½ oz. of the new growth from a spruce tree
1–10 Szechuan chile peppers (very optional)

¼ c. juniper berries (slightly crushed)

6 oz. unsweetened Baker's chocolate

And enough homebrew for you and your friends to enjoy while brewing!

O.G.: 1.050–1.060 (12.5–15)
F.G.: Your guess is as good as mine.

First of all, pop a homebrew and dissolve your anxieties.

Next, crush the grain malts and roasted barley and add
them to 1½ gallons of cold water and bring to a boil. Remove
the grains with a strainer when boiling commences. Then combine all of the ingredients (except the yeast, finishing hops and
bottling sugar) and continue to boil for 45 minutes. Add your
finishing hops during the final 2 minutes of boiling.

Have another homebrew.

You can't avoid sparging this potion, so sparge into your
fermenter and cold water. Add the yeast when cool. Bottle when
fermentation is complete.

When ready, chill, serve, close your eyes and slip back into
the eighteenth century. It is a good porter!

Sparrow Hawk Porter

If you'd like to treat yourself to a gloriously bittersweet black
porter, your heart will "soar like a hawk" when you part your
lips for this treat.

Sparrow Hawk Porter is brewed in the tastefully done tradition of the Anchor Brewing Company's "Anchor Porter." Its
character is complex: wonderfully black and bitter, yet sweet,
medium-bodied, rich and quenching. Served cold, the bitterness
will be enhanced; served at temperatures above 50 degrees F
(10 C) its sweet character will take the forefront. Its distinctly
bitter bite does not linger long enough to be cloying. Its sweetness is like an impatient songbird singing, hidden in the darkness
of midnight.

As Sparrow Hawk lingers it becomes wisely more enjoyable.

Ingredients for 5 gallons:

4½ lbs. German light or amber malt extract syrup
3.3 lbs. John Bull plain dark malt extract syrup
1 lb. black patent malt
1½ oz. Northern Brewer hops (boiling): 13 HBU
1 oz. Tettnanger hops (finishing)
1–2 pkgs. lager yeast
¾ c. corn sugar or 1¼ c. dried malt extract (for bottling)

O.G.: 1.058–1.062 (14.5–15.5)
F.G.: 1.014–1.020 (3.5–5)

Crush the black patent malt and add to 1½ gallons of cold water. Bring to a boil and boil the grains for 5–10 minutes, then remove them with a strainer. Add the malt extracts and boiling hops and continue to boil for 60 minutes. Add the finishing hops during the final 1–2 minutes of boiling. Sparge immediately into your fermenter and cold water. Pitch the yeast when cool and bottle when fermentation is complete.

BOCK

Doctor Bock

Whether you are on a starship or relaxing on your or someone else's couch, Doctor Bock will be sure to beam a smile of plea-

sure on your face. Doctor Bock is similar to a traditional German bock beer because it is brewed from a high original gravity. It consequently possesses the richness and alcoholic strength that German bock beers are meant to have. This brew is bitter but not sharp, malty but not overpowering. German varieties of hops and malt extract make this brew all the more authentic.

Ingredients for 5 gallons:

  8 lbs. German light or amber plain malt extract syrup
  ½ lb. chocolate malt
  2 oz. Hallertauer, Spalter or Tettnanger hops (boiling):
     10 HBU
  ½ oz. Hallertauer or Tettnanger hops (flavor)
  1–2 pkgs. lager yeast
  ¾ c. corn sugar or 1¼ c. dried malt extract (for bottling)

O.G.: 1.066–1.070 (16.5–17.5)
F.G.: 1.014–1.020 (3.5–5)

Add the crushed chocolate malt to 1½ gallons of cold water and bring to a boil. Remove the grains with a strainer when boiling commences. Add the malt extract and boiling hops and continue to boil for 60 minutes. Add the flavor hops during the final 15–20 minutes of boiling. Sparge immediately into your fermenter and cold water. Add yeast when cool. Bottle when fermentation is complete.

Purple Mountain Bock . . .

And forever waves of grain.
    Not forgetting that bock beer is brewed in America, here's a recipe that is more akin to an American bock; nowhere near as strong as a traditional bock, but every bit as tasty, it is in a class by itself.
    Purple Mountain Bock is much lighter in body than German styles of its namesake. It is lightly hopped and crisply refreshing, not quite as rich and dark, but characterfully malty.

Ingredients for 5 gallons:

4.4 lbs. Premier plain light malt extract syrup
½ lb. light dried malt extract
½ lb. toasted malted barley
¼ lb. chocolate malt
¼ lb. crystal malt
1 oz. Hallertauer or Tettnanger hops (boiling): 5 HBU
¼ oz. Hallertauer or Tettnanger hops (finishing)
1–2 pkgs. lager yeast
¾ c. corn sugar or 1¼ c. dried malt extract (for bottling)

O.G.: 1.038–1.040 (9.5–10)
F.G.: 1.008–1.012 (2–3)

Toast the whole malted barley in a 350-degrees F (177 C) oven for 10 minutes. Crush the warm malted barley and crystal and chocolate malts. Add them to 1½ gallons of cold water and bring to a boil. Remove the grains when boiling commences. Add the malt extract and boiling hops and continue to boil for 60 minutes. Add the finishing hops during the final 1–2 minutes of boiling. Sparge the hot wort immediately into the fermenter and cold water. Pitch the yeast when cool and bottle when fermentation is complete.

DUNKEL

Danger Knows No Favorites Dunkel

With a beer like this, hey, danger is my business. What a fantastic true German Dunkel flavor. And spiking the wort with flavor hops at 30 minutes and 15 minutes before the end of the boil really gives this brew a Continental flavor that is hard, hard, hard to beat. The character is a rich, dark smoothness and soft bitterness that typify a well-brewed German Dunkel (dark) beer. It has medium to full body, wonderful hop flavor and rich creamy head that make it freshly superior to St. Pauli Girl Dark, Beck's Dark or Heineken's Dark, all by a long shot.

Ingredients for 5 gallons:

3½ lbs. Munton & Fison plain amber malt extract syrup
3½ lbs. plain dark dried malt extract
¾ lb. crystal malt
¼ lb. chocolate malt
¼ lb. black patent malt
2 oz. Hallertauer hops (boiling): 10 HBU
1 oz. Hallertauer hops (finishing)
1–2 pkgs. lager yeast
¾ c. corn sugar or 1¼ c. dried malt extract (for bottling)

O.G.: 1.050–1.055 (12.5–14)
F.G.: 1.008–1.011 (2–3)

Crush the crystal, chocolate and black patent malts and add to 1½ gallons of cold water and bring to a boil. Remove the grains with a strainer when boiling has commenced. Add the malt extracts and boiling hops and continue to boil for 60 minutes. Add ½ oz. of flavor hops 30 minutes into the boil. Add final ½ oz. flavor hops at 45 minutes into the boil. Sparge immediately into your fermenter and cold water. Pitch the yeast when cool and bottle when fermentation is complete.

GERMAN SCHWARZBIER (BLACK BEER)

Limp Richard's Schwarzbier

As gentle as a calm night in the Black Forest, Limp Richard's Schwarzbier is a deep, dark, smooth, mild German lager with just a hint of dark malt expressing its black origin. It's a beer that few Germans have the opportunity to enjoy. That is the fantastic thing about homebrewing: You can have it for yourself anytime and any season. Schwarzbier is a brew for all seasons. It can make a dark beer drinker out of anyone.

Ingredients for 5 gallons:

    5 lbs. Bierkeller German dark malt extract
    1/3 lb. black patent malt
    3/4 oz. Perle hops (boiling): 6 HBU
    3/4 oz. Perle hops (flavor and some additional bitterness)
    1/2 oz. Tettnanger hops (flavor)
    3/4 oz. Tettnanger hops (aroma)
    1/4 oz. Cascade hops (aroma)
    2 tsp. gypsum
    1-2 pkgs. lager yeast
    3/4 c. corn sugar or 1 1/4 c. dried malt extract (for bottling)

O.G.: 1.008–1.012 (2–3)
F.G.: 1.036–1.040 (9–10)

Combine black malt with 1 1/2 gallons of water and bring to a temperature of 150–160 degrees F (65–71 C) and hold for 20 minutes. Strain out black grain and then add malt extract and boiling hops. Bring to boil for 30 minutes. Then add 1/2 oz. Perle hops and continue to boil for another 15 minutes. Then add another 1/4 oz. of Perle and 1/2 oz. Tettnanger and boil for another 15 minutes. During the last 2 minutes of your 1-hour boil, add the aroma hops.

Sparge and add the hot wort to your fermenter and cold water. Add yeast when wort has cooled. Bottle when fermentation is complete. Serve this one slightly chilled to bring out the gentle richness of malt and soothing bitterness of the black malt and hops.

STOUTS

Toad Spit Stout

Guinness Stout? I enjoy Guinness as much as any stout lover can imagine. It's easy to brew from malt extract. The only character that this recipe is lacking is the unique "tang" that the real stuff has. The Guinness Brewery achieves its tang by actually adding a small amount (3 percent) of pasteurized soured beer to all of

its stouts around the world. I enjoy my Toad Spit Stout as much as any Guinness I've ever tasted. It is bittersweet, full-bodied, dry and typifies the roasted barley character of all stouts.

Use only the best roasted barley. Roasted barley that is jet-black in appearance has been overdone; instead look for a deep dark brown color. Black patent malt is no substitute when you are making stout, especially when you are typifying Guinness.

Ingredients for 5 gallons:

    3.3 lbs. John Bull hopped dark malt extract syrup
    4 lbs. plain dark dried malt extract

¾ lb. crystal malt

⅓ lb. roasted barley

⅓ lb. black patent

1½ oz. Northern Brewer hops (boiling): 14 HBU

½ oz. Fuggles or Willamette hops (finishing)

8 tsp. gypsum

1–2 pkgs. ale yeast

¾ c. corn sugar or 1¼ c. dried malt extract (for bottling)

O.G.: 1.050–1.054 (12.5–13.5)
F.G.: 1.015–1.019 (4–5)

Add the crushed roasted barley, crystal and black patent malts to 1½ gallons of cold water. Bring to a boil and remove the grains after 5 minutes of boiling. Add the malt extracts and boiling hops and continue to boil for 60 minutes. Add the finishing hops for the final 10 minutes of boiling (Guinness-type stout does not have a hop bouquet, but in this recipe it will have a subtle hop flavor). Sparge the hot wort into the fermenter and cold water. Pitch the yeast when cool. Bottle when fermentation is complete.

You should be enjoying Toad Spit Stout within 3–4 weeks from the day you brewed it.

Dark Sleep Stout

Dark Sleep Stout is much heavier, richer and more bittersweet than a Guinness style of dry stout. It is akin to putting a fancy liqueur in your espresso. This homebrewed stout is extremely rich and creamy—a sipping stout that does extremely well with age.

It is a fun stout to taste over a period of time. Note that I don't use the word *fun* to belittle Dark Sleep; it is every bit a respectable stout.

Ingredients for 5 gallons:

6.6 lbs. John Bull plain dark malt extract syrup

1 lb. plain dark dried malt extract

2 oz. Northern Brewer hops (boiling): 18 HBU
½ lb. roasted barley
½ lb. black patent malt
½ lb. crystal malt
8 tsp. gypsum
1–2 pkgs. ale yeast
¾ c. corn sugar or 1¼ c. dried malt extract (for bottling)

O.G.: 1.060–1.064 (15–16)
F.G.: 1.024–1.028 (6–7)

Add the crushed roasted barley, crystal and black patent malts to 1½ gallons of cold water. Bring to a boil and remove the grains after 5 minutes of boiling. Add the malt extract and boiling hops and continue to boil for 60 minutes. Sparge the hot wort into the fermenter and cold water. Pitch the yeast when cool. Bottle when fermentation is complete.

Lip-smacking, black and stout!

Cushlomachree Stout

And for those who like a less assertive stout: Something a little more velvety and sweet (but not overly sweet), Cushlomachree Stout offers a style of stout that is as smooth as the finest silk, similar to Australia's Tooth Sheaf Stout and Ireland's Murphy and Beamish Stout.

Again, the ease of brewing such quality stuff is often mind-boggling.

Ingredients for 5 gallons:

7 lbs. Edme Stout kit hopped malt extract
¼ lb. roasted barley
1 oz. Fuggles hops (boiling): 5 HBU
½ oz. Cascade hops (finishing)
1–2 pkgs. ale yeast
¾ c. corn sugar or 1¼ c. dried malt extract (for bottling)

O.G.: 1.040–1.044 (10–11)
F.G.: 1.010–1.014 (2.5–3.5)

Add the crushed roasted barley to 1½ gallons of cold water. Bring to a boil and remove the grains with a strainer after 5 minutes of boiling. Add the malt extract and boiling hops and continue to boil for 60 minutes. Add the finishing hops during the final 10 minutes. Sparge into the fermenter and cold water. Pitch the yeast when cool. Bottle when fermentation is complete.

This beer should be ready to drink 21 days from when you started brewing.

Armenian Imperial Stout

One look at this recipe and you may think I've gone bonkers. Well I haven't, but you may after putting your ever-loving lips to this most royal of stouts. A nearly 8 percent alcohol, very bittersweet and hoppy stout with a full-bodied, creamy-headed sensation that is a definite treasure among stout lovers. This brew will age nicely for years, but believe it: This brew is velvet in glass within 4–6 weeks of bottling.

Lots of hops are called for in this recipe in addition to the hop-flavored malt extract kit used. High-alpha hops are used in the boil to minimize the amount of sparging that's done at the end of the boil.

Ingredients for 5 gallons:

6.6 lbs. Munton & Fison's Old Ale Kit (hopped malt extract syrup)

3.3 lbs. plain light malt extract syrup

½ lb. black patent malt

½ lb. roasted barley

3 tsp. gypsum

2 oz. Eroica, Galena, Nugget or Olympic hops (boiling): 22–25 HBU

1 oz. Cascade hops (aroma)

1–2 pkgs. ale yeast

¾ c. corn sugar or 1¼ c. dried malt extract (for bottling)

O.G.: 1.070–1.075 (17.5–19)
F.G.: 1.018–1.025 (4.5–6)

Add the crushed black malt and roasted barley to 1½ gallons of water and bring to a boil. When boiling begins, remove grains. Add gypsum, malt extract and boiling hops and return to a boil. Boil for 60 minutes. During the final 1–2 minutes add the aroma hops and then sparge into your fermenter and cold water. Add yeast when cool. Bottle when fermentation is complete and then wait until it's ready and continues to improve.

SPECIALTY BEERS

Rocky Raccoon's Crystal Honey Lager (Original)

This is the original and internationally acclaimed Rocky Raccoon's Honey Lager with only improved modifications. It is brewed with one of the lightest malt extracts available, fresh hops and light honey in place of malt or corn sugar. It is a clean, crisp, exceptionally light beer with a mellow, aromatic hop flavor. The use of honey encourages a very complete fermentation and subsequently high alcohol content. The lightness of flavor really can do justice to your finest hops. This recipe should be your foundation for a wide variety of experimenting with toasted

malts, hops, other grains and unusual ingredients. It is a real delight and numerous people have won first-place awards at state fairs around the United States with it.

This beer will change its character with age; most who have appreciated Rocky's consider age with respect and happily raised eyebrows of disbelief.

Rocky's has a slight resemblance to the character of some stronger types of Belgian Ales.

Ingredients for 5 gallons:

3½ lbs. plain light dried malt extract
2½ lbs. light clover honey
1½ oz. Cascade hops (boiling): 7.5 HBU
½ oz. Cascade hops (finishing)
1–2 pkgs. lager yeast
¾ c. corn sugar or 1¼ c. dried malt extract (for bottling)

O.G.: 1.048–1.052 (12–13)
F.G.: 1.004–1.008 (1–2)

Add the malt extract, honey and boiling hops to 1½ gallons of water and boil for 60 minutes. Add the finishing hops during the final 2–4 minutes of boiling. Sparge immediately into the fermenter and cold water. Add yeast when cool and bottle when fermentation is complete.

Linda's Lovely Light Honey Ginger Lager

Linda's Lovely is a variation of Rocky Raccoon's that offers the sparkle of fresh ginger to an already delicate and exquisite, finely balanced honey lager. The variation can easily be accomplished by adding 2–4 oz. of fresh grated ginger root to the boiling wort along with the malt extract, honey and hops.

It is easily brewed and offers great summertime or holiday satisfaction.

Bruce and Kay's Black Honey Spruce Lager

A heavenly delight for those who enjoy the rich taste of dark beers and the lighter body of light beers. A well-brewed Bruce and Kay's will impress even those friends who say they don't really like beer. Try this recipe if you see yourself as a homebrew missionary.

Bruce and Kay's Black Honey Spruce Lager does indeed have spruce essence as one of its ingredients, as well as honey, malt and hops. For a black beer it has a light body due to the use of honey. Its rich, dark appearance and creamy head lead deceivingly to a surprisingly refreshing and flavorful beer.

The recipe is for 5 gallons, but this is one time that you might consider doubling or tripling the recipe. You'll run out all too soon.

Ingredients for 5 gallons:

   3.3 lbs. John Bull plain dark malt extract syrup
   2 lbs. plain dried amber malt extract
   2 lbs. light honey
   ¾ lb. crystal malt
   ⅓ lb. black patent malt
   1½ oz. Cascade hops (boiling): 7 HBU
   ½ oz. Hallertauer hops (finishing)
   1 oz. spruce essence (available at homebrew supply stores)
   1–2 pkgs. lager yeast
   ¾ c. corn sugar or 1¼ c. dried malt extract (for bottling)

O.G.: 1.050–1.054 (12.5–13.5)
F.G.: 1.013–1.017 (3–4)

Add the crushed crystal and black patent malts to 1½ gallons of cold water. Remove the grains when boiling commences. Add the malt extract, honey and boiling hops and continue to boil for 45 minutes. Add the finishing hops and spruce essence during the final 2–4 minutes of boiling. Sparge immediately into the fermenter and cold water. Add yeast when cool and bottle when fermentation is complete.

". . . it was about spruce beer. Mr. Knightly had been telling him something about brewing spruce beer. . . . Talking about spruce beer—Oh! Yes—Mr. Knightly and I both saying we liked it and Mr. Elton's seeming resolved to learn to like it too. . . ."—*Emma*, **by Jane Austen**

Kumdis Island Spruce Beer

A spruce beer brewed in the tradition of authenticity, Kumdis Island Spruce was originally brewed with the fresh spring growth of tall Sitka spruce trees in the Queen Charlotte Islands of British Columbia, Canada. The aroma that filled the "brewhouse" cabin was as wonderful as gingerbread hot out of the oven. And the character of the beer when it was ready to drink? Well, let me tell you that it was a real surprise. It was a very light-bodied, brown ale that tasted very, very similar to Pepsi-Cola. Now, that may or may not sound appropriate for beer, but the fact is, it tasted fantastic, like an unsweetened Pepsi-Cola with a real beer character. It is a wonderfully refreshing and quenching beer.

Ingredients for 5 gallons:

   3½ lbs. Edme S.F.X. dark malt extract syrup
   2 lbs. plain dried dark malt extract

4 oz. new green growth of spruce trees
2 oz. Hallertauer hops (boiling): 10 HBU
1–2 pkgs. ale yeast
¾ c. corn sugar or 1¼ c. dried malt extract (for bottling)

O.G.: 1.040–1.044 (10–11)
F.G.: 1.010–1.014 (2.5–3.5)

Add the malt extracts, spruce tips and boiling hops to 1½ gallons of water and boil for 45 minutes. Sparge into the fermenter and cold water. Add yeast when cool and bottle when fermentation is complete.

Smokey the Beer—Rauchbier!

A golden brown lager with a smooth mellow body, medium hoppiness matched with a discernible sweetness and a rich smoked flavor that follows through with a quizzical smile. Holy smokes, what a drink!

German Rauchbier (smoked beer) is a distinctive tradition enjoyed by a privileged few in Bamberg, Germany (I was there in 1989—wow, it was like a fantasy dream come true!). The homebrewer can brew a remarkable rendition of German Rauchbier with the addition of smoked grains or a bit of liquid smoke. Rauchbier quite naturally had origins before the advent of hot air kilns. Primitive brewers discovered that fire was the most direct and simple means of "kilning" sprouted and malted barley. This tradition lent a smokey and slightly roasted flavor to the malted barley and beer brewed from these ingredients.

For the appreciator of smoked foods, Smokey the Beer is a phenomenally pleasant experience. For the homebrewer, a gratifying challenge.

Ingredients for 5 gallons:

7 lbs. Munton & Fison plain light dried malt extract
1½ lbs. smoked crystal malt (homemade) OR 2 tsp. liquid smoke
1½ oz. Hallertauer hops (boiling): 8 HBU

½ oz. Hallertauer hops (flavoring)
½ oz. Hallertauer or Tettnanger hops (finishing)
¼ c. chocolate malt
1–2 pkgs. lager yeast
¾ c. corn sugar or 1¼ c. dried malt extract (for bottling)

O.G.: 1.047–1.053 (12–13.5)
F.G.: 1.014–1.018 (3.5–4.5)

If you'd like to be authentic, you may smoke your own malted barley. Simply soak the grain in water for 5 minutes, then arrange your barbecue as a smoker. Use a brass screen (available at hardware stores) as a grill. Smoke, dry and lightly roast your malted barley over a bed of charcoal and hickory, apple, mesquite or other appropriate hardwood chips. As an alternative to "smoking your own," you may substitute commercially available liquid smoke (check your local supermarket's barbecue sauce section). Avoid liquid smoke indoctrinated with preservatives, vinegar and other peripheral ingredients. The brand I've used is Wright's Liquid Smoke (E.H. Wright Company, P.O. Drawer 899, Brentwood, TN 37027).

If smoked grains are used, add the crushed, smoked grain and chocolate malt to 1½ gallons of cold water and bring to a boil. Remove the grains when boiling has commenced. Add the malt extract and boiling hops (and liquid smoke if used instead of smoked grains) and boil for 40 minutes. Then add ½ oz. flavor hops and boil for 20 more minutes. Add the finishing hops during the final 2 minutes of boiling. Sparge into the fermenter and cold water. Pitch yeast when cool and bottle when fermentation is complete.

Vagabond Gingered Ale

Vagabond Gingered Ale is a deliciously dark, full-bodied ale, with the gentle essence of fresh ginger. The freshly grated ginger in this recipe offers a joyously refreshing balance to the sweetness of malt, counterbalanced by a judicious choice of hops. The blend of the main ingredients offers a complex triad of flavors—uniquely satisfying for the vagabond brewers who journey to places that have no boundaries.

A favorite of many who have tasted from cups of those who have dared.

You will not regret this experience. And you'll never know until you check it out.

Ingredients for 5 gallons:

3½ lbs. Munton & Fison plain dark malt extract syrup
2½ lbs. plain dark dried malt extract

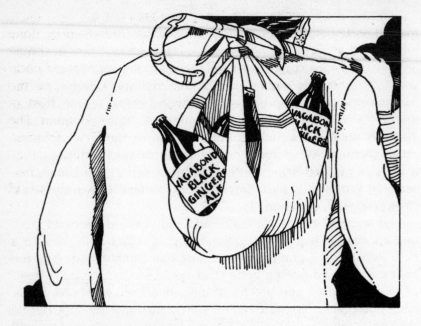

¾ lb. crystal malt
½ lb. chocolate malt
2 oz. Cascade hops (boiling): 10 HBU
1 oz. Willamette hops (finishing)
2–4 oz. freshly grated ginger root
1–2 pkgs. ale yeast
¾ c. corn sugar or 1¼ c. dried malt extract (for bottling)

O.G.: 1.040–1.044 (10–11)
F.G.: 1.012–1.016 (3–4)

Add the crushed crystal and chocolate malts to 1½ gallons of cold water and bring to a boil. When boiling has commenced, remove the grains and add malt extracts, boiling hops and freshly grated ginger root and continue to boil for 60 minutes. Add the finishing hops during the final 1–2 minutes of the boil. Sparge into the fermenter and cold water. Pitch yeast when cool and bottle when fermentation is complete.

Roastaroma Deadline Delight

Here's an unusual recipe and an unusual beer inspired by none other than an herb tea whose basic ingredients are crystal malt and roasted barley. Roastaroma Mocha Spice tea is a tea packaged by Celestial Seasonings. Its contents, besides having the above-mentioned traditional beer ingredients, have a host of other herbs and spices, including star anise and cinnamon. The hearty aroma of this tea suggested a worthwhile experiment. And indeed it was a favorite of my beer-drinking friends.

A rich, dark, heavy-bodied beer with the refreshing character of star anise and cinnamon. A wonderful oasis in the world of unusual brews.

Ingredients for 5 gallons:

6 lbs. Munton & Fison plain dark malt extract syrup
1 lb. light malt extract
2 oz. Fuggles hops (boiling): 10 HBU
1 oz. Cascade hops (finishing)
¾ lb. crystal malt
⅓ lb. black patent malt
2 oz. Roastaroma Mocha Spice Tea
1–2 pkgs. ale yeast
¾ c. corn sugar or 1¼ c. dried malt extract (for bottling)

O.G.: 1.042–1.046 (10.5–11.5)
F.G.: 1.008–1.012 (2–3)

Add the crushed crystal and black patent malts to 1½ gallons of cold water and bring to a boil. When boiling has commenced remove the grains and add malt extract and boiling hops and continue to boil for 45 minutes. Add the Roastaroma Mocha Spice Tea during the final 15 minutes of the boil, then add the finishing hops during the final 1–2 minutes of the boil. Sparge into the fermenter and cold water. Pitch yeast when cool and bottle when fermentation is complete.

Cherries in the Snow

A sinfully unique combination of sour cherries, malt extract, a mild blend of hops and patient aging conspires to celebrate the rites of spring with the luscious memories of summers past.

The acidity of sour cherries slices through the subtle malt sweetness to awaken the palate's winter remorse. Cherries in the Snow faintly resembles a Belgium Kriek, a style of beer brewed with sweet cherries, malt and a lactobaccilus bacteria for tartness. However, the tartness of Cherries in the Snow is not as explosive as a Belgium Kriek, Lambic or Gueuze (all sour-fermented beers); rather, it gently hints of a clean tartness, inspiring a call for more. The hops are subtle, not bitter, yet flavorful in the style of an awakening spring.

As does a good wine, Cherries in the Snow offers a wonderful potential to mature dearly with age (years)—called forth for sinfully special occasions.

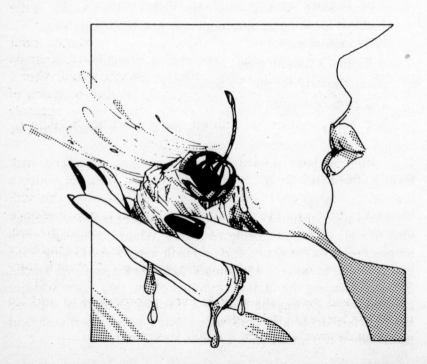

Ingredients for 5 gallons:

   6 lbs. light malt extract
   2 oz. Hallertauer or Tettnanger hops (boiling): 10 HBU
   ½ oz. Hallertauer or Tettnanger hops (finishing)
   10 lbs. sour cherries
   1–2 pkgs. ale yeast
   ¾ c. corn sugar or 1¼ c. dried malt extract (for bottling)

O.G.: 1.046–1.050 (11.5–12.5)
F.G.: 1.011–1.017 (2.5–4)

Add the malt extract and boiling hops to 1½ gallons of water and boil for 45 minutes. Add the crushed sour cherries and finishing hops to the boiling wort. The cherries should cool the wort to a temperature of about 160 degrees F (71 C). Let the cherries steep for a good 15 minutes at a temperature between 160–180 degrees F (71–88 C). These temperatures will pasteurize the cherried wort. Do not boil, as boiling will "set the pectin" in the fruit and will create a harmless haze in the finished beer.

After the cherried wort has steeped for 15 minutes, pour the entire contents of the wort (without sparging) into a sanitized plastic fermenter and cold water. Pitch yeast when cool. After 5 days of "primary" fermentation, carefully remove as much of the floating hops and cherries from the fermenter as humanly possible, but be sure that the strainer you use is sanitized by boiling or with a sanitizing solution.

After you have removed much of the floating debris, rack (siphon) the beer into a secondary fermenter. You will notice a sediment of spent cherries and hops. Avoid siphoning this sediment (don't worry). The pits create one hell of a nuisance once they get into your siphon hose. Attach an air lock to the secondary fermenter and continue with fermentation until the beer begins to show signs of clarity. Bottle when fermentation is complete.

Age and serve chilled. It is even appropriate to add ice cubes to Cherries in the Snow.

You deserve a kiss for brewing this one!

Cherry Fever Stout

"The best beer you've ever made."   —A.W.

The combination of cherries and stout is an experience too won-derful for any homebrewer to miss. If you like stout, this brew will cheer your very soul.

Its velvety roasted malt character, already perfectly bal-anced with a pungent bitterness offered by Northern Brewer hops, is wholly blessed with the soft kiss of ripe cherries. The complex blend of sweetness, bitterness and cherry tang is eu-phorically pursued with a fragrance of hops and cherry fever. Personally, it is my favorite stout to brew and enjoy—chilled in the heat of summer or at room temperature in the coldest of winter.

I have a difficult time describing the essence of this brew; so for now, at least until you've brewed it yourself, let it suffice to say Cherry Fever Stout is delightfully fine!

P.S. You can substitute red ripe raspberries and make an equally cosmic brew!

Ingredients for 5 gallons:

3.3 lbs. John Bull plain dark malt extract syrup

2½ lbs. Premier Malt hopped flavored light malt extract syrup

1½ lbs. plain dark dried malt extract

1 lb. crystal malt

½ lb. roasted barley

½ lb. black patent malt

1½ oz. Northern Brewer hops (boiling): 13 HBU

½ oz. Willamette hops (finishing)

8 tsp. gypsum

3 lbs. sour cherries

2 lbs. choke cherries OR, if not available, substitute with 2 more lbs. of sour cherries

1–2 pkgs. ale yeast

¾ c. corn sugar or 1¼ c. dried malt extract (for bottling)

5 gal. uncontrollable anticipation

O.G.: 1.064–1.068 (16–17)
F.G.: 1.018–1.026 (4.5–6.5)

Add the crushed roasted barley, crystal and black patent malts to 1½ gallons of cold water and bring to a boil. When boiling commences, remove the spent grains and add the malt extracts, gypsum and boiling hops and continue to boil for 60 minutes. Add the 5 lbs. of crushed cherries (pits and all) to the hot boiling wort. Turn off heat and let the wort steep for 15 minutes (at temperatures between 160–180 degrees F [71–88 C]) in order to pasteurize the cherries. Do not boil. Add the finishing hops 2 minutes before you pour the entire contents into a plastic primary fermenter and cold water. Pitch yeast when cool. After 4–5 days of primary fermentation, rack the fermenting beer into a secondary fermenter. Secondary fermentation should last about 10–14 days longer. Bottle when fermentation is complete.

Who's in the Garden Grand Cru

A most unusual brew that I love to love. In the style of a Belgian White beer flavored with coriander, orange peel and the spiciness of German hops, Who's in the Garden is a copy of Belgium's Hoegaarden Grand Cru Ale, but with a bit more intensity and freshness in flavor—because it's homemade and fresh from the brewery! Honey is a part of this recipe to help achieve a drier, less sweet and more refreshing brew.

For those who have never experienced the floral spiciness of freshly ground coriander seed, next time you're at the grocery store pick up a few ounces of this inexpensive spice in its whole form and grind some yourself. It'll make your special beer even that more special. I encourage you to give it a try.

Ingredients for 5 gallons:

5 lbs. light or extra-light dried malt extract
2¾ lbs. light honey

1 oz. Hallertauer hops (boiling): 5–6 HBU

⅓ oz. Hallertauer hops (flavor)

½ oz. Hallertauer hops (aroma)

1½ oz. freshly crushed (crush the whole seeds yourself) coriander

½ oz. dried ground orange peel

1–2 pkgs. ale yeast

¾ c. corn sugar or 1¼ c. dried malt extract (for bottling)

O.G.: 1.055–1.059 (14–15)

F.G.: 1.004–1.008 (1–2)

Add malt extract, honey and boiling hops to 1½ gallons of water and boil for 45 minutes. Then add ¾ oz. crushed coriander and flavor hops and boil for 10 more minutes. Then add ¾ oz. crushed coriander and orange peel and boil for 5 minutes. During the final 1–2 minutes add the aroma hops, then sparge immediately into your fermenter and cold water. Bottle when fermentation is complete.

For an added attraction, why not add one whole coriander seed to each bottle when bottling? Worried (heaven forbid) about bacteria on the seeds? Microwave them.

Holiday Cheer

A creation for the spirit of the holiday season and much better for you than a fruitcake.

Unusual as this recipe may be, if you think that you will enjoy it—brew it. This basic recipe has won the hearts of many, and prizes, too.

Ingredients for 5 gallons:

7 lbs. plain light malt extract (any brand)
1 lb. light honey (clover or alfalfa)
½ lb. crystal malt
⅛ lb. (½ c.) black patent malt
2 oz. Cascade hops (boiling): 10 HBU
½ oz. Saaz hops
1 oz. freshly grated ginger root
6-inch stick of cinnamon or 3 tsp. ground cinnamon
grated orange peels from 4 oranges
1–2 pkgs. ale yeast
¾ c. corn sugar or 1¼ c. dried malt extract (for bottling)

O.G.: 1.054–1.060 (13.5–15)
F.G.: 1.018–1.026 (4.5–6.5)

Add the crushed crystal and black patent malts to 1½ gallons of cold water and bring to a boil. When boiling commences remove the grains. Add the malt extract, honey, boiling hops and continue to boil for 45 minutes. Add the ginger, cinnamon, orange peels and continue to boil for another 10 minutes. Add the finishing hops during the final 2 minutes of the boil. Sparge immediately into your fermenter and cold water. Pitch the yeast when cool. Bottle when fermentation is complete.

INTRODUCTION TO GRAIN BREWING FOR THE MALT EXTRACT HOMEBREWER

With good techniques, brewing from malt extract offers the opportunity for simplicity and quality beer. There is no doubt that many homebrewers will remain with malt extract for exactly those reasons: simplicity and quality. But for others, the intrigue of brewing from scratch will tease your sense of creativity and the desire to dispel that mysticism attached to those beers brewed from scratch.

Indeed, the alchemy of converting starch molecules to fermentable sugars with the aid of little ''animals'' called enzymes has a romantic calling to homebrewers who have never experienced conversion! The missionary zealots, the all-grain fanatics, will tell you how much better their beer is . . . and then you watch, you read, you try to discover what all the brew-ha-ha is all about. Suddenly you are overwhelmed at the unlimited possibilities, the limitless opportunity to improvise, to manipulate, to fashion your own specialized equipment. . . .

But hey—wait a minute, not so fast, hold your donkeys. What about the malt extract brewers who are basically content but need to dabble in mash-mysticism just to understand a little bit more? Experiencing the mysteries of enzyme conversion and knowing that there are other horizons in the world of brewing is enlightenment.

Relax. Don't worry. Have a homebrew.

MASH-EXTRACT TRANSITION BREWS

Introduction to the world of grain brewing can be very simple, painless and rewarding. The recipes that follow are a combination of malt extract and grain mash. They serve to improve the quality of a homebrew and introduce you to the unlimited brewing versatility achievable with the use of grains.

Essentially, your introduction to all-grain brewing will be by mashing a small and very manageable amount of malted barley and other grains. The sweet liquid wort that you produce by converting starches to sugars is added to malt extract syrups or dry powders; from then on, the brewing process used in malt extract brewing continues without change.

This method offers some very significant advantages:

1) Mash-extract brewing retains the simplicity of malt extract brewing while developing your confidence and offering a sane introduction to new ingredients and the process of all-grain brewing.

2) Mash-extract brewing introduces you to the improvement in flavor that can be achieved with care and understanding that all-grain brewing can and should inspire.

3) You can learn how to mash your own grains without additional equipment or boiling huge volumes of wort.

A detailed theory of mashing and using grains is covered in the following section. This section will briefly introduce the theory of mashing and basic homebrewing-mashing procedures. Be aware that there are many methods used to convert and mash grains to fermentable sugars. The method used in this introduction is purposefully presented because of its simplicity, instructional potential and the absence of special equipment.

A SHORT COURSE ON THEORY

Mashing converts the soluble starch in grain to fermentable sugars and unfermentable "dextrins," each of which are present in most styles of beer wort. There are starch-to-sugar-converting "diastatic" enzymes in malted barley. These enzymes will become active under proper conditions. When the temperature of a water and malted barley "soup" reaches a certain range, the enzymes become active and literally break starch molecules into sugar molecules. Malted barley usually has more than enough enzymes to convert its own starches to sugars and convert additional soluble starches (adjuncts such as cooked rice, wheat, corn, etc.) to fermentable sugars.

For the mash-extract brewer, the sweet liquor that is produced from the following procedures is combined with malt extract and boiled with other beer ingredients.

MASH-EXTRACT EQUIPMENT AND PROCEDURE

Equipment

For a 5-gallon batch you will need:

- A 4–5-gallon brewpot.
- A means of crushing the grain.
  If preground malted barley is unavailable you may find it necessary to purchase a grain or flour mill in order to grind your grains. Many homebrew supply shops have a grain mill for their customers. The grinding plates of your mill should be set so that the grains are crushed or, rather, cracked into small pieces. They should retain their integrity as pieces rather than be pulverized to flour. The grinding should suffice to break the husks away from the grain.
- A lauter-tun.
  This is no more than a strainer that will have the capacity to hold the amount of grains that you mash and sparge. There are many varieties available in homebrew shops. If unavailable in your area, a clean 4–5-gallon food-grade plastic bucket can be easily converted into a lauter-tun by drilling hundreds of 1/8-inch holes in the bottom; there you have a homemade strainer, sparger, lauter-tun.
- Tincture of iodine.
  This will be used for testing for starch conversion.

Procedure

1) The grains are crushed.
2) Water and minerals are added to the crushed grains.
3) The temperature is raised to between 113–122 degrees F (45–50 C) and held for 30 minutes. This is called a protein rest and develops nutrients for the yeast.
4) The temperature is raised to 150 degrees F (65 C) and held for 10 minutes. This begins to develop fermentable sugars.

5) The temperature is raised to 158 degrees F (70 C) and held for 10–15 minutes. This completes conversion of all starches to fermentable sugars and unfermentable "dextrins" (dextrins contribute body to beer).

6) An iodine test is made to confirm that starch has been converted to sugars and dextrins. A drop of tincture of iodine in a starch solution will turn purple/black. If starch is not present, the iodine will not turn black. This test is simply done by removing a tablespoon of converted mash and pouring it onto a clean white plate. A drop of iodine into the solution will indicate whether conversion has been achieved.

7) Sparge grains to retrieve sweet wort and separate from spent grains. You will need an extra bucket or pot. A plastic fermenter can also be used for this purpose.

8) Add malt extracts, hops and other ingredients and continue to brew.

Relax. Don't worry. Have a homebrew.

MASH-EXTRACT RECIPES

Is It the Truth or Is It a Lie, Dutch Pilsener

This brew offers a striking resemblance to Heineken light pilsener beer. It has a nice hop bitterness balanced with a touch of sweetness. The quality and variety of hops lend a significant character to the beer. It is a delicious medium-bodied and very drinkable brew. Its head retention is superlative and a result of the mash.

Ingredients for 5 gallons:

3 lbs. Edme dry plain light malt extract
3 lbs. pale malted barley (preferably 2-row type)
1 oz. Saaz hops (boiling)
½ oz. Cascade hops (boiling)
½ oz. Saaz hops (finishing)
1 tsp. gypsum

¼ tsp. Irish moss powder
1–2 pkgs. lager yeast
¾ c. corn sugar (for bottling)

O.G.: 1.035–1.039 (9–10)
F.G.: 1.007–1.011 (2–3)

Heat 2½ quarts of water to 130 degrees F (58 C). Dissolve the gypsum in the water. Add the crushed malted barley and mix well. The temperature will stabilize between 115 and 120 degrees F (46–49 C). Add heat and hold the temperature at 120–122 degrees for 30 minutes, stirring every 5 minutes.

Raise the temperature of the mash to 130 degrees F (58 C) and add 1½ quarts of boiling water. This will raise the temperature to about or just below 150 degrees F (65 C). Hold at 149–152 degrees F (65–67 C) for 10 minutes, stirring occasionally. Then add more heat to raise the temperature to 158 degrees F (70 C) and hold for 15–20 minutes. Conversion should be complete at this stage. Test with iodine. Continue to mash (for up to 20 more minutes) until conversion is complete.

Pour your mash into your lauter-tun and sparge with 1 gallon of water at 170 degrees F (76 C).

Bring the sweet wort to a boil and add malt extract and boiling hops and continue to boil for 60 minutes. Add the finishing hops and Irish moss during the final 5 minutes of the boil. Sparge into your fermenter and cold water (approximately 2–2½ gallons). Pitch yeast when cool. Bottle when fermentation is complete.

Daisy Mae Dortmund Lager
Daisy Mae and Daisy may not. To get to Daisy, it takes a lot!

An exceptionally fine light Dortmund-style lager alludes to a very real German character. A rich gold luster is imparted to the brew by the toasted malt, while the bitterness and sweetness melt into Daisy Mae's full-bodiedness and rich creamy head. This deliciously satisfying beer is a beer worth brewing in any season. This relatively strong German lager is sometimes referred to as

"Export." The best exporting you'll be doing is exporting from your homebrewery to your dining room table.

Ingredients for 5 gallons:

   2½ lbs. malted barley (American 6-row type)
   ½ lb. dextrine malt
   ½ lb. toasted malted barley
   2 tsp. gypsum
   5 lbs. Bierhaus hopped lager kit malt extract syrup
   1 lb. light dried malt extract
   1½ oz. Hallertauer hops (boiling): 8–9 HBU
   ½ oz. Saaz hops (finishing)
   ¼ tsp. Irish moss powder
   1–2 pkgs. lager yeast
   ¾ c. corn sugar or 1¼ c. dried malt extract (for bottling)

O.G.: 1.046–1.050 (11.5–12.5)
F.G.: 1.008–1.012 (2–3)

Toast ½ lb. malted barley for 10 minutes in a 350-degree F (177 C) oven. Heat 2½ quarts of water to 130 degrees F (58 C). Dissolve the gypsum in the water. Add the crushed malted barley and dextrine malt and mix well. The temperature will stabilize between 115 and 120 degrees F (46–49 C). Add heat and hold the temperature at 120–122 degrees F (49–50 C) for 30 minutes, stirring every 5 minutes.

Raise the temperature of the mash to 130 degrees F (58 C) and add 1½ quarts of boiling water. This will raise the temperature to about or just below 150 degrees F (66 C). Hold at 149–152 degrees F (65–67 C) for 10 minutes, stirring occasionally. Then add more heat to raise the temperature to 158 degrees F (70 C) and hold for 15–20 minutes. Conversion should be complete at this stage. Test with iodine. Continue to mash (for up to 20 more minutes) until conversion is complete.

Pour your mash into your lauter-tun and sparge with 1 gallon of water at 170 degrees F (76 C).

Bring the sweet wort to a boil and add malt extract and boiling hops and continue to boil for 60 minutes. Add the Irish moss during the final 5 minutes of the boil. Add the finishing hops during the final 1–2 minutes of the boil. Sparge immediately into your fermenter and cold water (approximately 2–2½ gallons). Pitch yeast when cool. Bottle when fermentation is complete.

What the Helles Münchner

For all of you who have been and all of you who will go and all of you who wish you could go, What the Helles Münchner lager is the stuff of liters and liters. Under a big tent at a midsummer's fest or indoors at the Höfbrauhaus in Munich, liters and liters of this golden nectar are consumed all over southern Germany.

A mildly hoppy and extremely drinkable lager, Helles is best served on draft at chilled temperatures to express smooth carbonation and maltiness. The secret is in using fresh hops of German origin and infusing them at various points during the boil. A good lager yeast will further enhance the exceptionally true tradition of this jovial German lager.

Ingredients for 5 gallons:

3 lbs. 2-row American or German pale malt
4 lbs. light dried malt extract
¼ tsp. Irish moss powder
½ oz. Hallertauer Hersbrucker hops (boiling): 3 HBU
¼ oz. Czechoslovakian Saaz hops (boiling): 1–2 HBU
½ oz. Hallertauer Hersbrucker hops (flavor)
½ oz. Czechoslovakian Saaz hops (flavor)
½ oz. American Tettnanger hops (aroma)
½ oz. Hallertauer Hersbrucker hops (aroma)
1–2 pkgs. lager yeast
¾ c. corn sugar or 1¼ c. dried malt extract (for bottling)

O.G.: 1.046–1.050 (11.5–12.5)
F.G.: 1.009–1.013 (2–3)

Heat 3 quarts of water to 175 degrees F (79 C) and add the crushed pale malt. Stabilize at 155–157 degrees F (68–69 C) and let set for 30 minutes. Then add heat and raise the temperature to 160 degrees F (71 C) and let set for 15 more minutes. Conversion will be done at this point.

Strain and sparge with 1½ gallons of 170 degree F (77 C) water. Add the malt extract and bring the sweet wort to a boil. Add the boiling hops and continue to boil for 30 minutes. Then add ¼ oz. of Hallertauer and Saaz flavor (and some bitterness) hops and boil for 15 more minutes. Then add ¼ oz. each more of Hallertauer and Saaz hops, add Irish moss and boil for 15 more minutes. During the final 1–2 minutes add the aroma hops.

Sparge and add the hot wort to your fermenter and cold water. Add yeast when temperature has dropped. Ferment to completion and bottle.

Sayandra Wheat Beer

Sayandra Wheat Beer is a low-alcohol, light-bodied, fully carbonated wheat beer. Most or all of the enzymes for this mash-extract recipe are provided by Edme D.M.S. (''diastatic malt syrup'') malt extract. Wheat malt has some enzymatic potential but needs the help of either malted barley or diastatic malt extract. Edme D.M.S. is the only malt extract with active enzymes available to the homebrewer and can be added to any mash for extra natural enzymes.

Ingredients for 5 gallons:

> 3½ lbs. Edme D.M.S. light malt extract syrup
>
> 1 lb. malted wheat OR 1 lb. (dry weight) cooked ground wheat berries OR 1 lb. flaked wheat
>
> 2 tsp. gypsum
>
> 1½ oz. Hallertauer hops (boiling): 7 HBU
>
> ¼ oz. Hallertauer or Tettnanger hops (aroma)
>
> ¼ tsp. Irish moss powder
>
> 1–2 pkgs. ale yeast
>
> ¾ c. corn sugar or 1¼ c. dried malt extract (for bottling)

O.G.: 1.033–1.037 (8–9)
F.G.: 1.005–1.010 (1–2.5)

If wheat berries are used, crack them into pieces with a grinder or flour mill (do not grind into flour). Boil them for ½ hour in 3 quarts of water. Let cool to 145 degrees F (63 C) and add the malt extract and gypsum. Stabilize the temperature at about 122 degrees F (50 C). If either flaked wheat or malted wheat is used, heat 3 quarts of water to 130 degrees F (58 C). Dissolve the gypsum in the water. Add the crushed malted wheat or flaked wheat and malt extract and mix well. Stabilize the temperature at 120–122 degrees F (49–50 C) for 30 minutes, stirring every 5 minutes.

Raise the temperature of the mash to 130 degrees F (58 C) and add 1 quart of boiling water. Hold the mash at 149–152 degrees F (65–67 C) for 10 minutes, stirring occasionally. Then add more heat to raise the temperature to 158 degrees F (70 C) and hold for 15–20 minutes. Conversion should be complete at this stage. Test with iodine. Continue to mash (for up to 20 more minutes) until conversion is complete.

Pour your mash into your lauter-tun and sparge with 2 quarts of water at 170 degrees F (76 C).

Bring the sweet wort to a boil and add boiling hops and continue to boil for 60 minutes. Add the finishing hops and Irish moss during the final 5 minutes of the boil. Sparge into your fermenter and cold water (approximately 2–2½ gallons). Pitch yeast when cool. Bottle when fermentation is complete.

Lips Lager (India Pale Lager)

A rich white creamy head contrasts eloquently with the very deep copper-gold transparency of this well-hopped but softly balanced lager. The generous amount of hops adds an assertive bitterness, yet the equally generous amount of crystal malt brings the crescendo of bitterness to a soft alluring finale with full body and sweetness. A rich brew for the beer drinkers who enjoy having an affair with their beer.

Ingredients for 5 gallons:

    1 lb. malted barley (American 6-row type)
    1 lb. crystal malt
    ½ lb. dextrine malt

½ lb. toasted malted barley

2 tsp. gypsum

3½ lbs. plain light dried malt extract

2½ lbs. plain amber dried malt extract

1½ oz. Northern Brewer hops (boiling): 12 HBU

1 oz. Cascade hops (finishing)

¼ tsp. Irish moss powder

1–2 pkgs. lager yeast

¾ c. corn sugar or 1¼ c. dried malt extract (for bottling)

O.G.: 1.058–1.066 (12.5–14.5)
F.G.: 1.015–1.023 (4–6)

Toast ½ lb. malted barley for 10 minutes in a 350-degree F (177 C) oven. Heat 2½ quarts of water to 130 degrees F (58 C). Dissolve the gypsum in the water. Add the crushed malted barley, dextrine malt and crystal malt and mix well. The temperature will stabilize between 115–120 degrees F (46–49 C). Add heat and hold the temperature at 120–122 degrees F (49–50 C) for 30 minutes, stirring every 5 minutes.

Raise the temperature of the mash to 130 degrees F (58 C) and add 1½ quarts of boiling water. This will raise the temperature to about 150 degrees F (66 C). Hold at 149–152 degrees F (65–67 C) for 10 minutes, stirring occasionally. Then add more heat to raise the temperature to 158 degrees F (70 C) and hold for 15–20 minutes. Conversion should be complete at this stage. Test with iodine. Continue to mash (for up to 20 more minutes) until conversion is complete.

Pour your mash into your lauter-tun and sparge with 1 gallon of water at 170 degrees F (76 C).

Bring the sweet wort to a boil and add malt extract and boiling hops and continue to boil for 60 minutes. Add the Irish moss and finishing hops during the final 5 minutes of the boil. Sparge immediately into your fermenter and cold water (approximately 2–2½ gallons). Pitch yeast when cool. Bottle when fermentation is complete.

Uckleduckfay Oatmeal Stout

A legendary and almost forgotten stout enjoying a revival among homebrewers and small breweries in America. Uckleduckfay is a smooth stout with a medium bitterness, a chocolaty finish and a hint of roasted barley. Quaffing pints of oatmeal stout gives one the feeling of nourishment and why not. It's good for your soul.

Ingredients for 5 gallons:

1½ lbs. quick (cut and rolled) oats

2 lbs. 6-row pale malted barley

½ lb. crystal malt

¼ lb. dextrine malt

½ lb. chocolate malt

¼ lb. roasted barley

3.3 lbs. Edme D.M.S. (diastatic) malt extract

4 tsp. gypsum

2 oz. Willamette hops (boiling): 10–12 HBU

¼ tsp. Irish moss powder

1–2 pkgs. ale yeast

¾ c. corn sugar or 1¼ c. dried malt extract (for bottling)

O.G.: 1.042–1.046 (10.5–11.5)
F.G.: 1.011–1.015 (3–4)

Add 5½ quarts of 130-degree F (54 C) water to the malted grains, oats and 2 tsp. of gypsum. Stabilize temperature at 122 degrees F (50 C) and hold for a half hour. Add 3 quarts of boiling water to the mash (add additional heat if necessary) and stabilize mash at 150–52 degrees F (66–67 C) for 15 minutes. Then add heat and raise the temperature to 158 degrees F (70 C) and hold for 15 minutes.

In another pot combine the diastatic malt extract and 2 tsp. of gypsum with 2 quarts of water and raise temperature to 155 degrees F (68 C) and add to the grain mash and hold at 155–158 degrees F (68–70 C) for 15 more minutes. It's easier than it sounds and conversion will be assured.

Strain and sparge out grains with 1½ gallons of 170-degree F (77 C) water. Boil the resulting extract with boiling hops for 1 hour. Ten minutes before the end of the boil add the Irish moss.

Strain and sparge the hops and add the hot wort to your fermenter and cold water. Add yeast when cool. Ferment to completion and bottle.

Deliberation Dunkel

Deliberation Dunkel is a brown beer deliberately brewed for a dark flavor without the sweetness often associated with a beer that is as rich in appearance. The bitterness is neither excessive nor light; just right for a thirst-quenching darkness.

Ingredients for 5 gallons:

3 lbs. malted barley (American 6-row type)

½ lb. black patent malt

2 tsp. gypsum

5 lbs. Premier light hopped malt extract syrup

½ oz. Tettnanger hops (finishing)

¼ tsp. Irish moss powder

1–2 pkgs. ale yeast

¾ c. corn sugar or 1¼ c. dried malt extract (for bottling)

O.G.: 1.042–1.046 (10.5–11.5)
F.G.: 1.012–1.018 (3–4.5)

Heat 2½ quarts of water to 130 degrees F (58 C). Dissolve the gypsum in the water. Add the crushed malted barley and black patent malt and mix well. The temperature will stabilize between 115–120 degrees F (46–49 C). Add heat and hold the temperature at 120–122 degrees F (49–50 C) for 30 minutes, stirring every 5 minutes.

Raise the temperature of the mash to 130 degrees F (58 C) and add 1½ quarts of boiling water. This will raise the temperature to about 150 degrees F (66 C). Hold at 149–152 degrees F (65–67 C) for 10 minutes, stirring occasionally. Then add more heat to raise the temperature to 158 degrees F (70 C) and hold for 15–20 minutes. Conversion should be complete at this stage. Test with iodine. Continue to mash (for up to 20 more minutes) until conversion is complete.

Pour your mash into your lauter-tun and sparge with 1 gallon of water at 170 degrees F (76 C).

Bring the sweet wort to a boil and add malt extract and continue to boil for 60 minutes. Add the Irish moss and finishing hops during the final 5 minutes of the boil. Sparge immediately into your fermenter and cold water (approximately 2–2½ gallons). Pitch yeast when cool. Bottle when fermentation is complete.

Potlatch Doppelbock

The menagerie of malts blend together to outperform each other. A richly dark doppelbock (a stronger version of bock) in true German style, this brew possesses the sweetness, medium bit-

terness and alcohol content to make any homebrewer as proud as a German bockmaster.

Close your eyes, swallow, and imagine that velvety darkness sliding down your throat, a warm glow inspiring a smile and a sense of satisfaction. It's yours and only you the brewmaster can experience and offer to share it.

Ingredients for 5 gallons:

    2 lbs. malted barley (American 6-row type)
    6 oz. toasted malted barley
    6 oz. Munich malt (for malt sweetness)
    4 oz. crystal malt (for caramel sweetness)
    4 oz. chocolate malt (for smooth black flavor)
    4 oz. black patent malt (for a burnt bite)
    6 oz. dextrine malt (for additional body and head stability)

2 tsp. gypsum

7 lbs. dried plain amber malt extract

1 oz. Northern Brewer hops (boiling): 9–10 HBU

½ oz. Hallertauer hops (finishing)

¼ tsp. Irish moss powder

1–2 pkgs. lager yeast

¾ c. corn sugar or 1¼ c. dried malt extract (for bottling)

O.G.: 1.072–1.078 (18–19.5)

F.G.: 1.018–1.026 (4.5–6.5)

Toast 6 oz. malted barley for 10 minutes in a 350-degree F (177 C) oven. Heat 3 quarts of water to 130 degrees F (58 C). Dissolve the gypsum in the water. Add the crushed malts and mix well. The temperature will stabilize between 115–120 degrees F (46–49 C). Add heat and hold the temperature at 120–122 degrees F (49–50 C) for 30 minutes, stirring every 5 minutes.

Raise the temperature of the mash to 130 degrees F (58 C) and add 2 quarts of boiling water. This will raise the temperature to about 150 degrees F (66 C). Hold at 149–152 degrees F (65–67 C) for 10 minutes, stirring occasionally. Then add more heat to raise the temperature to 158 degrees F (70 C) and hold for 15–20 minutes. Conversion should be complete at this stage. Test with iodine. Continue to mash (for up to 20 more minutes) until conversion is complete.

Pour your mash into your lauter-tun and sparge with 5 quarts of water at 170 degrees F (76 C).

Bring the sweet wort to a boil and add malt extract and boiling hops and continue to boil for 60 minutes. Add the Irish moss and finishing hops during the final 5 minutes of the boil. Sparge immediately into your fermenter and cold water (approximately 2–2½ gallons). Pitch yeast when cool. Bottle when fermentation is complete.

Limnian Wheat Doppelbock

It often takes all the skill a brewer can muster to brew a high-alcohol, well-balanced doppelbock; a doppelbock that will be recollected as a malty brew with just enough bitterness to

briefly retain a linger of sweetness. Doppelbock is not a bitter beer even when the strength gets up to 9–10 percent alcohol as Limnian Wheat Doppelbock does.

The recipe for Limnian Wheat Doppelbock makes choosing

the right ingredients for this aberration of a legendary style of German lager a sure thing. I've never heard of a wheat doppelbock being brewed in Germany. Have you? But sure as shootin' malted wheat lends a wonderful toastiness to the character of this brew.

What you as a brewer need to attend to is getting hold of a good-quality lager yeast that will ferment to 9–10 percent alcohol and create a cool fermentation environment to inhibit the formation of warm-temperature, alelike fruity esters. Worried? Don't be. Give it your best shot and you'll be gallons ahead of everyone else who never tried.

Limnian Doppelbock is a high-alcohol doppelbock, best reserved for special occasions and perhaps a quiet, peaceful afternoon on the shores of your favorite lake, gazing up at the heavens and contemplating your accomplishments and the 6½ gallons of Limnian Doppelbock you've got back home. That's 6½ gallons because 5 just isn't enough and it ages so well.

Ingredients for *6½* gallons:

For the mash:
2½ lbs. malted wheat
3½ lbs. pale malted barley
1 lb. Munich malt
6 oz. dextrine malt
5 oz. chocolate malt
5 oz. crystal malt

(Note: 3 lbs. of wheat malt extract syrup and 2 lbs. of dried amber malt extract may be substituted for the above malts.)

For the boiling pot:
12 lbs. dried light malt extract
2½ oz. Eroica hops (boiling): 25 HBU
1 oz. Tettnanger hops (flavor)
1 oz. Hallertauer hops (aroma)

lager yeast (healthy and strong liquid culture or 2 pkgs. of
  dried yeast)
¾ c. corn sugar or 1¼ c. dried malt extract (for bottling)

O.G.: 1.100 (25)
F.G.: 1.022–1.030 (5.5–7.5)

For the mash heat 2 gallons of soft water to 130 degrees F
(54 C) and add crushed malts. Let stabilize at about 122 degrees
F (50 C) and steep for 30 minutes. Then add 1 gallon of boiling
water and stabilize temperature at about 150 degrees F (66 C)
and hold for 15 minutes. Apply heat and raise temperature to
158 degrees F (70 C) while stirring constantly to prevent hot
spots. Let steep at 158 degrees F (70 C) for 15 minutes to complete conversion.

Strain out and sparge your mashed grains with 3 gallons of
170 degrees F (77 C) water and collect sweet malt liquor. Add
12 lbs. of light dried malt extract and boiling hops and bring to
boil for 1 full hour. (Note: the total volume of the boil will be
close to 4 gallons, requiring a very large brew kettle.)

After 1 hour of boiling add flavor hops and boil for another
15 minutes. Then add the aroma hops and steep for 1–2 minutes.

Strain and sparge your hot wort into your fermenter and 2
gallons of cold water. Let the wort cool to yeast-pitching temperatures. Before you add yeast be sure to aerate the wort well
by shaking your stoppered glass fermenter from side to side.
Add a well-cultured yeast and ferment to completion. Bottle and
hold your breath. A good time to celebrate is during the rituals
of springtime. Prosit.

Colonel Coffin Barley Wine Ale

"A barley wine before its time is like a mountain without a peak."

If ever there were a style of beer to brew then glow with pride
over, then it must be barley wine ale. If ever there were ale truly
distinct, a flavor and bouquet worth savoring slowly, then it would
be barley wine ale. If you ever had dreams of brewing an ale so
memorable it would linger for a lifetime, then try Colonel Coffin

Barley Wine Ale, a perfect beer brewed to alcoholic strength up to 11 percent by volume.

Colonel Coffin is powerfully alcoholic, stunningly hopped, estery with hints of strawberry, raspberry, pear and other tantalizing characters. The abundance of hops proliferates first in the bouquet. The alcohol vapors warm the nostrils, titillate the lungs. First sweetness turns to a wonderfully complex and compensating bitterness.

It's expensive and demands patience and aging. But what a reward. Life's other rewards should be so grand.

Ingredients for 5 gallons:

For the mash:
3 lbs. pale malted barley
½ lb. dextrine malt
½ lb. crystal malt

For the boiling kettle:
12 lbs. light dried malt extract
6–7 oz. Eroica, Galena, Nugget, Chinook or Olympic hops
  (boiling): 70 HBU
1½ oz. Willamette or Cascade hops (flavoring)
1½ oz. Cascade hops (aroma)
2 pkgs. ale, lager or champagne yeast
¾ c. corn sugar or 1¼ c. dried malt extract (for bottling)

O.G.: 1.100 (25)
F.G.: 1.022–1.035 (5.5–9)

For the mash heat 1 gallon of soft water to 130 degrees F (54 C) and add crushed malts. Let stabilize at about 122 degrees F (50 C) and steep for 30 minutes. Then add 2½ quarts of boiling water and stabilize temperature at about 150 degrees F (66 C) and hold for 15 minutes. Apply heat and raise temperature to 158 degrees F (70 C) while stirring constantly to prevent hot spots. Let steep at 158 degrees F (70 C) for 15 minutes to complete conversion.

Strain out and sparge your mashed grains with 2 gallons of 170 degrees F (77 C) water and collect sweet malt liquor. Add 12 lbs. of light dried malt extract and boiling hops and bring to a boil for 1½ hours. (Note: the total volume of the boil will be close to 4 gallons, requiring a very large brew kettle.) After the 1½ hours of boiling remove most of the boiling hops with a strainer (rinse off the good stuff with boiling water) and then add the flavor hops and continue to boil for 15 more minutes. Finally add the aroma hops and steep for 1–2 minutes.

Strain, sparge and transfer the hot wort into a closed fermenter with 1 gallon of cold water in it. Seal the fermenter and let cool gradually in the fermenter until yeast-pitching temperatures are reached. Caution: If you use a glass fermenter it may be too hot to bathe in cold water for fear of cracking due to cold/hot stress. To alleviate this situation somewhat, you may immerse your hot brewpot in cold water (with the lid securely on) to help cool the wort before you transfer it into your fermenter.

Ferment to completion and bottle. Age will transform this ale dramatically. The initial sharp bitterness of Colonel Coffin Barley Wine Ale will mellow with age. Just remember: "A barley wine before its time is like a mountain without a peak." I said that.

Advanced Homebrewing for the Practical Homebrewer

"Beer does not make itself properly by itself. It takes an element of mystery and of things that no one can understand. As a brewer you concern yourself with all the stuff you can understand, everywhere."

—Fritz Maytag, President
Anchor Brewing Company

INTRODUCTION

Making your own homebrew from essential ingredients is only part of what advanced homebrewing is all about. Yes, a homebrewer does have the option of processing ingredients the same way as commercial breweries do. But how sophisticated and elaborate does the brewing process need to get for a homebrewer to be classified as advanced? Is it brewing beer solely from grains? Is it cultivating your own yeast? Is it treating your water with the perfect combination of minerals? Or, is it just being able to make perfectly delicious beer every single time, with malt extract or all-grain?

For me, advanced homebrewing means appreciating and being involved on an intimate level with the entire brewing process, considering each phase singularly and as part of a whole. Advanced homebrewing is that effort to cultivate an understanding of the limitless variability of the brewing process and the versatility of ingredients.

With experience and labor come rewards and a special satisfaction. A reward that is the glass of beer you created and know something more about. A satisfaction of creating something special for yourself and your friends.

The essence of this book is to provide fundamentals from which to grow. No one completely understands what goes on in the brewing process. As brewers, we observe, take note and base our next batch of beer on our own experience and that of others. It is sheer folly to be taken by the hand and led down the path of better brewing by someone who says that they know it all. No, it is your experience that counts most. It is your experience that will always lead you to more questions.

> *"Always the beautiful answer who asks a more beautiful question."*
> —e.e. cummings, i

ADVANCED HOMEBREWING AND THE ALL-GRAIN HOMEBREWER: What Have You Gotten Yourself Into?

For the homebrewer who is inclined to brewing beer from all-grains, rather than malt extract syrups and powders, the most significant area of brewing that you will become involved in is with enzymes—how they behave and influence the taste of beer.

Enzymes are like organic catalysts that are influenced by environmental conditions of time, temperature, raw ingredients and minerals, among other things. They significantly alter the raw ingredients of beer to a more desirable and useful form for fermentation into quality beer.

Numerous enzymes are present in the ingredients of beer; some are more significant than others. The two types of enzymes that are most important to the practical homebrewer are those that break down proteins into yeast nutrients and those that break down soluble starches to fermentable (sugars) and unfermentable (dextrins) carbohydrates.

The all-grain homebrewer becomes aware of these variables and physically deals with separating desirable from undesirable materials. The all-grain homebrewer, in contrast to the malt extract homebrewer, deals with the entire wort (rather than a concentrated wort of syrup and water) throughout the brewing process, boiling and quickly cooling the beer wort, while simultaneously maintaining sanitary brewing conditions.

WHAT SPECIAL EQUIPMENT WILL YOU NEED?

Because of the volumes of liquid that are used in brewing 5 gallons of all-grain beer you will find it necessary to purchase or fashion a mash-tun, a vessel that holds the grains during controlled-temperature mashing. You'll also need to purchase or fashion a lauter-tun (a sparging system) for separating your spent grains from the sweet liquid. You will certainly find the need to have a brewpot that has at least an 8-gallon capacity and a system for cooling your boiling wort as quickly as possible.

Relax. Don't worry. Have a homebrew!

Of course, all-grain brewing is much more involved but, believe me, once you've thought out the process and gathered the extra equipment you will develop a system that gets easier with every batch of beer. My very first batch of all-grain beer left my kitchen looking like the aftermath of a Civil War battle: Every strainer, pot, pan, spoon and measuring device was impulsively used. Needless to say I had not thought out my system. I learned about many things that I should not do. But that first batch of all-grain beer, my very first, well, it won me a Best of Show in an International Homebrew Competition in 1980. You can be a winner, too.

Remember that you are a homebrewer! Don't look upon variability negatively. Quality beer can vary in flavor. If your brewing sanitation is attended to and your starch conversion is complete, you are much more likely to brew great beer every time, beer you can be proud of, no matter what the variables are. Your persistence and experience will pay off.

THE MASH!

Mashing is the process of physically combining water with crushed malted barley, specialty malts and prepared starchy adjuncts. The process is continued over a period of time with controlled temperature adjustments that activate different enzymes in order to break down soluble starches and proteins.

But before we get into the nitty-gritty of mashing, it helps to understand what malted barley is. By now you should know that malting is a natural process. Briefly, whole unmalted barley is germinated to a certain degree and then dried to make malted barley. The process of malting not only develops enzymes but also develops a small amount of fermentable sugar (mostly maltose) and unfermentable dextrins and very significantly converts rock-hard insoluble starch to a very crushable, convertible and soluble starch. About 80 percent of malted barley is soluble starch that awaits conversion by enzymes.

The enzymes that are developed in the malting process act directly to degrade nitrogen-based proteins (amino acids) and soluble starches.

ENZYMES AND MYSTICISM

Perhaps the most mystifying part of brewing is the behavior of enzymes. They aren't living organisms, yet like animals they are triggered to react under appropriate conditions. They can also be "deactivated" or, more properly put, "denatured" by conditions that cannot be tolerated. Invisible to the eye and influenced by dozens of factors, enzymes magically convert a soup of starchy liquid to a delicious sweetness.

There are many variables that can influence the behavior and efficiency of enzymatic activity; these variables, in turn, directly influence the flavor of the beer.

There are two types of enzymes whose behavior a homebrewer can significantly control. They are: 1) proteases or proteolytic enzymes (protein degrading), and 2) diastase or diastatic enzymes (starch degrading).

Protein degradation by proteolytic enzymes

Proteolytic enzymes break down long, complex chains of protein molecules into forms of protein which improve the quality and fermentation characteristics of beer.

At temperatures ideally 113–122 degrees F (45–50 C), certain proteolytic enzymes break down nitrogen-based proteins into amino acid proteins, which in turn can be used by yeast as a valuable nutrient. The degree to which yeast can ferment and convert fermentable sugars to alcohol and carbon dioxide is referred to as the attenuation of the wort. Nutrients that are developed by proteolytic enzymes are very significant in determining how well attenuated the beer wort will be. The process of developing these nutrients in the mash is not necessary in fully modified (usually English-grown 2-row) malts, as the nutrients are developed in a specialized malting process (more on modified malts later).

At temperatures ideally 122–140 degrees F (50–60 C), other proteolytic enzymes break down proteins into forms that improve the foam potential of the beer and aid in clarity.

The process and stage at which a brewer activates proteolytic enzymes is called the *protein rest*.

Starch degradation by diastatic enzymes

Diastatic enzymes convert starch molecules into fermentable sugars and unfermentable dextrins (responsible for giving beer fuller body).

There are two diastatic enzymes that become active during the mashing process. They are alpha-amylase and beta-amylase. The combination of their action literally breaks down very long chains of soluble or gelatinized (cooked to a necessary degree) starch molecules into shorter chains of sugars and dextrins. During the mashing process the brewer wants to convert all starches to dextrins or sugars. This yield is called *extract*.

In order to clarify what these diastatic enzymes do it will be helpful to explain the molecular structure of starches, sugars and dextrins:

- Starch molecules are basically a very long chain of very fermentable glucose molecules (the simplest of sugars), but because they are all attached they are not fermentable.

- Maltose is a chain of two glucose molecules linked together and is very fermentable.

- Dextrins are chains of four or more glucose molecules that result from a breakdown of starch. They are not fermentable. They are tasteless, yet add body and "mouthfeel" to beer.

Keep these molecular points in mind as you begin to understand how enzymes work.

Alpha-amylase

Alpha-amylase breaks down very long chains of glucose molecules (starch) by literally "chopping" them at the middle and reducing them into shorter and shorter chains. Until these secondary chains are reduced to chains of one, two or three molecules of glucose, they are unfermentable and called dextrins. The process of reducing the very large chains of starch molecules is called *liquefication* or *dextrinization*.

Beta-amylase

Beta-amylase breaks down both long and very long chains of glucose molecules (starch or dextrins) by literally "nibbling" at the ends, rather than chopping at them from the middle. When the beta-amylase has achieved the reduction of long chains of glucose molecules to chains of one (glucose), two (maltose) or three (maltotriose) glucose molecules, the starch has been finally converted to fermentable sugar. This process is called *saccharification*.

Nibbling & chopping

Keeping the preceding points in mind, one can imagine that the conversion to fermentable sugars by the beta-amylase will be quicker if the chains that get nibbled at from the ends are more numerous. If alpha-amylase were not present, it would take too long for the beta-amylase to nibble its way through the very long chain of glucose (starch) molecules. Thus, with alpha-amylase chopping up the starch molecules, these two enzymes—alpha- and beta-amylase—work together in the mashing process to produce a yield of both unfermentable and fermentable malt extract. Proportionally, diastase is made up of approximately 25 percent alpha-amylase and 75 percent beta-amylase.

Variables, variables. . . . Nothing's perfect

Unfortunately, many variables interfere with the perfect enzymatic progression. Let's take a look at some of them.

TEMPERATURE

Alpha-amylase works best (but not exclusively!) at temperatures between 149–153 degrees F (65–67 C). It will become deactivated within 2 hours at a temperature of 153 degrees F (67 C).

Beta-amylase works best (but not exclusively!) at temperatures between 126–144 degrees F (52–62 C). It will become deactivated within 40–60 minutes at a temperature of 149 degrees F (65 C).

It is important that the all-grain homebrewer realize that both enzymes generally work well together at temperatures between 145–158 degrees F (63–70 C). In general, the higher mash temperatures will produce dextrinous (heavy-bodied beer) worts in a very short, active period, while lower temperatures produce more fermentable (lighter-bodied, more alcoholic beer) worts over a longer period.

When mashing, the brewer, especially the homebrewer, must compromise with regard to the equipment at hand and the degree of sophistication that is practical.

TIME ($E = mc^2$: Time Is Relative)

The time it takes to fully convert starch to dextrins and fermentable sugars varies with temperature, amount of enzymes and amount of starch to be converted.

Generally, higher temperatures will inspire quicker conversions but will produce more dextrins.

In practice, most homebrewers will experience conversion within 15–25 minutes at temperatures of about 158 degrees F (70 C) and conversion within 45–90 minutes at temperatures of about 150 degrees F (65 C). These times are based on mashes consisting of malt with a proportion of adjuncts no greater than 25 percent.

pH

pH is a numerical measure of either acidity, neutrality or alkalinity. Neutral is 7.0, less than 7.0 is acid, and greater than 7.0 is alkaline. The optimum pH for diastatic enzymes is 5.2–5.8. The optimum pH for proteolytic enzymes is 4.2–5.3. Usually a compromise is made at 5.2. Fortunately, a pH of about 5.2 is naturally achieved when water is mixed with the grains, because there are enzymes (not discussed in this book) and chemical reactions that occur almost immediately upon mixing. These reactions lower the pH of the mash even when the water is neutral.

A small amount of calcium sulfate ($CaSO_4$, gypsum) present or added to the brewing water is helpful in achieving a mashable pH.

In practice, monitoring the pH of the mash is not a high priority for a homebrewer, unless extremely soft or distilled water or water high in bicarbonates is used for brewing (see the section on water, page 267).

THICKNESS OF THE MASH

The ratio of water to malt will have an effect on the activity of enzymes. Generally, thicker mashes favor proteolytic activity and thinner mashes favor diastatic activity.

MINERAL CONTENT OF BREWING WATER

The most significant mineral that should be considered by the homebrewer is the calcium ion. The most natural and common source is calcium sulfate (gypsum). Its presence in the mash aids in acidifying the mash and helps inhibit alpha-amylase from deactivation caused by high temperatures.

Excessive amounts of bicarbonates can adversely affect mash yield.

INGREDIENTS: VARIETIES OF BARLEY AND HOW MALTED

The type of malted barley a brewmaster chooses is a significant factor in the mashing procedures. Generally, there are three factors that the brewer needs to consider:

1) The variety of barley used: 2-row or 6-row.
2) The degree to which they have been malted: fully modified or undermodified.
3) Enzymatic power: high or low.

Varieties of barley

Until about 1970, most American brewers used a 6-row variety of barley for the brewing of beer. One of the major factors for this choice was that the farmer could produce more yield per acre (approximately 160 bushels per acre) than from a 2-row variety (approximately 80 bushels per acre). Due to the many agricultural changes in the past years, agriculturists have been able to develop strains of 2-row barley that are beginning to approach yields comparable to 6-row varieties.

2-row—Physically, 2-row barley appears to be a plumper kernel, having less husk than 6-row varieties. Because of its plumpness there is more starch and potential yield (extract) per weight of the kernel. Some brewers believe that the thinner husk associated with 2-row varieties of malted barley makes for mellower beers due to the reduction in the amount of tannins and "phenolic" flavors which are derived from husk material. However, the lesser amount of husk creates some problematic considerations in that the husk material is utilized by the brewer as a filter bed during the sparging process (separation of the sweet liquid from the spent grains). Extra care is often required by professional brewers to ensure adequate filtering by the husks.

The enzyme potential of 2-row malted barley varies with the strain being used. Generally, 2-row malt has less enzyme potential than 6-row varieties. American 2-row has more enzyme potential than English varieties. And new strains are always being developed to try to match 6-row enzyme potential.

In summary, the brewer can achieve greater extract per weight of 2-row malted barley. The brewer should realize that the types of sugars and dextrins produced during mashing are not influenced by the type of malted barley used as long as the mashing procedures are identical.

6-row—A higher percentage of the entire weight of 6-row varieties of malted barley is attributable to the husk and embryo. Generally, 6-row varieties have a greater enzyme potential and are able to convert as much as 30 to 40 percent extra starch (adjuncts) to sugars and dextrins. The greater amount of husk material enables easier filtering during the sparging and lautering process. Brewers often are concerned with the amount of husk tannins that may be leached out during excessive or improper sparging techniques.

In summary, 6-row varieties of malted barley will yield less extract per weight of kernel but are desirable for mashing with adjuncts due to their generally higher enzyme content.

MALTING AND MODIFICATION

To the maltster, *modification* is defined as the degree to which the "meaty part" or starchy "endosperm" is converted to soluble malt starch (and usable amino acids). Modification begins near the embryo and progresses through the kernel.

Full modification is at the expense of malt yield because as time progresses toward full modification a lot of waste (weight of kernel, potential yield) goes into the growth of the acrospire (the growing shoot). The maltster has the choice of producing fully modified or undermodified malt depending on the needs of the brewer.

Full modification also results in the conversion of very long chains of proteins to usable yeast nutrients (amino acids). If fully modified malt is used in the brewing process, a protein rest (see Proteolytic enzymes) during the initial phases of mashing is not necessary.

Undermodification will result in the potential for more yield per weight of barley but necessitates a protein rest during the mash in order to develop amino acids to be utilized by the yeasts as nutrients.

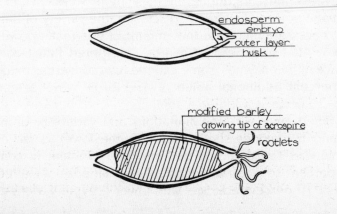

endosperm
embryo
outer layer
husk

modified barley
growing tip of acrospire
rootlets

Note: Modification does not have anything to do with high or low enzyme content. There are strains of 2-row and 6-row barley possessing either high or low enzyme content.

After barley has been malted its composition will be approximately:

soluble starches	82–88 percent
fermentable sugars	12–18 percent
glucose	1–2 percent
maltose	8–11 percent
maltotriose	3–5 percent
sucrose	less than 1 percent

In summary

Highly modified malt has fewer complex proteins and more free amino acids available to the yeast as nutrients. The brewer who uses highly modified malt has less concern about haze problems created by the raw proteins that are in undermodified malt. The degree of attenuation is largely dependent on mash temperatures.

Undermodified malt has more complex proteins and fewer free amino acids (yeast nutrients). If this type of malt does not go through proteolytic conversions (proteins) during the protein rest, then yeast nutrients may be lacking and attenuation will not be optimal. Slower or stuck fermentations may result. Protein haze problems in the finished beer may also occur. The degree of attenuation is dependent on mash temperatures and development of yeast nutrients during the mashing process.

Enzymatic power—As already discussed, the variety of barley will not necessarily indicate the amount of enzymatic power malt will have. But in general, it can be considered that 6-row varieties have more enzymes; some varieties can convert as much as 30–40 percent additional adjuncts. The 2-row varieties can convert 10–20 percent additional adjuncts.

The homebrewer with the limitations and variability of ingredients and techniques should consider the lower range of percent adjuncts. There should be very little problem in converting 20 percent adjuncts with high enzyme varieties of malted barley and 5–10 percent adjuncts with lower enzyme varieties.

THE USE OF ADJUNCTS (STARCH)

Fermentable sugars other than those derived from malt can be used in the brewing process. Although the traditional ingredients in beer are malt, hops, yeast and water, brewers have found that economy will often require that locally grown starchy foods be utilized in the beer process. Until the late 1980s Germany was the only country in the world that had a strict law against using anything but the four basic ingredients. They still consider beer to be their national drink, but the law, called the *Reinheitsgebot*, is an option now that Germany has become a member of the EEC (European Economic Community).

All forms of starch can be converted to fermentable sugars. Often the abundance of certain cereal grains or vegetable starches in a particular region will provide a cheaper source of a beer ingredient than malted barley. Some of the unmalted cereal grains and vegetables that can be used in the brewing process are: barley, corn (maize), oats, potato, rice, rye, sorghum (millet, milo maize), tapioca (cassava, manioc), triticale and wheat.

Adjuncts are often used to achieve in the finished beer certain characteristics such as flavor, visual appearance and stability (flavor and foam). The use of properly prepared adjuncts will usually contribute a neutral flavor to the beer and promote a lighter body. Variability in processing adjuncts can produce unique flavors, both desirable and undesirable.

Commercial brewers using sophisticated brewing techniques may use up to 40 percent adjuncts in their mashes. Homebrewers, with proper processing, attention to mashing techniques and quality ingredients, can effectively utilize 10–20 percent adjuncts in their homebrews.

Although economy and distinctiveness can be achieved with adjuncts, there are some problems that can be encountered by the professional brewer and homebrewer. With attention to proper processing many problems can be overcome. For the homebrewer some of the problems are not as easily overcome. However, these problems should never deter you from using adjuncts if you are so inclined to use them. It is easy to homebrew quality beer with the use of adjuncts. Your endeavors will lead you to some very classic and unique styles of beer.

The most common problem that you will likely encounter is a stuck runoff during the lautering and sparging process. Stuck runoffs are due to the presence of vegetable gums that serve to clog the filter bed created by spent grains. Another problem often caused by the use of adjuncts is haze in the finished beer. Haze problems are due to insoluble proteins that were not or could not be fully degraded by proteolytic enzymes during the mashing process. Still another problem that may be encountered is poor foam stability due to vegetable oils that may be present in whole unprocessed grains.

Most problems can be alleviated or avoided by using properly prepared adjuncts.

Preparation of Adjuncts

All starch adjuncts must go through a process called "gelatinization" before they can be utilized and converted by enzymes to fermentable sugars and nonfermentable dextrins. Gelatinization describes the process of cooking insoluble starch to a degree that allows it to "swell" and become soluble and vulnerable to enzyme degradation. Some starches will gelatinize at temperatures below 140 degrees F (60 C) while others require prolonged boiling. The necessity to gelatinize starch adjuncts means that the homebrewer must often cook cereal grains or vegetable starches before they are added to the mash.

Grains are available to homebrewers in a variety of forms, some of which are precooked (gelatinized) and can be added directly to the mash. The following list provides a short description of the various ways cereal grains are available to the homebrewer. They are listed in order of the degree of processing.

1) *Whole grains*—Whole grains are often the easiest and cheapest to find; however, their use presents problems for the homebrewer. Husks, bran and the germ of the grain will still be intact. When whole grains are milled and cooked, undesirable flavors and other characteristics will be imparted to the beer. The husks will contribute phenolic and harsh flavors because of the presence of tannins. The bran and germ will contribute

to poor head stability and inhibition of fermentation due to the presence of oils and fats. Old or improperly stored grain will have rancid (oxidized) oils that may detract from beer flavor.

Whole grain, if used, must be ground into granules and cooked.

2) *De-husked grains*—Barley, rice (brown), rye, oats, millet, triticale and wheat (berries) often are available in the de-husked form. The harsh flavors produced by the husk are eliminated. However, oils and fats are still present, and with grains that have a great amount of oils the flavor of the beer will be influenced. De-husked grains are not gelatinized.

3) *De-branned grains*—Pearled barley and white rice are good examples of this degree of processing. With proper grinding or milling, these forms of grains can be easily utilized by the homebrewer. De-branned grains are not gelatinized.

4) *Grits*—Grain that has been de-husked, de-branned, de-germed and then milled into small granules is called grits. Grits are useful to the homebrewer in that milling is not required. Grits are not gelatinized.

5) *Flakes* —Grits or forms of grains that have been moistened and passed between rollers are described as being flaked. The massive pressures involved in rolling wet grains creates heat. This heat along with the heat that is added to the rollers instantly gelatinizes these grains. Because flaked grains are gelatinized they can be added directly to the mash without precooking. The appearance of flaked grains is similar to uncooked oatmeal.

6) *Torrefied grain*—Grains that have undergone a process that gives them a character similar to puffed wheat or puffed rice are called torrefied. These grains are gelatinized and can be added directly to the mash.

7) *Refined starch*—Grain that has undergone extensive processing, including gelatinization, is called refined

starch. A common example is cornstarch. Refined starch can be very easy for the homebrewer to use and can be added directly to the mash.

Adjuncts commonly used and available to homebrewers

Barley—As an adjunct, unmalted barley will contribute to foam (head) retention in the finished beer. The nitrogenous and complex proteins that contribute to head retention also contribute to chill haze problems. It is a classic ingredient used in the world-famous Guinness Stout. Clarity problems make it inappropriate for light beers.

Flaked barley is the easiest to use. If pearled or de-husked barley is used, it should be milled into small granules. Barley is gelatinized at low mashing temperatures, but homebrewers should cook all forms of barley (other than flaked barley) to ensure gelatinization and complete conversion during the mashing process.

Barley has a significant amount of vegetable gum and can inhibit runoff during lautering and sparging.

Corn (maize)—Fermentables that are derived from cornstarch will theoretically provide a neutral flavor to the beer. Their use will lighten the body and flavor of the finished beer. Some brewmasters claim that the use of corn (10–20 percent) will help stabilize the flavor of beer.

Regular cornstarch is the easiest form of corn to use (but usually the most expensive). It is easily converted in the mash without precooking. Flaked corn, if available (not the breakfast cereals that have other ingredients added), can also be easily utilized in the mash. If corn grits are used they must be boiled in water for 30 minutes. After gelatinization, the starches may be added to the mash.

Oats—The high protein, fat and oil content of oats is theoretically a deterrent to their use in brewing, but I have enjoyed many a fine brew with oats as an ingredient.

Oats have been used in the brewing process, particularly in the brewing of Oatmeal Stout. The character of this stout lingers mostly in memories. There are several oatmeal stouts commercially produced today. It has been popularized by homebrewers. Add 1–2 pounds into your mash.

Potato—Potatoes are a cheap and easily gelatinized form of starch. However, their use is discouraged by beer drinkers justifiably or unjustifiably prejudiced against "potato beer." Fermentables produced from potato starch do not contribute significantly to the character or flavor of beer, other than providing fermentables to be converted to alcohol. Sliced or chopped potatoes may be added directly to the mash. They are gelatinized at mashing temperatures. The homebrewer may choose to precook his potatoes to ensure complete conversion.

Rice—Rice is one of the more common adjuncts used by commercial breweries. It offers a clean source of fermentables, neutral flavor and beer body lighteners.

White rice or rice grits are commonly available and are easily used. Whole white rice should be ground into small granules before cooking. It is absolutely necessary to cook the rice for 30 minutes in boiling water in order to gelatinize it.

Rye—The character that rye contributes to beer can be dry and crisp with unmalted rye or similar to wheat malt when it is malted. Rye is used in the process of making rye whiskey, but seldom in brewing. It is a starch that can be gelatinized at mashing temperatures and converted to fermentable sugars, but the malting and mashing process can also produce "gooey" substances that promote "stuck" runoffs. Its use in brewing, particularly by homebrewers, seems inviting and well worth trying.

Sorghum (millet, milo maize)—Sorghums contain a great amount of oils and fats. These oils will go rancid with age or improper storage. Old millet can detract from the flavor of the finished beer. The oils and fats can detract from the overall profile of the beer. Experiments have been done with special processing of millet to remove oils and fats, making it more suitable for brewing.

A homebrewer is more likely to be able to utilize quality millet because the beer is fresh when consumed. My adventurous spirit has long invited me to experiment with this grain.

Traditional beers are made with millet in regions of the

world where it grows in abundance, particularly the Himalayas, Pakistan and Nepal.

Tapioca (cassava, manioc)—This may be the one ingredient listed here that is not readily available to the American home-brewer. Tapioca is a starchy root easily grown in tropical cli-mates. Its starchy character resembles potatoes.

I have tasted a native homebrew brewed with cassava in the Fiji Islands: *vale vakaviti!* It was a 24-hour concoction of boiled cassava root, sugar, water and yeast. Although cloudy and yeasty, its flavor was not all that objectionable. What sur-prised me the most was the announcement made in my honor the day before: "You want homebrew? Then tomorrow we will have homebrew." And so it was—brewed to Pacific potency in 24 hours. (I wonder what the Pacific gravity was?)

If the opportunity ever presents itself to you and you are inspired, cook and physically crush the cassava before adding it to the mash for conversion.

Triticale—Triticale is a trademarked name of a grain hybrid that is a cross between rye and wheat. It has a low gelatinizing temperature. Its use by the homebrewer is largely unexplored. Anyone interested in pioneering?

Wheat—Both malted wheat and unmalted wheat are used in the brewing process.

Malted wheat can be milled and added to the mash grist in the same manner as malted barley. Because there are very few enzymes in malted wheat it is desirable but not necessary to mash it with a malted barley of high enzymatic power.

Unmalted wheat in the form of wheat flakes or wheat flour is often used as an adjunct by brewers who wish to economize, enhance head retention and foam stability or lighten flavor and body. The variety of wheat that is preferred as an adjunct is usually of the soft type (rather than "hard wheat"), low in protein (low gluten, low nitrogen).

Both flaked wheat or wheat flour can be added directly to the mash. Flaked wheat is already gelatinized; however, because of wheat's low gelatinizing temperatures, it can be added directly to the mash. But again, I would advise homebrewers to precook any form of wheat in order that protein and starch conversion be assured during the mashing process.

Some chill haze problems may be experienced with the use of wheat as an adjunct. Relatively great amounts of wheat will inhibit runoff during the lautering and sparging process.

Quinoa, Tef, Buckwheat, Dinkel, Amaranth—These grains and others have continued to allure me as a homebrewer. An adventure in the waiting, but I am sure history would uncover a somewhere and a sometime people who have already done it. But do you know anyone who has? Dare I say ''Be the first on your block . . .''?

Quinoa, from Peru; tef, from Ethiopia; buckwheat, from Asia; dinkel, an ancient form of wheat; amaranth, a nutritional grain from South American Indian cultures, and others offer some very interesting possibilities and the excitement of coming up with a truly unique beer. When in doubt, it will do little harm to cook by boiling these and other grains to gelatinize their starches.

This just in: Wild rice beer is brewed by two small brewers in Wisconsin and Minnesota. Who'll be the first to brew with the starchy root of the cattail plant?

ADVANCED HOMEBREWING AND HOPS

Advanced homebrewers may choose to deal with fancy mathematical formulas to calculate bittering units and stage balancing acts, but by no means should any brewer substitute anything for quality, freshness, accurate information and most important—experience. Experience, more than anything else, will improve your ability to refine the artful balancing act between hop bitterness, flavor, aroma and beer's sweetness and body.

There are methods by which homebrewers can match the bitter qualities of commercially made beer throughout the world, just by knowing the amount of International Bitterness Units in a given recipe. But before we get into these methods, a brief account of how hop bitterness can be lost in the beermaking process would be helpful.

Not all of the bitterness potential from the alpha acid in the hop is utilized during the brewing and fermentation process. Under ideal conditions, when one boils all 5 gallons of a 5-gallon batch of beer (as opposed to boiling a malt-extract-based concentrated wort, then adding cold water in the fermenter later), only 50 percent of the chemical conversion of alpha acid to isomerized (iso- for "short") alpha acid occurs. *The higher the specific gravity of your boiled wort the less efficient the extraction of bitterness will be.*

There is further loss of isoalpha acid bitterness as yeast and protein sediment have a natural tendency to attract isoalpha acid molecules. Bitterness compounds can ride on foam and be carried out or left behind during fermentation or transfer. After all is said and done, one can hope for about 30 percent utilization of the available potential bitterness in hops.

Percent utilization is equal to the amount of alpha acid present divided by the amount of alpha acid used times 100:

$$\% \ U = (\text{Isoalpha acid present/alpha acid used}) \times 100$$

If you are following a recipe and the desired bitterness is stated in terms of IBUs you may use the following formula to calculate how much bittering hops to use when boiling your wort. (Note: percentages are expressed as whole numbers, i.e., 15% = 15. Volumes are total volumes for recipe.)

Metric Units:

$$\text{Weight}_{grams} = \frac{\text{Volume}_{liters} \times \text{IBU} \times 10}{\% \text{ Utilization} \times \% \text{ alpha acid of hops}}$$

Likewise:

$$\text{IBU} = \frac{\text{Weight}_{grams} \times \% \text{ Utilization} \times \% \text{ alpha acid of hops}}{\text{Volume}_{liters} \times 10}$$

English Units:

$$\text{Weight}_{ounces} = \frac{\text{Volume}_{gallons} \times \text{IBU} \times 1.34}{\% \text{ Utilization} \times \% \text{ alpha acid of hops}}$$

Likewise:

$$IBU = \frac{Weight_{ounces} \times \% \text{ alpha acid of hop} \times \% \text{ Utilization}}{Volume_{gallons} \times 1.34}$$

For example, if I add 1 ounce of 5 percent alpha acid Hallertauer hops during the last 15 minutes of the boil to a malt extract and water boil (I used 6 pounds of extract to 2 gallons of water for the boil, which gives me 6 percent utilization as indicated in the Hop Utilization Chart on page 268; but remember there are 5 gallons total for the recipe), then I would add bitterness to my beer in the amount of:

$$IBU = \frac{1 \times 5 \times 6}{5 \times 1.34} = 4.5 \text{ IBUs}$$

When using the International Bitterness Units equations, HBUs may be conveniently substituted in the formula for $Weight_{ounces} \times \%$ alpha acid of hop.

$$IBU = \frac{HBUs \times \% \text{ Utilization}}{Volume_{gallons} \times 1.34}$$

For 5 gallons the formula is simplified to:

$$IBU = \frac{HBUs \times \% \text{ Utilization}}{6.7}$$

ADVANCED HOMEBREWING AND WATER

The science of water and its significance in the brewing of beer can become extremely involved. All of the important factors such as mineral content, pH, acidity, alkalinity, hardness and temperature are influenced by each other.

HOP UTILIZATION CHART BASED ON DENSITY OF BOILED WORT AND BOILING TIME

In Percent Utilization

Approx. Specific Gravity of Boil	1.040 (10)	1.070 (17.5)	1.110 (28)	1.130 (32.5)	1.150 (37.5)
Lbs. of malt extract per gallons of boiling water	1 lb./gal.	2 lbs./gal.	3 lbs./gal.	4 lbs./gal.	5 lbs./gal.
Time of Boil					
15 minutes	8%	7%	6%	6%	5%
30 minutes	15%	14%	12%	11%	10%
45 minutes	27%	24%	21%	19%	18%
60 minutes	30%	27%	23%	21%	20%

The importance of brewing water becomes significant when brewing all-grain beer. Malt extract beers have already been properly balanced with minerals during the manufacturer's mashing process. When malt extract is made, evaporation removes only the water. However, when homebrewing all-grain beers, the important mineral balance necessary for proper enzyme activity may not be present; therefore, it would be prudent to learn the fundamentals of water and brewing. And for the homebrewer who wishes to duplicate traditional and world-classic beers, an even more thorough understanding of water chemistry is required.

Most homebrewers (even all-grain homebrewers) need not work themselves into a hydraulic frenzy over perfecting their water. There are so many other more important variables that require attention to ensure quality beer; the most important are sanitation and quality ingredients. Relatively speaking, so long as the water you use is potable and not extremely hard, then water becomes a lower priority. Where hard water (111 parts per million total hardness) and certainly very hard water (in excess of 200 parts per million total hardness) are used, mashing can be a frustrating affair. pH measurements of 8 and above are indications of both temporary and permanent hardness: a poor environment for diastatic enzymes to convert starches to sugars. Brewers with hard water will experience poor yields from their mash. To improve mash yields you may treat the water with the addition of certain food-grade acids or naturally produce them and add them to the mash.

If you use municipal water that is treated with chlorine, one of the most dramatic and simplest things you can do to improve your beers is to pass all brewing water through a countertop or more elaborate charcoal-type filter to remove chlorine. Chlorine will combine with organic compounds (beer worts included) and produce chlorophenols that even in parts per billion can lend a harsh flavor and aroma to your brew.

When the time comes and inspiration has evolved a desire for you to understand water and its relation to brewing, then you will need to know about the fundamental principles that concern water and beer brewing.

What is hard water? What is soft water?

The terms "hard" and "soft" were derived a long, long, long time ago when people began using soap. The ability of soap to lather is affected by the mineral content of the water. Generally, a high mineral content in water will inhibit lathering of soap; thus, it is "hard" to lather, ergo: hard water! Water having low mineral content is generally considered "soft" water.

Water hardness is measured in two ways: temporary hardness and permanent hardness. Total hardness is the combined effect of the two measurements. In the United States, total hardness is expressed in parts per million (ppm) of certain minerals and determines the degree of softness or hardness. Generally:

0–50 ppm is considered soft water

51–110 ppm is considered medium hard water

111–200 ppm is considered hard water

greater than 200 ppm is considered very hard water

What is measured to determine total hardness?

Essentially, total hardness is the measure of the bicarbonate, magnesium (Mg) and calcium (Ca) ions present in the water.

What is temporary hardness? How does it affect the brewing process?

In the United States temporary hardness is determined by a measure of bicarbonates $[2(HCO_3)]$. The hardness that bicarbonate ions contribute is temporary because it is easily precipitated (becomes solid) and is removed when water is boiled or treated with certain acids.

A measure of bicarbonates (temporary hardness) greater than 100 ppm is undesirable because of its contribution to the alkalinity (higher pH) of water and the harsh, bitter flavor that it imparts to beer. Alkalinity will inhibit the proper acid pH balance necessary during mashing, resulting in inadequate conversion of starch to fermentables. If used for sparging grains, alkaline water will extract undesirable harsh grainy flavors.

What is permanent hardness? How does it affect the brewing process?

In the United States, permanent hardness is determined by a measure of calcium and magnesium ions, the calcium being more significant. It is that portion of total hardness remaining after the water has been boiled.

Generally, permanent hardness and the calcium ion raise the acidity (lower the pH) of water. A certain amount of permanent hardness is desirable in the homebrewing of all-grain beers. Enzyme conversion (starch to sugars) works best at a mash pH of 5.2 (acid).

What is pH and what is its significance in brewing?

pH is a measure of acidity and alkalinity of solutions and is measured on a scale of 0–14: 7.0 is neutral; less than 7.0 is acid; greater than 7.0 is alkaline.

Its measurement *is* affected by temperature. The pH of a solution at 150 degrees F (66 C) will be .35 less than at 65 degrees F (18 C). In other words, if a 150-degree mash measures 5.2, then a reading at 65 degrees F would indicate a pH of 5.55.

A measure of the pH of the brewing water *does not* give an indication of what the mash pH will be. The mineral content, particularly calcium, is more influential than the apparent pH of the water.

pH can be approximately measured with "pH papers" that are available at homebrew or chemical supply stores or pharmacies.

What minerals influence the brewing process?

The calcium ion is by far the most significantly influential mineral in the brewing process. Its influence begins when the water in which it is dissolved is mixed with the malt grist. The calcium ion reacts and acidifies the mash with phosphates that are naturally present in malted barley. When calcium is present in quantities of 50 ppm or more, it will acidify the mash, usually dropping the pH to about 5.2. This process of "acidification" is often referred to as "buffering." The presence of the calcium ion is influential even in very small amounts. The small amount of calcium that is present in the malt will result in the acidification of distilled water (pH = 7.0) and malt grist to a pH value of 5.8.

The calcium ion also aids in protecting alpha-amylase from heat inactivation. It also helps extract tannin and husk flavors from beer wort.

If there is an excessive amount of calcium, a harsh, thin flavor may characterize the beer. There also will be poor hop utilization due to inhibition of the necessary isomerization process (making hop-bittering resins soluble) during the boiling of the wort.

The bicarbonate $[2(HCO_3)]$ ion (temporary hardness) counters the positive effects of calcium ions. Its presence in excess of 100 ppm will alkalize the mash.

How can pH of the mash be adjusted?

The addition of calcium in the form of calcium sulfate ($CaSO_4$, gypsum) is the most acceptable way of influencing mash pH. If this is not available or if you would like to brew with very soft water (as some of the classic pilsener beers are), then a more sophisticated technique of adding lactic acid can accomplish acidification in the mash. A technique calling for an "acid rest" at about 90 degrees F (32 C) will also develop varying degrees of acidity. Additional information should be sought by the homebrewer in order to use the latter techniques.

Where can I find information about my water?

Consult your local town, city or county water board. They will usually supply you with free information about the contents of your water.

What kinds of water are used in some of the famous (and not so famous) brewing areas of the world?

Here's a limited sampler:

Mineral (ion)	Pilsen	Munich	Dublin	Dortmund	Burton-on-Trent	Milwaukee	Your Water
Calcium (Ca)	7	70–80	115–120	260	260–352	35	
Sulfates (SO_4)	5–6	5–10	54	283	630–820	18	
Magnesium (Mg)	2–8	18–19	4	23	24–60	11	
Sodium (Na)	32	10	12	69	54	?	
Chloride (Cl)	5	1–2	19	106	16–36	5	

Numerical values represent parts per million (ppm)

Can I adjust my water?

It is much easier to add a mineral than to remove a mineral. The homebrewer who desires to make a variety of adjustments and has access to very soft or distilled water is most fortunate because adjustments are only a matter of adding certain minerals. If you have hard water and desire soft or mineral-free water, it is easiest to buy distilled, deionized or R/O (reverse osmosis) water and add minerals. For the waterlogged homebrew enthusiast there are a number of relatively inexpensive home water treatment systems; look in the Yellow Pages of your phone book under Water Purification and Filtration Equipment. Other types of water filters are available that will remove select compounds including undesirable chlorine. These systems can be very cost-effective over the long term and can be used for other household water consumption.

Various minerals can be added to water; however, caution and knowledge of water chemistry should be pursued by the homebrewer before adding *any* chemical to water used for consumption. The following information will give you some indication of the amounts of minerals needed in order to achieve an increase in ion concentrations.

1 teaspoon of gypsum ($CaSO_4$) in 5 gallons of water will increase (approximately) concentration of:

Calcium (Ca^{++}) ion . . . . 55 ppm
Sulfate [$(SO_4)^{--}$] ion . . . . 135 ppm

1 teaspoon of pure table salt (NaCl) in 5 gallons of water will increase (approximately) concentration of:

Sodium (Na^+) ion . . . . 135 ppm
Chloride (Cl^-) ion . . . . 209 ppm

1 teaspoon of Epsom salt ($MgSO_4$) in 5 gallons of water will increase (approximately) concentration of:

Magnesium (Mg^{++}) ion . . . . 52 ppm
Sulfate [$(SO_4)^{--}$] ion . . . . 207 ppm

1 teaspoon of calcium chloride flakes ($CaCl_2$) in 5 gallons of water will increase (approximately) concentration of:

Calcium (Ca^{++}) ion . . . . 95 ppm
Chloride [$2(Cl)^{--}$] ion . . . . 84 ppm

ADVANCED HOMEBREWING AND YEAST

The homebrewer who has given proper attention to sanitation will be pleased with the results obtainable by using dried cultures of beer yeast. However, there is room for significant improvement in your homebrews if you choose to undertake the culturing of your own liquid beer yeasts. But as with undertaking any new procedures that will improve your beer, more effort is needed on your part not only to do so, but also to understand and have a feeling as to what is going on with your homebrew. If you haven't done so already, read the section in this book entitled "The Secrets of Fermentation."

There are various sources of cultured pure liquid beer yeasts. Your local homebrew supply shop or local brewery will be able to help you find a source.

Once you have obtained a live culture of beer yeast you will want to do the following:

1) Prepare a culturing medium
2) Propagate the yeast for storage
3) Propagate the yeast for beer fermentation

Culturing your own yeast and keeping it healthy is easier than you probably expected. Granted, it is an extra effort some may choose not to bother with, but for those of you who are inspired, the rewards will be satisfaction and an untold multitude of smiles.

CULTURING YEAST

There are many methods of culturing yeast; all of them stress sanitation and sterile procedures. The method that I have been using and will describe is extremely easy and requires no extra equipment other than a butane cigarette lighter, cotton swabs (Q-Tips), ethyl "grain" alcohol and rubber corks that will allow fermentation locks to be affixed to beer bottles.

Equipment and ingredients necessary to culture yeast:

12 clean 12-oz. beer bottles*
12 bottlecaps
2–3 fermentation locks with rubber corks that will allow them
    to be used on a beer bottle
6 oz. dried light malt extract
¼ oz. bitter whole hops
2½ qts. water
household bleach (for sanitizing)
ethyl "grain" alcohol or high-proof vodka
small fine strainer
cotton swabs (Q-Tips)
glass (kitchen) measuring cup with pouring spout

*You will be preparing and bottling small amounts of sterile beer wort and propagating yeast in these bottles as required.

PREPARATION OF CULTURING MEDIUM (WORT)

1) Boil 6 oz. of malt extract, ¼ oz. hops and 2½ quarts of water for 30 minutes. This wort is highly hopped in order to help inhibit bacterial growth. Do not substitute other sugars for malt extract.

2) While wort is boiling sanitize the already clean beer bottles. Place ¼ tsp. of household bleach in each bottle and fill with cold water. Allow to sit for 15 minutes. Rinse well with hot tap water. Then preheat bottles by filling with hot tap water. Meanwhile . . .

3) Boil bottlecaps and glass measuring cup for at least 15 minutes, in order to sterilize.

4) After wort has boiled for ½ hour, remove hops by pouring wort through a strainer into another pot or saucepan. Bring to a boil again and continue to boil for at least 10 more minutes.

5) Drain the hot water from the beer bottles.

6) Using the sterile measuring cup, pour about 6 oz. of boiling hot sterile wort into each sanitized beer bottle. Don't breathe, and work in a dust-free and draft-free room.

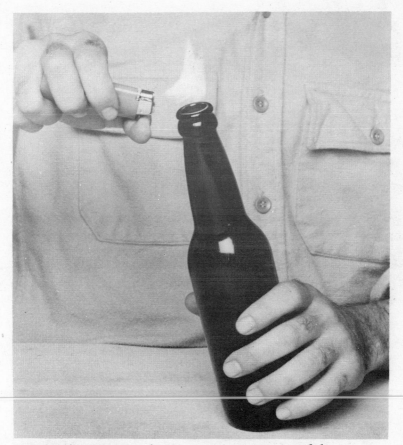

Burning lips! Yeast culturing requires very careful attention to sanitation and contaminant-free procedures. All surfaces that come in contact with yeast cultures and sterile wort must be contaminant-free. A butane lighter burns off surface contaminants while boiling or chlorine bleach sanitizers have been used to disinfect the insides of the culturing bottles. Using these procedures yeast can be successfully cultured in bottles of sterile beer wort.

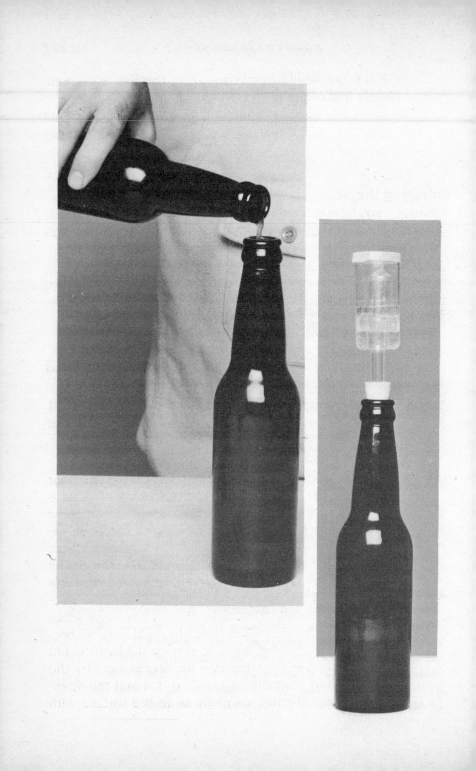

7) Place the sterile bottlecaps atop the bottle immediately and cap.

8) Label the bottles "Sterile Beer Wort" and let cool slowly at room temperature, after which you should store in your refrigerator for use as needed.

Culturing the yeast

Whenever you are in the process of culturing your own yeast, sanitation is extremely important. It is essential that you work in a draft-free, dust-free environment. If you are using your kitchen, do not expose yeast to air that is smoky or filled with cooking oil vapors. Bacteria will "ride" on dust and other solids that are suspended in air and *will* contaminate your yeast should they be offered the opportunity.

In the proper environment:

1) Remove the bottled sterile beer wort from storage and shake vigorously in order to aerate the wort.

2) Prepare a solution of household bleach and water (1 teaspoon per quart of water) and immerse rubber corks and fermentation locks in order to sanitize.

3) Carefully remove cap from bottle of wort.

4) Carefully open container of pure yeast culture and pour into the beer wort. Note: If your container of yeast is glass (beer bottle?) and the surface of the opening through which the yeast will be poured has been exposed to the air, swab the lip and surrounding surfaces with disinfecting ethyl "grain" alcohol. Use the cotton swabs for this purpose, then use your butane cigarette lighter to "torch" the surface. (CAUTION: Grain alcohol is dangerously flammable. Do not use flame when containers are open.) This procedure will burn off bacteria that have surely come to rest on the surface and would have been carried into the sterile wort by the yeast. If your container is plastic or foil and the opening was unprotected, carefully swab the surface with alcohol.

5) After the yeast has been added to the beer wort, shake the excess sanitizing solution from the fermentation lock and cork and place atop the bottle. Appropriately fill the fermentation lock with a weak sanitizing solution.

6) Allow the inoculated wort to sit at room temperature until a good healthy fermentation is visible (usually seen within 6 to 18 hours, or less). Then place fermenting culture in a cold refrigerator. *Do not place in the refrigerator unless fermentation is active*; otherwise, the cooling of the air space in the bottle may create a vacuum and suck the liquid in the fermentation lock into the wort. If fermentation is active, the carbon dioxide gas produced is always pushing air out of the bottle.

   Refrigeration will slow fermentation and provide a better environment for the yeast to go dormant. You can be assured that the yeast will remain healthy and active for at least 2–4 weeks, after which time you should propagate the yeast in another bottle of sterile beer wort. My experience has shown me that some beer yeasts can survive for over a year using this method—and still make excellent beer; much to the disbelief of yeast experts.

   At no time should the fermenting wort be fully capped.

Your kitchen refrigerator is probably the most bacterially contaminated place in your house. Be absolutely certain to swab with alcohol and flame the pouring surfaces of your bottles of cultured yeast before transferring them anywhere.

Culturing yeast for pitching into wort

As a homebrewer, you want enough yeast to pitch into your wort for quick, active fermentation. Ideally, the "rate" at which you would like to pitch into a 5-gallon batch of beer would be 4–8 fluid ounces of yeast slurry (sediment)—that's a lot of yeast! You can obtain this amount of yeast either by carefully removing and repitching the sediment from a primary fermentation (or less ideally from a secondary fermentation) or pitching your yeast into an ever-increasing amount of wort and harvesting the sediment; starting with ½ pint to 1 pint to 1 quart to 1 gallon to 2½ gallons to 5 gallons.

Harvesting yeast from active primary (or secondary) fermentations is an easy way to obtain enough yeast for pitching into your beer. However, you must be certain that the yeast is not and will not get contaminated in the process. If in doubt, don't use it.

"Step-culturing" is laborious, time-consuming and very effective! However, on a practical level I have found that pitching active yeast that has been cultured from a bottle containing 16–20 ounces of fermenting wort has provided me with excellent results. Theoretically, I am certainly underpitching, but with the yeast that I am using the results are very satisfactory, even though visible fermentation is not evident for 12–18 hours. If the proper amount of yeast is pitched, visible fermentation will be evident within hours—an ideal situation.

Let it be your choice and your experience that determine to what degree you want to "step-culture" your yeast.

Prolonged storage of yeast

Once the yeast has gone through its fermentation cycle and its source of food is exhausted, the yeast will go through a limited period of dormancy. This period will vary with the strain of yeast. After a prolonged period the yeast will begin to die.

Yeast can be stored for long periods by freezing. In order to freeze yeast without destroying the cell walls, glycerol should be added to the slurry in an amount equal to 10 percent of the total volume. If this is done correctly, the yeast may be frozen for up to one year before reculturing is necessary.

Contaminated yeast

Your yeast can become contaminated with bacteria or wild yeast. The easiest and best solution is to return to the original source of yeast and start over.

There are methods of "washing" yeast in weak acid solutions. These washes will inhibit or kill bacteria, but because yeast is more acid resistant it will survive (though its qualities may suffer a little). If your yeast is contaminated with wild yeast it is virtually impossible for the homebrewer to separate the good from the bad. Your best bet is to replace the yeast. If this is not possible, sob (but don't let the tears fall into the beer).

ADDITIONAL YEAST INFORMATION RESOURCES FOR THE HOMEBREWER

The 1989 Special Issue of *Zymurgy* is an 80-page magazine devoted to the subject of yeast and homebrewing. It is an excellent resource for further reading on the subject of yeast, its culture and its use in homebrewing. It is available from the American Homebrewers' Association, P.O. Box 1679, Boulder, CO 80306, USA.

LET'S GET PRACTICAL: Special Equipment for the Advanced Homebrewer

So, after all of this brew-ha-ha you still want to brew your own from scratch. I admire your persistence. With that kind of attitude you are certainly more than likely to succeed.

You'll need some specialized equipment, some of which you may already have; otherwise, all are available for purchase. The necessary equipment is simple enough so that it will be within your means to fabricate if necessary. If you can't personally do it, I am sure that some homebrew-appreciating friend will be happy to trade some brew for fabrication.

There are four essential pieces of equipment unique to all-grain mashing that you will have to procure:

1) A mill to grind your malt
2) A mash-tun to contain the malt grist and water at controllable temperatures
3) A lauter-tun to strain and separate the sweet wort from the spent grains

4) A cooling coil to "chill" the hot wort to fermentation temperatures as quickly as possible

This section will first describe what kind of equipment to use or how to make it. The actual use of the equipment will be described in detail later in this section.

THE MILL

Grinding the grain

The purpose of a mill is to grind malted barley into small pieces so that the inner starches, sugars and enzymes are exposed and accessible to the water that is added during the mash. At the same time, it is desirable to remove the husks from the grain, keeping them as intact as possible in order that they can help serve as a natural filter during the lautering process. The grain mill can double as a grinder of adjuncts such as rice, wheat, barley, etc.

By no stretch of the imagination should the malted barley be ground into flour.

Malted barley cannot be appropriately ground with a rolling pin. Save the rolling pin for crystal, black patent and chocolate malts, roasted barley and pies. Commercial breweries use what is called a "roller mill" to grind all of their grains. Grain is crushed between two rotating, grooved rollers. This system enables the commercial brewer to retain the integrity of the husk as it is torn from the grain and crushed at the same time into granules with a minimal amount of dust.

For most homebrewers, a roller-type mill is impractical to obtain or build. The next best thing is a household hand-driven flour mill (not a meat grinder!). A flour mill works on the principle that grains are forced between two plates, one of which is rotating. The grain is crushed as it passes between the plates. Adjustment of the space between the plates allows one to grind grain into flour or, for the homebrewer, to grind the grain into granules appropriate for brewing.

Some homebrew supply shops sell preground malt. Other shops will often have an in-store grinder available that can be used to grind the malt that you purchase.

Having a crush! It may not be love at first sight, but with proper adjustments, the grinding plates on this type of flour mill can serve your malt grinding needs.

Flour mills can be bought in most communities.

For the more mechanically oriented homebrewer, an electric motor or electric drill can be rigged to drive the grinder, saving you the effort of hand-turning the mill.

Whatever you do, don't grind your grains in the same area in which you brew. The dust that is created in the milling process is rich in beer-spoiling, lactobacillus bacteria.

Going against the grain! Before and after: malted barley must be crushed into granular-size pieces, while maintaining the integrity of the husk.

THE MASH-TUN

Holding the water and malt grist at controlled temperatures

A mash-tun is a container whose purpose is to hold the combination of malt (and adjuncts), grist and water at desired temperatures. There are a variety of ways to mash and many systems and specialized equipment designed for the homebrewer. Visit your local homebrew supply shop to see what is available or pick up a copy of a homebrewing magazine.

The methods of mashing that are useful and practical for the homebrewer are called:

> 1) Infusion system of mashing
> 2) Temperature-controlled ("step") system of mashing

The *infusion mashing system* is a one-temperature mash, best used with fully modified malts that do not require a protein rest. It is essentially a process that involves the combination of a predetermined amount of grist and water (at a specific temperature). When combined, the temperatures of the grist and water stabilize. The object is to stabilize at the temperature and sustain a near-constant temperature during conversion of starch to sugar and dextrin. For the practical homebrewer, this will usually take 30–60 minutes.

The homebrewer can devise a system of infusion mashing in many different ways. Here are three methods which I have personally found to be practical, efficient or economic.

> 1) The grist and water mash can be combined in an insulated "picnic cooler" (the inner lining of which is food-grade plastic). Picnic coolers will sustain nearly constant temperatures inside for the period of time required for enzyme conversion of starch to dextrins and sugars.
>
> 2) The "monitored brewpot method" offers economy and satisfactory results to the homebrewer who would rather not have to buy any additional equipment. In

A grin reminder—Relax. Don't worry. Have a homebrew!
Temperatures are easily maintained within insulated
"picnic coolers" when undertaking an all-grain mash.
Grain bag is easily fitted inside, while the sweet wort can
be drawn out the spout upon starch-to-sugar conversion.

this method the grist and water are combined in the brewpot. The temperature is carefully monitored every 5–10 minutes over a period of 30–60 minutes. The volume of mash that you are working with will maintain a fairly constant temperature. Any temperature drop will be very gradual. Heat can be easily added while stirring. When the temperature that you want to achieve is reached, remove the brewpot from the heat.

There are some commercially available systems that work on this principle. Essentially, they are a brewpot with a thermostatically controlled heating element that automatically maintains the desired temperature of the wort. The pioneer system in this area is the renowned Bruheat manufactured in England.

3) Another very ingenious (if I say so, myself) way to maintain the temperature of the mash while it is in the brewpot is to place the entire brewpot in an insulated container large enough to accommodate it. An insulated container can be very inexpensively made by lining a large cardboard box with sheets of Styrofoam. You will be surprised at how effective and convenient this system is in maintaining controlled temperatures.

Prefabricated Styrofoam boxes can be often found in metropolitan area seafood restaurants. These types of boxes are used to ship fresh seafood.

THE LAUTER-TUN

Separating the liquid from the spent grains

The object of the vessel called a lauter-tun is to separate the spent grains (and adjuncts) from the sweet liquor that has been created, leaving behind the grains and husks.

Some mash-tuns are designed so that they can be adapted with what is called a "false bottom." A false bottom is a strainer that is positioned 1 or 2 inches above the real bottom of a container (the mash-tun).

An outlet or spigot is positioned between the false bottom and real bottom. This false bottom creates a system whereby

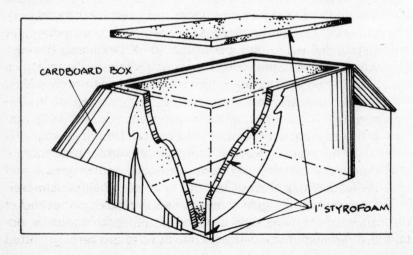

CARDBOARD BOX

1" STYROFOAM

the grains are held 2 inches above the real bottom of a vessel, allowing sweet liquor to pass into the space below and flow out of the spigot (outlet) without the risk of clogging the ''plumbing.''

A false bottom can be created in any mash-tun or lauter-tun by containing the grains in a grain bag. Grain bags are made from cloth or synthetic fabric and have a screenlike weave for a bottom that allows liquid to flow from the bag while retaining the grains. But of course there must be a means of draining the mash-tun or lauter-tun of the liquid. Many picnic coolers have a convenient spigot that is perfect for the practical homebrewer.

An alternative to the picnic cooler and grain bag lautering system can be easily constructed from a 4- or 5-gallon plastic food-grade bucket. The bottom of a bucket can be drilled with hundreds of holes ⅛ inch in diameter, thus creating a strainer that will hold up to 15 pounds of grain. Grains and liquid can be added to this giant strainer and a brewpot placed below can handily catch the sweet liquor.

THE ''ZAPAP'' LAUTER-TUN

A most versatile lautering system

With a little bit more effort, a most versatile lautering system can be made with materials that are available anywhere. The ''Zapap'' lauter-tun is essentially constructed of two 5-gallon plastic food-grade buckets (available from restaurant kitchens). The bottom of one of the buckets is drilled with ⅛-inch-diameter holes, enough to give the appearance of a handmade strainer. The other bucket is fitted with a spigot or plastic hose 1 inch from the bottom of the bucket. The bucket whose bottom is filled with holes is inserted inside the bucket with the spigot. Voilà— you have just constructed a lauter-tun, complete with false bottom and controllable flow. You will need an electric drill to drill holes. You will need a ''spigot'' (a ⅜-inch MPT [male pipe thread] drain cock—available at any hardware store—works great!) and a rubber gasket (inside diameter: ⅜ inch; outside diameter: ½ inch; thickness: ¼ inch) that will line the hole in the bucket through which the spigot is inserted. If a spigot cannot be obtained, a ⅜-inch outside diameter plastic hose can be easily fitted

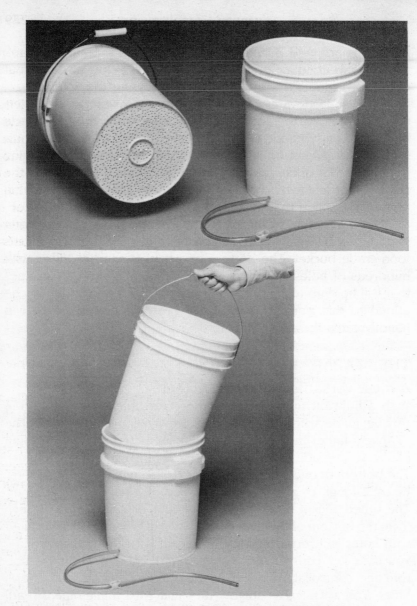

There's a hole in the bucket! The Zapap lauter-tun;
hundreds of holes are drilled in one of two 5-gallon-size
plastic food buckets. When inserted into the second
bucket a "false bottom" is created, allowing grains to be
suspended 2 to 3 inches above the outlet. The plastic
clamp controls flow.

into a ⁵⁄₁₆-inch hole drilled in the bucket. A clamp can be put on the hose to control flow.

The use of this lauter-tun is explained on page 288.

As homebrewers we can't claim, by any means, exclusivity on our handmade creativeness. I once discussed lautering systems with masterbrewers from the Anheuser-Busch and Heileman brewing companies. They explained a system that they fabricated in their pilot brewery to duplicate the hydrodynamics of sparge water flow through a 4- or 5-foot bed of grain in their brewery mash-tun. They removed the lids from both ends of 9 or 10 coffee cans, taped them together end to end with waterproof electrical tape, and attached a bottom can that had been punctured with holes. Voilà—your basic 5-foot-tall lautering system! They said that it worked well, too.

WORT CHILLERS
Cooling the boiled wort as quickly as possible
When brewing all-grain beers, the brewer must boil the entire wort. It is always important to cool the wort as quickly as possible, pitch the yeast and maintain sanitation.

The principle behind various configurations of wort chillers is that cold water is used to cool the hot wort without directly adding the water to the wort. This can be done in principle by immersing the container of hot wort in a bath of cold water so that the heat of the wort can be reduced by the cold water. Immersion of a brewpot in cold water, while effective, is awkward and slow. Many homebrewers devise a "closed" system by which the hot wort passes through copper tubing on its way to the fermenter. A portion of the copper tubing is coiled and that portion is immersed in a cold bath of water. Boiling hot wort enters in one end and exits at temperatures between 50–70 degrees F (10–21 C), chilling 5 gallons of wort within 15 minutes.

There are a variety of wort chillers that are available commercially. They are often advertised in homebrew magazines or available at homebrew supply shops. Some systems are fabricated from copper tubing that is inserted into a 15–20-foot length of garden hose. Various plumbing fittings allow hot wort to pass through the copper tubing while allowing cold water to pass through the garden hose that envelops the copper tubing. Other systems are configured in such a manner that 15–25 feet of coiled copper tubing is immersible in a moving cold water bath.

By far, the easiest way to have a wort-chilling system is to buy one. If you are inclined to make your own, you'll need a length of soft copper tubing that has an inside diameter of ¼, ⅜ or ½ inch. You do not want to even consider bending the copper tubing without a tube bender (see your local plumber).

If you can't get a wort-chilling system together, don't let that deter you. You can still make all-grain beers by letting the wort cool to temperatures below 160 F (71 C) while in the brewpot, then sparge the hot wort directly into your fermenter. BUT if you use a glass fermenter, make absolutely sure that you preheat your fermenter; otherwise, the addition of hot wort will shock the cooler glass fermenter and cause it to break. When sparging hot wort directly into the fermenter, you will have to allow it to cool overnight or bathe or shower it in cool water. It is essential that your fermentation system be a closed one, allowing you to seal the cooling wort away from the air and contaminants.

You may also cool your wort while it is in the brewpot by immersing it in a tub of cold water or in a snowbank outside.

REMEMBER THAT MAINTAINING SANITATION IS EXTREMELY IMPORTANT WHEN THE TEMPERATURE OF THE WORT DROPS BELOW 160–170 DEGREES F (71–77 C).

LET'S MASH!

Hold your horses. Not so fast, buster, and you, too, toots. I want to remind you of a few things.

Don't forget that you are a homebrewer and that the reason you are one is that you enjoy good beer and somehow have grown to enjoy the process of making beer. Some will even profess that since you are now going to mash your own grains it is time to get serious! Give yourself a break, and allow yourself to get concerned, but please, *not serious*. Being concerned will allow you to creatively work out the problems you may encounter. Being concerned will allow attention to quality. Being con-

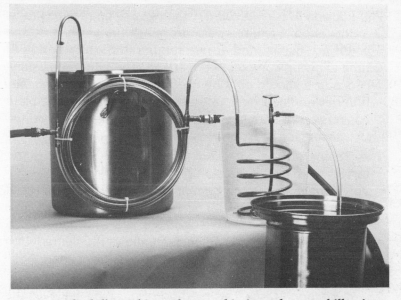

Not a sci-fi chiller! This rather sophisticated wort chiller is a commercially available homebrew system that utilizes a two-stage coolant system. First, the hot wort exits the brewpot and flows through copper tubing that is inserted in a plastic hose. Cold water counterflows around the copper. As the cooler wort exits the first stage it enters another copper coil that is immersed (cutaway) in an ice-water bath. The temperature can be read as it exits into a fermenter or other receptacle. This system is made by Andrews Homebrewing Accessories, Riverside, California.

cerned will allow you to improve your skills with every batch of beer. Being concerned means allowing yourself to Relax, Not Worry and Have a Homebrew. Becoming serious will muddle your mind and mislead you from the real reason you are a home-brewer—enjoyment!

Enjoy the process, appreciate it, savor it. Don't forget—you are a homebrewer.

INTRODUCTION

There are three mashing procedures worth mentioning, two of which are of practical use to the homebrewer. Briefly they are:

The Infusion Mash—Infusion mashing is often referred to as a "one-step," one-temperature mash, in which grist and water are maintained at one temperature for a period of time allowing complete conversion. The infusion-mashing procedure should only be used with fully modified malts. If undermodified malts are used in this system, complete conversion of starches to dextrins and sugars will result, but necessary yeast nutrients will not be developed.

The Temperature-Controlled (Step) Mash—Sometimes referred to as "step-infusion," this mashing procedure involves maintaining the combination of grist and water at various temperatures for specific periods of time. This procedure is particularly suited for use with undermodified malted barley and adjuncts. It allows the degradation of proteins when held at temperatures lower than those that are later necessary for starch conversion.

The Decoction Mash—This method of mashing achieves the same end as the temperature-controlled mash. The distinction of this method is that portions of the water and

Mix and mash!

grist are brought to a boil and added to the main mash in order to raise the temperature through steps similar to the temperature-controlled mashing system. This system seems to have been developed in days predating the thermometer, when there was no accurate means of measuring temperature. Brewmasters devised this system in order to achieve much more consistency in their mashing process. This system still is widely used in Germany to get maximum extraction and perpetuate an age-old tradition. In the rest of the brewing world it is rarely used.

For those interested in learning more about the art and science of decoction mashing, Gregory Noonan's *Brewing Lager Beer*, published by Brewers Publications, P.O. Box 1679, Boulder, CO 80306, USA, is the most comprehensive resource on the subject written in the English language.

The infusion and the temperature-controlled mashing procedures are the most practical for the homebrewer. The time involved in mashing with either method is about the same. If you organize your brewing session, you can figure that from mashing to boiling to sparging to cleaning will involve 4–5 hours of your time. Remember that cleaning both before and *afterwards* is an unavoidable part of the brewing process and will take a considerable amount of your brew time.

THE INFUSION MASH

If the malt you are using is highly modified, then this is the mash for you. It is the simpler of the two mashing systems and requires less attention. Once you've primed yourself with the preceding background information, you'll be surprised at how simple this process can be.

The situation that you want to achieve during the infusion mash is stabilizing the grist and water mash at a temperature between 150–158 degrees F (66–70 C) for 30–60 minutes. The higher temperatures will convert the starches more quickly but at the same time will be more dextrinous, resulting in a more full-bodied beer. The lower temperatures will convert starches more slowly, resulting in a less full-bodied beer.

Desired temperatures are achieved by adding a measured amount of grain to water that is at a predetermined temperature. The following information will help you determine changes in temperature that will occur when the room-temperature grain is added to the hot water.

Here are some facts that will make your life as an infusion masher as easy as eating pie.

- The amount of water needed for every pound of grain is 1 quart.
- There will be a temperature drop of 16–18 degrees F (−9 to −7 C) when the measured amount of water and grain are combined. For example, if 4 quarts of water at a temperature of 168 degrees F (76 C) is added to 4 pounds of grain the temperature of the mash will stabilize at 150–152 degrees F (66–67 C). If adjustments are necessary then heat can be added to raise the temperature or a small amount of cold water can be added to lower the temperature.
- One-half gallon of sparge water is (ideally) needed to sparge each 1 pound of grain. You will lose water along the way from mash to finished beer.
- Each 1 pound of grain will absorb and retain approximately .1 (one-tenth) gallon of water.
- Boiling will evaporate approximately ½–1 gallon of water in 60 minutes. This depends on the vigor of the boil.
- Sediments will account for ¼–½ gallon of losses in volume.

Most homebrewers will brew in 5-gallon increments. You will use between 6 and 10 pounds of grain (including adjuncts) for each 5 gallons of homebrewed beer. The following chart provides practical information for the brewing of all-grain beers using an infusion mash procedure.

GUIDELINES FOR INFUSION MASHING

Gain and adjunct (lbs.)	Mash water (gal.)	Water absorbed by grain (gal.)	Sparge water at 170 °F (77 °C) (gal.)	Water added to boil (gal.)	Water evapor. in boil (gal.)	Initial yield to primary (gal.)	Yield to secondary (gal.)
6	1.5	.6	3.0	2.0	.5	5.5	5.0
7	1.75	.7	3.5	1.5	.5	5.5	5.0
8	2.0	.8	4.0	.75	.5	5.5	5.0
9	2.25	.9	4.5	.25	.5	5.5	5.0
10	2.5	1.0	5.0	0	1.0	5.5	5.0

NOTE: The "water added to boil" is added to the brewpot in order to obtain 6 gallons of wort. You will eventually boil this down to 5.5 gallons as indicated.

THE TEMPERATURE-CONTROLLED MASH

"Step mashing"

A temperature-controlled mash is the most desirable method of mashing when undermodified malted barley is used. A temperature-controlled mash allows the homebrewer to more closely control the temperature of the mash. It promotes the development of yeast nutrients, more poetically referred to as "free amino nitrogens." Also, the controlled temperatures can aid in giving the beer more stability, less of a haze problem and a more controllable balance of dextrins and fermentable sugars with starch conversion.

The practical method described here is easy to follow and also has the advantage of having a desirably thicker mash during the protein rest at 122 degrees F (50 C)—a condition that proteolytic enzymes enjoy. The conversion of starch to dextrin and sugar occurs in a more diluted mash, more appropriate for diastatic enzyme activity.

The temperature-controlled method of mashing will take the grist and water combination to a temperature of 122 degrees F (50 C) and maintain it for 30 minutes, while stirring at intervals of 5 minutes. The temperature is then raised to 150–158 degrees F (66–70 C) by adding a measured amount of boiling water. This temperature is held for 20–30 minutes. The temperatures that are chosen for starch conversion will determine the dextrin–sugar balance of the wort. Higher temperatures will produce beers with a fuller body. Lower temperatures will result in a beer with more alcohol and less body. A temperature rest at 150 degrees F (66 C) for 10 minutes followed by a boost in temperature to 158 degrees F (70 C) held for an additional 10–15 minutes (or until conversion) will produce a medium-bodied beer.

For every pound of grains and adjuncts used, 1 quart of water at a temperature of 130 degrees F (54 C) is necessary to decrease and stabilize the temperature of the mash to 120–124 degrees F (49–51 C). If the adjuncts that you are using need to be cooked, the water that is used to cook them should be figured into the total volume of water. The cooked adjunct and water should be allowed to cool to 130 degrees F (54 C) and then added to the grist with the water.

Stirring of the mash is helpful during each phase of the temperature-controlled procedure.

In order to initiate starch conversion, the temperature of the mash needs to be raised to at least 150 degrees F (66 C). For every pound of grain (and adjunct) that is in the mash ½ quart of water at 200 degrees F (93 C) will be needed to raise the temperature of the mash about 18 degrees F (10 C). (Note: In Colorado I brew at an altitude of 5,300 feet. Water boils at 200 degrees F [93 C]. It would be safe to guess that water at 212 degrees F [100 C], which is boiling at sea level, would increase the temperature by about 25 degrees F [14 C]. Try it and record your observations for later use.) For example, if the temperature of the mash at the end of the protein rest is slightly raised to 132 degrees F (56 C), the 200-degree F (93 C) water that is added will raise the temperature to 150 degrees F (66 C).

After the temperature is held at 150 degrees F (66 C) for 10–15 minutes a simple addition of heat (turn on the stove and stir) can raise the temperature to 158 degrees F (70 C) in a short time.

Most homebrewers will brew in 5-gallon increments. You will use between 6 and 10 pounds of grain (including adjuncts) for each 5 gallons of homebrewed beer. The chart on page 300 provides practical information for the brewing of all-grain beers using a temperature-controlled procedure.

You may have thought that you've missed something, but all the practical essentials are here.

IODINE TEST FOR STARCH CONVERSION

After you have finished your mashing procedures you may wonder whether or not you have completed the starch-to-sugar/dextrin conversion. You can do a simple test for starch by using tincture of iodine as an indicator. The test is based on the fact that tincture of iodine (available at any pharmacy) will turn a starch solution purple or black in color. If all of the starches in your mash have been converted to sugars or dextrins, the iodine will not display any color change.

GUIDELINES FOR TEMPERATURE-CONTROLLED MASHING

Grain and adjunct (lbs.)	Mash water at 130 °F (gal.)	Water at 200 °F to raise to 150 °F (gal.) [qts.]	Water absorbed by grain (gal.)	Sparge water at 170 °F (gal.)	Water added to boil (gal.) [qts.]	Water evapor. in boil (gal.)	Initial yield to primary (gal.)	Yield to secondary (gal.)
6	1.5	.75 (3)	.6	3	1.35 (5.5)	.5	5.5	5
7	1.75	.875 (3.5)	.7	3.5	.575 (2.5)	.5	5.5	5
8	2.0	1.0 (4)	.8	4.0	.25 (1)	.5	5.5	5
9	2.25	1.125 (4.5)	.9	4.5	—	1.0	5.5	5
10	2.5	1.25 (5)	1.0	5.0	—	1.75	5.5	5

NOTE: The "water added to boil" is added to the brewpot in order to obtain 6 gallons of wort. You will eventually boil this down to 5.5 gallons as indicated.

To perform this test remove 1 tablespoon of the liquid mash and place it on a cool white saucer. Drip a drop of iodine into the puddle and observe. If there is a change in color to black or purple, then you should continue to mash until a repeat of this test indicates no change in color.

LAUTERING

Wort separation and sparging

Now that you've successfully converted your grains to the better things in life, it is necessary to stop the conversion process and separate the sweet liquor from the particulate matter: the spent grain and husk material. You accomplish this by raising the temperature of the mash to 170 degrees F (77 C) in order to deactivate enzymes, and then contain the spent grains in an oversized strainer while allowing the liquid to drain from the bottom. A measured amount of "rinse" (sparging) water is added to the surface of the grains to trickle through and carry remaining sugars away.

The major problem that you want to avoid is a "stuck runoff." A stuck runoff results from a compaction of the bed of grains in your lauter-tun and/or the clogging of the holes in the strainer section of the lauter-tun. In any case, the flow of liquid through the grains is hindered when a stuck runoff occurs. The possibility of a stuck or restricted runoff can be minimized by providing "foundation water" to the lauter-tun. Foundation water will provide a means of gently "floating" the grains onto the false bottom, avoiding compaction of the grain and clogging of the false-bottom strainer.

The principle of using foundation water in the lautering process can be demonstrated with an explanation of a double-bucket lauter-tun system (see Let's Get Practical: The Lauter-tun). The main points to remember are: 1) the sparge water should be 170–180 degrees F (77–82 C); 2) the level of liquid (sparge/foundation water and mash) should always be maintained above the surface of the grains that are gradually being added.

To begin, add enough hot water (170 degrees F [77 C]) so that the surface level exceeds the level of the false bottom by a good 3 or 4 inches. Then alternately add the mash (grains and sweet liquor) and reservoir of sparge water while maintaining a level of liquid that is visibly above the surface of the grain bed. After all of the mash has been added to the lauter-tun, draining can commence.

If the mash were added to a dry lauter-tun, it would be more likely that the weight of the unsuspended grains would compact and clog the straining system.

When you begin, slowly drain the sweet wort, and continue to gently add hot sparge water until the supply of sparge water is depleted. Avoid pouring the sparging water onto the surface of the grains with abandonment; rather, gently spray or sprinkle the hot water over the top of the surface. As the water gently flows through the "filter bed" of grains it carries with it the desired sugars and dextrins.

If you are not using a double-bucket or false-bottom lautering system, do the best you can. There are a variety of ways to provide foundation water to the simplest lautering system, even if it is only temporarily. The principle remains the same: Float the grains into your lautering system and retain a level of liquid above the grain bed.

As you direct your sweet runoff into your brewpot, avoid aeration of the hot liquid as this could lead to the development of oxidized flavors later in the beermaking process.

BOILING THE WORT

You are boiling a much greater volume of liquid because the wort is not concentrated. You will be able to boil your wort more vigorously, allowing for more or less evaporation, as required. The more vigorous boil will facilitate protein coagulation (the hot break) and more precipitation of sediment. The removal of this precipitate can be dealt with later.

COOLING THE WORT

From 212 degrees F (100 C) to 70 degrees F (21 C) in 15 minutes!

In order to ensure healthy and contaminant-free fermentation (and beer), it is desirable to cool the hot wort as quickly as possible so that yeast can be pitched.

The cooling systems that have been described in the equip-

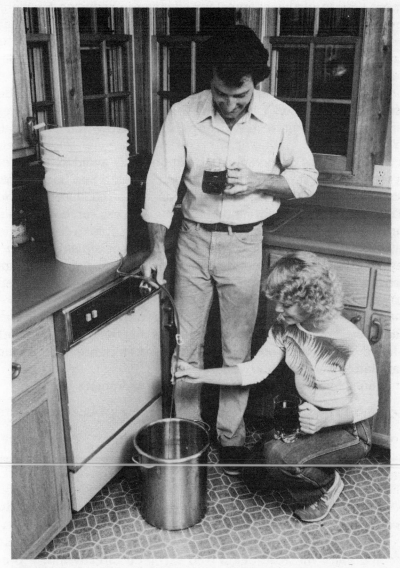

*It takes two hands! The Zapap double-bucket lauter-tun
demonstrates the ease of separating and sparging grains in an
all-grain mash. The double-bucket configuration shown in
operation strains the sweet wort from the spent grains. The
flow is directed into the brewpot. The next step is boiling the
wort with hops.*

ment section of this chapter are effective in reducing 5 gallons of wort from boiling temperatures down to 60 degrees F (17 C) within 15–30 minutes.

The problems that need to be avoided are bacterial contamination and clogging due to the presence of hops.

It is extremely important that any piece of equipment be thoroughly sanitized if it is going to be in contact with the beer after the temperature has been reduced below 160 degrees F (71 C).

Clogging of cooling systems can be easily avoided if the hot wort is passed through a lauter system (called a hop-back at this stage of the process) and then introduced to the chiller system. The lauter-tun used during the mashing process can double as a hop-back with the added advantage of being able to connect the drain spigot to the wort chiller with a piece of tubing.

If a lauter-tun system is unavailable, you must strain, sparge and remove hops from the hot wort before the wort is allowed to enter the chilling system.

Once the wort enters the chilling system, the cold water that envelops the plumbing which is carrying the flow of hot wort should always be in motion for maximum efficiency. This is true no matter what method you devise.

In summary, the essential points to remember are:

- You must remove the hops from the wort before it enters the chilling system.
- Once temperatures drop below 160 degrees F (71 C), it is imperative that all equipment that comes in contact with the beer be sanitized.

If you simply do not want to deal with chilling systems you may "prechill" your hot wort by immersing your covered brewpot in a bath of cold water. Then you can sparge the warm wort (temperature must be below 160 F [71 C]) directly into a preheated fermenter. It is almost essential that your fermentation system be a closed system—one that allows you to lock the wort away from air and potential contaminants. After the hot wort has been put into your fermenter, you may have to wait many hours (perhaps overnight) in order that the wort drops to tem-

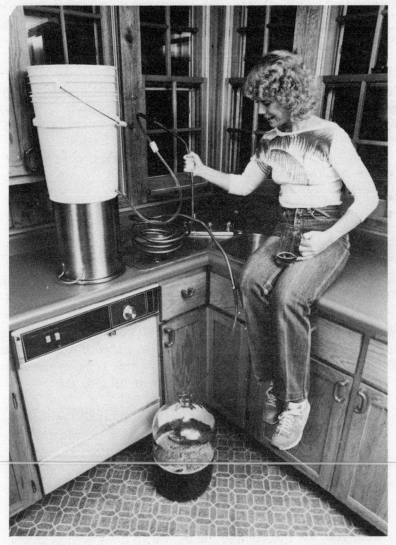

A counterbalanced wort chiller! Leather hands hold what normally would be boiling hot copper tubing. (I don't know how she does it.) Boiling hot wort is added to the Zapap lauter-tun which now serves as a "hop-back." As the hot wort separates from the hops, it passes into the coiled copper tubing which is immersed in a bath of cold water. The wort is cooled when it exits the tubing.

peratures suitable for pitching yeast. Be forewarned that this procedure can result in beers that have a flavor character reminiscent of sweet corn (really dimethyl-sulfide). It is best to chill as quickly as possible. If a carboy fermenter is used, it may be immersed in a bath of cool water once temperature is below 110 degrees F (43 C). CAUTION: If you are using a glass carboy for your fermenter, you must heat the glass sufficiently before adding boiling hot wort to it. The shock of hot wort to cool glass will break the carboy.

NOTE: Remember that aeration of the cooled wort is important for healthy fermentation. Splashing the wort into your fermenter will accomplish adequate aeration.

THE PROTEIN SEDIMENT—TRUB

Once your wort has been added to the fermenter and allowed a quiet period of 30 minutes or so, you will notice the formation of sediment called "trub" on the bottom of the fermenter. This protein sediment was coagulated and precipitated (the hot-break) during the boil and further precipitated upon cooling (called the cold-break). The use of a hop-back will filter out a significant amount of trub, in much the same way as the grains acted as a filter in your lauter-tun. If you wish, you may remove the wort from the trub by siphoning the clear wort off into another carboy, leaving the sediment behind.

In theory, the trub will inhibit fermentation and reduce the production of esters, often desirable in beer. In practice, the effect on fermentation is not significant to the homebrewer. If it bothers you, siphon the clear wort off and have a homebrew. If you can't be bothered, just have a homebrew.

FERMENTATION

Ferment your beer to completion as you've done with all of your beers and don't forget to relax . . . don't worry . . . have a homebrew!

"It is not through knowledge, but through experience of the world that we are brought into relation with it."

—Albert Schweitzer
My Life's Thoughts

ALL-GRAIN RECIPES

Amaizeing Pale Ale

This fresh-tasting, all-grain, medium-bodied British-style ale blends golden sweetness with a refreshing bitterness of hops. A dry crisp clean aftertaste embellishes the soul with the amaizement that you, a homebrewer, can brew truly fine beer from "scratch."

Fermentable sugars converted from cornstarch are married with malted barley and English hops to make this an exciting ale that should be able to please anybody's beer palate.

Ingredients for 5 gallons:

7 lbs. malted barley (6-row, high enzyme)
1 lb. crystal malt
1 lb. cornstarch
1 tsp. gypsum
1 oz. Fuggles or Willamette hops (boiling): 5 HBU
1 oz. Cascade hops (boiling): 5 HBU
½ oz. Hallertauer hops (aroma)
¼ tsp. Irish moss powder
1–2 pkgs. ale yeast
¾ c. corn sugar or 1¼ c. dried malt extract (for bottling)

This recipe calls for using a "temperature-controlled" procedure for mashing 9 lbs. of grains and adjuncts (see chart, page 300).

Combine the crushed grains, cornstarch and gypsum with 2.25 gallons of 130-degree F (54 C) water and proceed with a protein rest. Raise the temperature by adding 4½ quarts of 200-degree F (93 C) water and continue with starch conversion at about 150 degrees F (66 C) for 10–15 minutes. Complete conversion by raising the temperature to 158 degrees F (70 C) and holding for 10–20 minutes or until an iodine test indicates complete conversion.

Sparge with 4½ gallons of 170-degree F (77 C) water.

Bring the wort to a boil, add boiling hops and continue to boil for 1 hour. Add the Irish moss during the final 10 minutes of the boil. Add the aroma hops during the final 1–2 minutes of boiling. Remove the spent hops and sparge. Cool the wort as quickly as possible.

Final yield should be 5–5½ gallons of wort.

Pitch the yeast and ferment to completion. Bottle with ¾ cup corn sugar or 1¼ c. dried malt extract.

This ale can be brewed, bottled and enjoyed within 3 weeks.

Hesitation Red Märzen

I have no idea why this beer ever got to be named Hesitation. After one small sip any hesitation that you may have had will vanish! A blend of home-toasted malt serves to accent this wonderfully balanced bittersweet brew—one that rejoices in the character of a true continental lager. Saaz, the classic Czechoslovakian hop, serves to uniquely complement the reddish glow of this homebrewed Märzen.

Ingredients for 5 gallons:

        5 lbs. malted barley (6-row, high enzyme)
        2 lbs. Munich malt
        1 lb. toasted malted barley
        1 tsp. gypsum
        2 oz. Saaz hops (boiling): 7 HBU
        ½ oz. Saaz hops (aroma)
        ¼ tsp. Irish moss powder
        1–2 pkgs. lager yeast
        ¾ c. corn sugar or 1¼ c. dried malt extract (for bottling)

This recipe calls for using a "temperature-controlled" procedure for mashing 8 lbs. of grains (see chart, page 300).

First, toast 1 lb. malted barley in a 350-degree F oven for 10 minutes. Combine the crushed grains and gypsum with 2 gallons of 130 degree F (54 C) water and proceed with a protein rest. Raise the temperature by adding 4 quarts of 200-degree F

(93 C) water and continue with starch conversion at about 150 degrees F (66 C) for 10–15 minutes. Complete conversion by raising the temperature to 158 degrees F (70 C) and holding for 10–20 minutes or until an iodine test indicates complete conversion.

Sparge with 4 gallons of 170-degree F (77 C) water.

Bring the wort to a boil, add boiling hops and continue to boil for 1 hour. Add the Irish moss during the final 10 minutes of the boil. Add the aroma hops during the final 1–2 minutes of boiling. Remove the spent hops and sparge. Cool the wort as quickly as possible.

Final yield should be 5–5½ gallons of wort.

Pitch the yeast and ferment to completion. Bottle with corn sugar or malt extract.

High-Velocity Weizen
(Wheat Beer)

Originally brewed on a windy night, this alcoholically low wheat beer offers a refreshing sparkle to your beer cellar. The subtleness of German hops blesses this light ale with an authentic German character. The uniqueness of malted wheat contributes a refreshing and very drinkable lightness to this beer.

Ingredients for 5 gallons:

   5 lbs. malted barley (6-row, high enzyme)

   3 lbs. malted wheat

   1 tsp. gypsum

   ½ oz. Hallertauer hops (boiling): 3 HBU

   ¼ oz. Hallertauer hops (aroma)

   ¼ tsp. Irish moss powder

   1–2 pkgs. Red Star ale yeast or Weizen/wheat beer yeast

   ¾ c. corn sugar or 1¼ c. dried malt extract (for bottling)

This recipe calls for using a "temperature-controlled" procedure for mashing 8 lbs. of grains and adjuncts (see chart, page 300).

Combine the crushed grains, malted wheat and gypsum with 2 gallons of 130-degree F (54 C) water and proceed with a protein rest. Raise the temperature by adding 4 quarts of 200-degree F (93 C) water and continue with starch conversion at about 150 degrees F (66 C) for 10–15 minutes. Complete conversion by raising the temperature to 158 degrees F (70 C) and holding for 10–20 minutes or until an iodine test indicates complete conversion.

Sparge with 4 gallons of 170–180-degree F (77–82 C) water.

Bring the wort to a boil, add boiling hops and continue to boil for 1 hour. Add the Irish moss during the final 10 minutes of the boil. Add the aroma hops during the final 1–2 minutes of boiling. Remove the spent hops and sparge. Cool the wort as quickly as possible.

Final yield should be 5–5½ gallons of wort.

Pitch the yeast, ferment to completion and bottle.

Olde 33

Yep, I was born and bred in a brewpot. The original version of this here recipe celebrated my 33rd birthday (too long ago!). Every year I have wanted to brew another batch and aim for an original specific gravity that matches my years. I'm looking forward to 1.090!

Olde 33 is a relatively pure and simple light lager. A good beginning for the all-grain brewer, it allows you the experience of discovering how the essential ingredients of all-grain beers contribute to the flavor of beer. This one is light, simple and delicately hopped.

Ingredients for 5 gallons:

7 lbs. malted barley (American 2-row or 6-row)
1 tsp. gypsum
1 oz. Cascade hops (boiling): 5 HBU
¼ oz. Hallertauer hops (aroma)
¼ tsp. Irish moss powder
1–2 pkgs. lager yeast
¾ c. corn sugar or 1¼ c. dried malt extract (for bottling)

This recipe calls for using a "temperature-controlled" procedure for mashing 7 lbs. of grains (see chart, page 300).

Combine the crushed grains and gypsum with 1.75 gallons of 130-degree F (54 C) water and proceed with a protein rest. Raise the temperature by adding 3½ quarts of 200-degree F (93 C) water and continue with starch conversion at about 150 degrees F (66 C) for 10–15 minutes. Complete conversion by raising the temperature to 158 degrees F (70 C) and holding for 10–20 minutes or until an iodine test indicates complete conversion.

Sparge with 3½ gallons of 170-degree F (77 C) water.

Add 2½ quarts of water and bring the wort to a boil. Add boiling hops and continue to boil for 1 hour. Add the Irish moss during the final 10 minutes of the boil. Add the aroma hops during the final 1–2 minutes of boiling. Remove the spent hops and sparge. Cool the wort as quickly as possible.

Final yield should be 5–5½ gallons of wort.

Pitch the yeast and ferment to completion. Bottle with corn sugar or malt extract.

Catch Her in the Rye

A German Pils style with a twist that lends a brilliantly dry crispness and lightness to this innovative brew. I'm sure German brewmasters would cringe at the thought of naming a beer after a Pils if it had rye in it. But then again, I'm not a German brewmaster. I'm a homebrewer who can do it my way and I don't have to answer to anyone but my taste angel.

Ingredients for 5 gallons:

6½ lbs. pale malted barley
2½ lbs. flaked rye
1½ oz. Hallertauer hops (boiling): 7 HBU
1 oz. Hallertauer hops (flavor)
½ oz. Saaz hops (aroma)
½ oz. Tettnanger hops (aroma)
1–2 pkgs. lager yeast
¾ c. corn sugar or 1¼ c. dried malt extract (for bottling)

This recipe calls for a "temperature-controlled" procedure for mashing 9 lbs. of grains (see chart, page 300).

Combine the grains with 2.25 gallons of 130-degree F (54 C) water and proceed with a protein rest. Raise the temperature by adding 1.25 gallons of 200-degree F (93 C) water and continue with starch conversion at about 150 degrees F (66 C) for 15 minutes. Complete conversion by raising the temperature to 158 degrees F (70 C) and holding for 10–20 minutes or until an iodine test indicates complete conversion.

Sparge with 4 gallons of 170-degree F (77 C) water. Bring to a boil and add boiling hops. Boil for 30 minutes, then add ½ oz. flavor hops and boil for 15 minutes more. Then add remaining ½ oz. flavor hops and boil for 15 minutes more. Add aroma hops during the last 1–2 minutes of boiling. Remove the spent hops and sparge. Cool the wort as quickly as possible.

Final yield should be 5 gallons of wort.

Pitch the yeast, ferment to completion and bottle.

Un-American Light Beer

What's so un-American about this beer (no, it isn't red)? It is American because it uses rice to lighten the body, but it's typically un-American in that there's real beer flavor despite its lightness. Now, why didn't they ever think of that back at the brewery?

The contribution that crystal malt makes to this beer is one of fulfillment. The Cascade hops contribute to making a true-brew American product.

Ingredients for 5 gallons:

    5 lbs. malted barley (6-row, high enzyme)
    1 lb. cooked white rice (weight is dry weight)
    ½ lb. crystal malt
    1 tsp. gypsum
    1 oz. Cascade hops (boiling): 5 HBU
    ¼ oz. Cascade hops (aroma)
    ¼ tsp. Irish moss powder

1–2 pkgs. lager yeast

¾ c. corn sugar or 1¼ c. dried malt extract (for bottling)

This recipe calls for using a "temperature-controlled" procedure for mashing 6.5 lbs. of grains and adjuncts (see chart, page 300).

Cook the rice in 6½ quarts of water for ½ hour. Let the temperature drop to 130 degrees F (54 C) and then combine the crushed grains and gypsum and proceed with a protein rest. Raise the temperature by adding 3½ quarts of 200-degree F (93 C) water and continue with starch conversion at about 150 degrees F (66 C) for 15–20 minutes. Complete conversion by raising the temperature to 158 degrees F (70 C) and holding for 10–20 minutes or until an iodine test indicates complete conversion.

Sparge with 3½ gallons of 170-degree F (77 C) water.

Add 2½ more quarts of water to the brewpot and bring the wort to a boil. Add boiling hops and continue to boil for 1 hour. Add the Irish moss during the final 10 minutes of the boil. Add the aroma hops during the final 1–2 minutes of boiling. Remove the spent hops and sparge. Cool the wort as quickly as possible.

Final yield should be 5–5½ gallons of wort.

Pitch the yeast, ferment to completion and bottle.

Monkey's Paw Brown Ale

A rich, satisfying chocolaty brown ale. A pleasing sweetness that is cleaned by a crisp finish of English hops. Monkey's Paw will make you wish you had another, but that won't be necessary because this recipe, like all the others, is for 5 gallons. Five gallons of medium-bodied brown ale in the English tradition.

Ingredients for 5 gallons:

7 lbs. malted barley (English highly modified malt)

¼ lb. chocolate malt

¼ lb. black patent malt

½ lb. crystal malt

1 tsp. gypsum

1 oz. Fuggles hops (boiling): 5 HBU

½ oz. Northern Brewer hops (boiling): 5 HBU

½ oz. Fuggles hops (aroma)

¼ tsp. Irish moss powder

1–2 pkgs. ale yeast

¾ c. corn sugar or 1¼ c. dried malt extract (for bottling)

This recipe calls for using an "infusion" procedure for mashing 8 lbs. of grains (see chart, page 297).

Combine the crushed grains and gypsum with 1.75 gallons of 168-degree F (76 C) water. The mash will stabilize at 150–155 degrees F (66–67 C). Hold this temperature for 30–60 minutes.

Sparge with 4 gallons of 170-degree F (77 C) water.

Add 3 additional quarts of water to the brewpot and bring the wort to a boil. Add boiling hops and continue to boil for 1 hour. Add the Irish moss during the final 10 minutes of the boil. Add the aroma hops during the final 1–2 minutes of boiling. Remove the spent hops and sparge. Cool the wort as quickly as possible.

Final yield should be 5–5½ gallons of wort.

Pitch the yeast and ferment to completion. Bottle with corn sugar or malt extract.

Silver Dollar Porter

The best porter either side of a silver dollar can buy—but you can't buy it because it ain't for sale. It's homebrew and it's yours. Lucky for you because there won't be enough to go around as it is.

A full-bodied, sharply bittersweet version of black heaven, this is the homebrewer's best shot at duplicating the famous Anchor Porter of San Francisco fame.

Ingredients for 5 gallons:

8 lbs. malted barley (American 2-row or 6-row)

1 lb. Munich malt

½ lb. crystal malt

½ lb. black patent malt

½ lb. chocolate malt

1 tsp. gypsum

1 oz. Northern Brewer or Perle hops (boiling): 9 HBU

½ oz. Cascade hops (boiling): 3 HBU

½ oz. Cascade hops (aroma)

¼ tsp. Irish moss powder

1–2 pkgs. ale yeast

¾ c. corn sugar or 1¼ c. dried malt extract (for bottling)

This recipe calls for using a "temperature-controlled" procedure for mashing 10 lbs. of grains (see chart, page 300).

Combine the crushed grains and gypsum with 2.5 gallons of 130-degree F (54 C) water and proceed with a protein rest. Raise the temperature by adding 5 quarts of 200-degree F (93 C) water and continue with starch conversion at about 150 degrees F (66 C) for 10–15 minutes. Complete conversion by raising the temperature to 158 degrees F (70 C) and holding for 10–20 minutes or until an iodine test indicates complete conversion.

Sparge with 5 gallons of 170-degree F (77 C) water.

Bring the wort to a boil, add boiling hops and continue to boil for 1 hour. Add the Irish moss during the final 10 minutes of the boil. Add the finishing hops during the final 1–2 minutes of boiling. Remove the spent hops and sparge. Cool the wort as quickly as possible.

Final yield should be 5–5½ gallons of wort.

Pitch the yeast, ferment to completion and bottle.

Propentious Irish Stout
(A La Guinness)

The real thing—the real recipe. The only difference is that you make it. A wonderful experience for the aficionado of real stout. A rich brown head tops off a deep black liquid—bittersweet and satisfying.

Ingredients for 5 gallons:

7 lbs. malted barley (British 2-row)

1 lb. flaked or cooked pearled barley

1 lb. roasted barley

1 tsp. gypsum

2½ oz. Goldings hops (boiling): 12 HBU

¼ tsp. Irish moss powder

1–2 pkgs. ale yeast

¾ c. corn sugar or 1¼ c. dried malt extract (for bottling)

This recipe calls for using an "infusion" procedure for mashing 9 lbs. of grains (see chart, page 297).

Combine the crushed grains and gypsum with 2.25 gallons of 168-degree F (76 C) water. The mash will stabilize at 150–155 degrees F (66–67 C). Hold this temperature for 30–60 minutes.

Sparge with 4.5 gallons of 170-degree F (77 C) water.

Add 1 additional quart of water to the brewpot and bring the wort to a boil. Add boiling hops and continue to boil for 1 hour. Add the Irish moss during the final 10 minutes of the boil. Remove the spent hops and sparge. Cool the wort as quickly as possible.

Final yield should be 5–5½ gallons of wort.

Pitch the yeast, ferment to completion and bottle.

Dream Export Lager

If it's a luscious body you're after, this is your fermentation. This full-bodied light lager is the rich version of German beer—with a sweetness that is turned inside out by an adequate supply of bitterness. From German Hallertauer, of course. The addition of dextrine malt to this recipe (as it would be with any recipe) enhances the head retention of this satisfying real beer!

Dream Export Lager is by no means a fairy ale.

Ingredients for 5 gallons:

9½ lbs. malted barley

½ lb. dextrine malt

1 tsp. gypsum

1½ oz. Hallertauer hops (boiling): 7.0 HBU

½ oz. Hallertauer hops (flavor)

½ oz. Hallertauer hops (aroma)

¼ tsp. Irish moss powder

1–2 pkgs. lager yeast

¾ c. corn sugar or 1¼ c. dried malt extract (for bottling)

This recipe calls for using a "temperature-controlled" procedure for mashing 10 lbs. of grains (see chart, page 300).

Combine the crushed grains and gypsum with 2.5 gallons of 130-degree F (54 C) water and proceed with a protein rest. Raise the temperature by adding 5 quarts of 200-degree F (93 C) water and continue with starch conversion at about 150 degrees F (66 C) for 10–15 minutes. Complete conversion by raising the temperature to 158 degrees F (70 C) and holding for 10–20 minutes or until an iodine test indicates complete conversion.

Sparge with 5 gallons of 170-degree F (77 C) water.

Bring the wort to a boil, add 1½ oz. of boiling hops and boil for 40 minutes. Then add ½ oz. of flavor hops and continue to boil for 20 minutes. Add the Irish moss during the final 10 minutes of the boil. Add the aroma hops during the final 1–2 minutes of boiling. Remove the spent hops and sparge. Cool the wort as quickly as possible.

Final yield should be 5–5½ gallons of wort.

Pitch the yeast and ferment to completion. Bottle with corn sugar or malt extract.

Spider's Tongue German Weiss-Rauchbier

As fine as the finest gossamer, Spider's Tongue smoked lager will be one of your crowning achievements if you like smoke-flavored foods. In the tradition of Bamberg, Germany, this brew is an attempt at duplicating their best. A sweet smoke flavor lending itself to the Märzen or Oktoberfest tradition with a homebrewer's twist of wheat malt.

Ingredients for 5 gallons:

6 lbs. pale malted barley (German or American 2-row)

2 lbs. smoked Munich malt

1 lb. wheat malt

1 lb. crystal malt

2 tsp. gypsum

⅛ tsp. plain and pure 100% noniodized table salt (sodium chloride)

1¼ oz. Hallertauer hops (boiling): 6 HBU

1 oz. Tettnanger hops (aroma)

1–2 pkgs. lager yeast

¾ c. corn sugar or 1¼ c. dried malt extract (for bottling)

Immerse the 2 lbs. of Munich malt in water. Remove and drain water off the grains. You must have a charcoal barbecue grill that can be covered, such as a Weber-type kettle. Get the coals white-hot. Place pieces of apple, hickory, cherry, beech, mesquite or other hardwoods suitable for barbecuing food on the hot coals. Place the wet Munich malt on a clean wire screen atop the grill (which has been degreased by wire brushing and heat) and cover with the air vents open, allowing the wood to smolder. Stir the malt every few minutes to prevent burning. When the malt has dried and smoked for about 15 minutes, remove and cool.

This recipe calls for a "temperature-controlled" procedure for mashing 10 lbs. of grains (see chart, page 300).

Combine all of the grains with 2.5 gallons of 130-degree F (54 C) water and proceed with a protein rest. Raise the temperature by adding 1.5 gallons of 200-degree F (93 C) water and continue with starch conversion at about 150 degrees F (66 C) for 15 minutes. Complete conversion by raising the temperature to 158 degrees F (70 C) and holding for 10–20 minutes or until an iodine test indicates complete conversion.

Sparge with 4 gallons of 170 degree F (77 C) water. Bring to a boil and add boiling hops. Add aroma hops during the last 1–2 minutes of boiling. Remove the spent hops and sparge. Cool the wort as quickly as possible.

Final yield should be 5 gallons of wort.

Pitch the yeast, ferment to completion and bottle.

Appendices
Appendix 1
Homebrewer's Glossary

A.A.U.—Alpha acid units. A measurement of potential bitterness in hops. The numerical value is equivalent to the percentage of alpha acid.

Adjuncts—Any fermentable ingredient added to beer other than malted barley.

Aerobic—Processes requiring oxygen.

Ale—A style of beer. Traditionally a "top-fermented" beer brewed at temperatures between 60–70 degrees F (16–21 C) using ale yeast.

Ale Yeast—*Saccharomyces cerevisiae* type of yeast. Generally speaking, it does best at fermentation temperatures between 55–70 degrees F. It is also known as "top-fermenting yeast" because of some varieties' ability to form a layer of yeast on the surface during primary fermentation. Top-fermenting yeast is anaerobic and will always form a sediment on the bottom.

Alpha Acid—The bittering acid of hops, usually measured in percent by weight: 2–4 percent is low; 5–7 percent is medium; 8–12 percent is extremely high.

Alpha-amylase—One of two principal diastatic enzymes that convert starches to fermentable sugars. Often referred to as the "liquefying" enzyme, converting soluble starch to dextrin.

Anaerobic—Processes that do not require dissolved oxygen.

Aroma—The smell of beer associated with malt and grain character.

Attenuation—The measure of how much of the dissolved solids in beer wort is converted by the fermentation process to alcohol and CO_2, indicated by the difference between starting specific gravity and final specific gravity.

Barm—Verb: To add yeast; pitch. Noun: the foam or froth atop fermenting beer (kraeusen) or foam on top of a glass of beer.

319

Beer—Any alcoholic beverage made from the fermentation of sugars derived from grain. That which is meant to be enjoyed.

Beta-acid—A bitter acid of hops. It does not contribute to beer's bitterness due to its insolubility.

Beta-amylase—One of the two principal diastatic enzymes. Often referred to as the saccharifying enzyme, converting dextrins and soluble starches to fermentable sugars.

Body—The "mouth-feel" of beer; "thicker" beers are said to have a fuller body.

Bottom-fermenting—See Lager yeast.

Bouquet—The smell of beer associated with hop character.

Break—The phase during the boiling and cooling of beer wort when proteins precipitate. Also hot-break, cold-break.

Bung—Cork that serves to seal kegs.

Carboy—5- or 6½-gallon glass bottle with a narrow opening on top. Properly cleaned, carboys can be used as primary or secondary fermenters.

Cold-break—See Break.

Conditioning—The process of developing CO_2 (carbonation) in beer.

Copper—An old term that refers to the brewpot which used to be made from copper; some brewers still use coppers.

Dextrins—Unfermentable and tasteless carbohydrates that contribute body to beer. Technically, 4 or more glucose molecules linked together.

Dextrinization—The enzymatic process of degrading soluble starch molecules to dextrin molecules.

Diastase (diastatic)—Referring to enzymes in malt that convert starch to sugars and dextrins.

Diacetyl—A chemical naturally produced during fermentation; characterized by a butterscotch flavor.

Drunk—Past participle of "drink."

Dunkel—German word for "dark" (as in color).

Ester—Term used to describe the "fruity" aromatics and flavors of beer. Apple, pear, grapefruit, strawberry, raspberry and banana esters are often produced during the respiration cycle of yeast.

Fermentation—The conversion of sugar to alcohol and carbon dioxide by yeast. It is an anaerobic process.

Fermentation Lock—A simple water and bubble-type device used during closed or secondary fermentation that prevents ambient air from coming in contact with the fermenting brew. At the same time, the fermentation lock permits the escape of carbon dioxide (a by-product of fermentation). It fits into a rubber cork atop a carboy being used as a secondary fermenter.

Fining—A procedure used by some brewers to aid in the clarification of their brews. Usually a gelatinous ingredient such as gelatin, Irish moss or isinglass is added in the brewing process, thus facilitating clarification.

Finishing Hops—Fresh aromatic hops that are added to the boiling wort during the final 1–2 minutes of boiling. Clean hops can be added during secondary fermentation. This is called dry hopping. Care should be taken to ensure cleanliness. "Finishing" or "dry hopping" impart hop aroma and flavor to beer.

Flocculation—The tendency of yeast to gather and migrate to the surface or bottom of fermenting beer. Usually refers to the sedimentation phase of fermentation that follows yeast suspension.

Gelatinization—In mashing, the process of making starch soluble, usually in reference to cooking (boiling) adjuncts.

Grist—Ground (milled) malt and/or adjuncts.

Gyle—That portion of unfermented beer wort that is reserved for or added to finished beer for conditioning (carbonation).

Helles—German word for "light" (as in color).

Homebrew—That which is to be enjoyed.

Homebrew Bitterness Units—HBUs or Homebrew Bitterness Units are a measure of the total amount of bitterness potential in a given volume of beer. Homebrew Bitterness Units are calculated by multiplying the percent of alpha acid in the hops by the number of ounces. For example, if 2 ounces of Northern Brewer hops (9% alpha acid) and 3 ounces of Cascade hops (5% alpha acid) were used in a 10-gallon batch, the total amount of bitterness units would be 33: $(2 \times 9) + (3 \times 5) =$

18 + 15. Bitterness units per gallon would be 3.3 in a 10-gallon batch or 6.6 in a 5-gallon batch, so it is important to note volumes whenever expressing Homebrew Bitterness Units. HBUs are not related to IBUs (International Bitterness Units) except that they both measure bitterness in beer.

Hydrometer—A very simple device to measure the specific gravity of liquids.

Hot-break—The time at which the protein trub coagulates during boiling.

International Bitterness Units—One Bitterness Unit is equal to 1 milligram of iso(merized) alpha acid in 1 liter of wort or beer. This is a system of measuring bitterness devised by brewing scientists and is an accepted standard throughout the world. Homebrewers usually do not have the sophisticated equipment to measure actual BUs and often use a system of Homebrew Bitterness Units to closely approximate the desired bitterness in their beer.

Kraeusen—The billowy, rocky, foamy head that develops on the surface of wort during the first days of fermentation.

Kraeusening—A priming process that substitutes unfermented wort for sugar at bottling time.

Lager—From the German word: to store. A style of beer. Traditionally a "bottom-fermented" beer brewed at temperatures of 40–50 degrees F (4–10 C) and stored for a period of time at temperatures as low as 32 degrees F (0 C).

Lagering—The period during which lager beer is aged.

Lager Yeast—*Saccharomyces uvarum* (formerly known as *S. carlsbergensis*) type of yeast. Generally speaking, true lager yeast does best at fermentation temperatures of 33–50 degrees F. It is also known as "bottom-fermenting yeast" because of its tendency not to flocculate, or form a head of yeast on the surface of the brew.

Lambic—A style of Belgian beer that is brewed with wild yeast and beer-souring bacteria.

Lauter-tun—The brewing vessel that is used to separate grains from sweet wort by a straining process.

Lautering—Process of removing spent grains or hops from wort. This is simply done by the utilization of a strainer and a subsequent quick, hot water rinse (sparging) of the caught spent grains and hops.

Liquefication—See Dextrinization.

Malt—See Malted Barley.

Malt Extract—A sugary liquid, syrup or powder that has been derived by mashing malted barley (grain) and dissolving evolved sugars in water. This malt extract can be reduced to a syrup or a dry form by removing water by evaporation.

Malted Barley—Barley that has been partially germinated (sprouted) and then dried. Sugars, soluble starches and starch-converting enzymes are developed during the malting process.

Mashing—The process of converting grain starches to fermentable sugars by carefully sustaining a water and grain "soup" at temperatures ranging from 140–160 degrees F for a period of time.

Pitch(ing)—The "throwing in" or addition of yeast to the wort.

Primary Fermentation—Process of initial fermentation. It is generally considered to be the first 60–75 percent of the fermentation process.

Primary Fermenter (The Primary)—Any vessel in which primary fermentation occurs.

Priming—The process of adding sugar at bottling time. Three-fourths cup of corn sugar to 5 gallons is standard.

Protease (Proteolytic)—Referring to enzymes in malt that degrade proteins.

Rack (Racking)—Process of transferring unfinished homebrew from a primary fermenter to a secondary fermenter. A siphon is always used so yeast sediments remain undisturbed in the primary.

Relax—To ease the mind. Homebrew helps.

Respiration—An aerobic and metabolic cycle which yeast performs prior to its fermentation cycle, during which oxygen is stored for energy and later use.

Secondary Fermentation—Closed fermentation which occurs

after the brew has been transferred from the primary fermenter into a second (or secondary) fermenter, usually a carboy. It is the final 25–40 percent of fermentation which precedes bottling. The later stage of fermentation is much less active. It is desirable to protect the brew with a fermentation lock.

Secondary Fermenter (The Secondary)—Any vessel in which secondary fermentation occurs. It is desirable to use a carboy. Carboys have the advantage of a small opening on the top to which a fermentation lock can easily be secured.

Sparge (Sparging)—See Lautering.

Specific Gravity—A measure of the density of a liquid as compared to water. Readings above 1.000 indicate a density higher than plain water. Adding fermentable sugar to water will increase density. Fermentation will decrease density. Degrees Balling or Degrees Plato are other scales of measuring the density of wort.

Sterile—Impossible condition to achieve. There will always be micro-organisms in your wort. Sanitization is the best situation that can be achieved.

Top-fermenting—See Ale Yeast.

Trub (pronounced: troob)—Proteins that precipitate out of malt wort during boiling with hops. They are removed from wort by professional and sophisticated brewers. Its presence in homebrewing is less significant and should not be worried about.

Worry—Something to be avoided. Homebrew helps in avoiding this.

Wort (pronounced: wert)—Lovingly prepared liquid which will ferment to homebrew.

Yeast—Micro-organisms that convert fermentable sugars to alcohol, CO_2 and various by-products that contribute to the taste of beer. All yeast fermentation is anaerobic. And all yeast types will suspend themselves throughout the fermenting beer.

Zymurgy—The science/art of yeast fermentation. Also, the last word in my dictionary.

Appendix 2
Kegging Your Beer

Yes, you can put your beer in kegs and serve it "on draft." There are many advantages to kegging your beer, the best being that there are no bottles to wash. Kegging beer is an incredibly simple process, but it does require an investment in kegs and tapper systems. The cash you will spend in order to get set up may bother you a bit, but once that expenditure is a memory, you'll wonder why you didn't do it sooner.

The actual process of kegging is simple. Finished beer is siphoned directly into a sanitized keg; then priming sugar is added at a rate of ⅓ cup corn sugar per every 5 gallons. (NOTE: Less priming sugar is required for draft beer. Excessive foaming will result if the normal rate of ¾ cup of corn sugar per 5 gallons is used.) The keg is then sealed and set aside for conditioning for 1–2 weeks.

The beer can be dispensed with tapper systems that are designed for the type of keg used. The first few glasses will contain a small amount of sediment; after that, it's all clear aleing. If a CO_2-dispensing system is used, the beer can be dispensed over a period of weeks or even months (if it lasts that long). CO_2 tapper systems allow you to draw a pint whenever you like because the beer is being displaced with carbon dioxide. The pressure required to dispense beer is only 5 pounds (per square inch). The valves and pressure gauges that come with a CO_2 system are adjustable and will indicate the amount of pressure being used. CO_2 does not adversely react with the beer inside the keg. If a hand pump is used to push out the beer, the beer will be displaced with air (containing oxygen and potential airborne contaminants). The oxygen will oxidize the beer over a short period of time. So, if a hand-pump tapper system is used, invite your friends over and drink it up.

KEGGING SYSTEMS

THE BREWERY KEG

Commercial breweries use half (15½ gallons) or quarter (7¾ gallons) barrels to keg their beer. Most of these types of kegs (and there are many) can be used by a homebrewer to package homebrew. The easiest type to clean is the Golden Gate keg. Empty kegs can usually be borrowed through your local friendly liquor store for the price of the deposit. Hand-pump tapper systems can be borrowed for the price of the deposit. If you want to buy a hand pump or CO_2 tapper system, a local bar supply outlet will cheerfully sell you any system that you desire.

Kegs must be thoroughly cleaned and sanitized. In order to accomplish this, you must remove the wooden (or in some cases, plastic) bung from the keg, empty the remaining contents, clean and sanitize with 2 ounces per 5 gallons of household bleach solution for at least an hour. The solution must then be drained through the keg's internal plumbing. This will sanitize everything that comes in contact with the beer.

Priming sugar is boiled with a small amount of water and added directly to the empty keg. Beer is siphoned directly into the keg with a minimum amount of aeration. The keg is then rebunged with a new bung. You will have to find a source of new bungs. They are often accessible through your local homebrew supply shop or through mail-order outlets advertised in homebrew magazines.

THE CORNELIUS "KEG"

The Cornelius draft system is one of the most versatile systems for the homebrewer. Cornelius "kegs" are actually stainless steel canisters that serve as containers for the soft drink industry. They come in 2½-, 3-, 4- and 5-gallon sizes—perfect for your 5-gallon batch of beer and small enough to fit in a refrigerator. They are very easy to clean and sanitize. Beer can be dispensed as needed with a CO_2 tapper system.

As always, sanitation is important. All the fittings should be

Don't roll out this barrel! Brewery kegs can be used to hold draft homebrew. The sediment will be drawn off with the first pint of brew. A hand pump or CO_2 tapper system can be attached.

Better than soda pop! This draft beer system uses a
canister normally used for soft drinks, is dispensed with
CO_2 pressure and conveniently fits in most refrigerators.
Canisters come in 2½-, 3-, 4- and 5-gallon sizes.

taken apart and sanitized (as well as the inside of the keg itself)
after it is empty. There is only one small, though solvable, problem that I have encountered in using these containers. The gasket that seals the top of the container will sometimes leak unless
a small (5 lbs.) amount of pressure is injected immediately after
the keg is filled. The small amount of pressure will force a seal
and prevent CO_2 from escaping while the beer is conditioning.
The Cornelius draft system is a joy to use.

   The containers and tapping fixtures are available through
some homebrew supply shops, while others will be able to direct
you to sources where you can obtain them. If all else fails, contact
your friendly local soft drink distributor.

OTHER DRAFT SYSTEMS

There are many plastic keg systems that are becoming available to the homebrewer. They are specifically designed for the home-brewer and provide a system that requires a minimum effort in setting up. Drop by your local homebrew supply shop to see what is available.

QUICK DRAFT BEER

Need carbonated draft beer in a hurry and all you have is beer finished, but resting in carboys? Need sediment-free beer for traveling? Here's a way to do it that is so easy you'll wonder why you didn't think of it yourself.

Simply siphon unprimed, clear, finished beer from your fer-menter into your Cornelius or stainless steel keg. Seal it off. Chill to below 40 degrees F (4 C) and apply 25–30 pounds per square inch of CO_2 pressure to the flat, cold beer. Shake it vigorously for 5–10 minutes with live pressure on or let set for 2 days. The carbon dioxide gas will dissolve into the beer and you'll have sediment-free, artificially carbonated draft beer.

POINTS TO REMEMBER

- Prime at a rate of ⅓ cup corn sugar for every 5 gallons of beer.
- A small amount of sediment will be drawn off with the first few glasses of beer–after that, it's clear aleing!
- Sanitize all equipment.
- Only 5 pounds of CO_2 pressure is required to dispense beer and should be applied only after the initial natural pressure is relieved.
- Do not aerate beer as it goes into the keg. Siphon quietly. For added protection, you may wish to ''purge'' (displace) the air with CO_2 from your tapper system. This will elim-inate oxygen from inside the keg and prevent its combi-nation with the beer.
- Kegs should be allowed to condition at temperatures no less than 60 degrees F (16 C) for quick carbonation. If

pure lager yeast cultures are used and you know that the yeast works well at lower temperatures, then kegs can be conditioned at lower temperatures; otherwise keep the keg at room temperature for 1-2 weeks before refrigeration.

* Excessive pressure may inhibit yeast activity during conditioning period.

Appendix 3
Kraeusening Your Beer

NATURAL CARBONATION WITHOUT CORN SUGAR

Kraeusening (besides being difficult to spell) is the process of priming beer with a measured amount of gyle. Gyle is the amount of unfermented wort a brewer uses to prime the finished beer for carbonation purposes. Gyle can be used instead of the simpler homebrewing procedure of adding ¾ cup corn sugar for every 5 gallons of finished beer. It allows the homebrewer to make a brew from 100 percent barley malt, hops, water and yeast.

Kraeusening is a process using natural ingredients and is used by many commercial brewers to naturally condition beer. On any given day, breweries are always brewing and packaging one batch of beer or another. It is convenient for commercial breweries to add a small amount of the new beer to the finished beer. But for the homebrewer, brewing and bottling in the same day is often more time-involving than desirable (it doesn't leave you with as much time to relax and enjoy . . .).

A PRACTICAL METHOD FOR THE HOMEBREWER

Aha! You don't have to brew the same day as you are bottling in order to kraeusen your beer. There is an easier, more convenient way. A homebrewer only has to save a measured amount of unfermented sterile wort and store in a sealed container in the refrigerator. The gyle must be taken from the wort *before* yeast has been added. When it is time to bottle, the stored gyle is added to the finished beer.

331

The big question is: How much wort should be saved as gyle? The sugar content and specific gravity of worts will vary with every batch. Keeping that in mind, I have reduced an involved mathematical equation to a simple formula that anyone can use. This formula will allow you to calculate accurately the amount of gyle to save in order to prime any amount of beer being brewed. There is one assumption that I make: that priming is based on a priming rate of about ¾ cup corn sugar per 5 gallons.

The formula is:

$$\text{Quarts of gyle} = \frac{(12 \times \text{gallons of wort})}{(\text{specific gravity} - 1) \times 1000}$$

For example, for 5 gallons of wort that has a specific gravity of 1.040:

$$\text{Quarts of gyle} = \frac{12 \times 5}{(1.040 - 1) \times 1000}$$

$$\text{Quarts of gyle} = \frac{60}{40}$$

NOTE: The denominator is simply equal to the last 2 digits of the specific gravity.

$$\text{Quarts of gyle} = 1\frac{1}{2}$$

If the Balling scale is used instead of specific gravity, then the formula becomes:

$$\text{Quarts of gyle} = \frac{3 \times \text{gallons of wort}}{\text{degrees Balling}}$$

NOTE: It is emphasized that the gyle must be removed from your batch of wort before yeast is pitched. It is important that it be sealed in a sterile jar and kept cold in the refrigerator.

Appendix 4
Alcohol, Your Beer and Your Body

The purpose of this section is to make you aware of the effect of alcohol on your body, particularly with overindulgence.

Brewer's yeast is one of the richest and most complete sources of the vitamin B complex. Homebrewed beer and ale are not filtered products. They contain live brewer's yeast minutely in suspension and as sediment.

So what else is new?

Well, it just so happens that those of us who have made the switch from commercial to homebrewed beer have come close to unanimously agreeing that, compared to commercial overindulgence, homebrew overindulgence leaves one with a minimal hangover.

There are many reasons. I suspect that one of them is the intake of brewer's yeast and the vitamin B complex that is naturally in homebrew. It is a known fact that alcohol consumption depletes our body of the vitamin B complex (B complex refers to all of the B vitamins). The vitamin B complex is immensely responsible for the metabolism of fats, carbohydrates and protein. In other words, without it we cannot convert the food we eat into usable energy. The energy or fuel our body synthesizes from food is glucose (blood sugar). Ever wonder why you have a hangover headache? It's due in part to the lack of glucose reaching your brain. Ever wonder why you feel shaky or have very low energy? It's due in part to a deficiency of the vitamin B complex which, in turn, decreases the digestion of food and inhibits the orderly functioning of the nervous system. Ever feel dehydrated? That's in part due to the deficiency of vitamin B complex. The B complex helps maintain fluid levels in our bodies.

It seems to me that there is an advantage to drinking homebrew as opposed to commercial beer. It is my hypothesis that the yeast in homebrew helps balance our body's deficiencies and helps in its quest for normalcy.

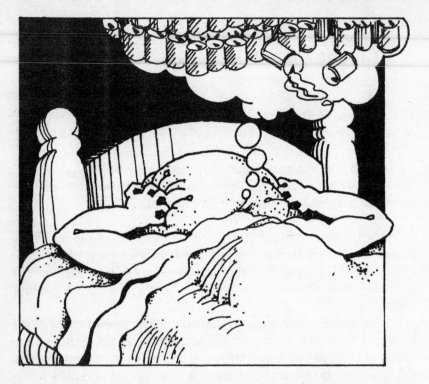

It's quite obvious that the cure for a hangover, no matter how bad, is not the consumption of more homebrew. What follows are a few effective suggestions and the reasoning behind them.

First of all, we need to know that our bodies do not enjoy the presence of a lot of alcohol—our minds may, but our bodies certainly do not! When healthy, we have a built-in chemistry that is exceptionally efficient in the elimination of alcohol. Bless your bottles, otherwise, we'd remain forever inebriated. Our body's metabolic systems burn a considerable amount of energy in the process of elimination and use an inordinate quantity of water. Furthermore, the wastes from this process shellac our feelings.

What follows is a surefire means of helping our bodies rid themselves of alcoholic wastes and replace essential vitamins that have been destroyed.

    1) Before drinking, retiring, or as soon as possible, partake of the vitamin B complex. Two teaspoons of brew-

er's yeast in a glass of juice is the cheapest and most effective way to provide oneself with the B complex. Vitamin B complex pills are simpler and can also be taken.

If you have a notion that doesn't jibe with what I'm saying about vitamin B or it's not convenient at the time, take two aspirin before retiring. This doesn't really help your body, but it will hide some of the pain.

2) Drink at least a pint of water *before* retiring. One of the reasons for feeling lousy is dehydration. After downing several quarts of homebrew, it may not make much sense that you need more liquid, but believe me (!) you need water. Much of this water will be used in the process of waste elimination other than through urination, so don't worry about necessary midnight trips to the potty.

3) In the morning, shower. Your skin pores are clogged with waste by-products from the breakdown of alcohol. It's as though your body were wrapped in dirty plastic wrap. When your skin can breathe, you will feel exceptionally better.

4) Eat breakfast. Settle your stomach. This is especially effective if you've replaced some of those B complex vitamins that you've lost the night before.

So take heed. Vitamin B complex (brewer's yeast or vitamin pills), lots of water, a shower and a light breakfast.

MAGIC?

Yeast produces alcohol. When we consume alcohol it destroys our body's store of the vitamin B complex. The yeast that made the alcohol that depletes the vitamin B complex replenishes the vitamin B complex. Think about that. Isn't this part of the magic that we are all involved in?

Appendix 5
Making Honey Mead

Mead—the mere mention of the word conjures visions of drinking vessels swaying high in the air; it is the nectar of nectars and one of the most natural drinks ever surmised by man.

Predating all other forms of concentrated sugars, honey, diluted to honey water, was in all probability one of the first fermented beverages ever concocted by man. With its fermentation came the alcoholic drink we know as mead.

The ancient Greeks, Romans, Egyptians, Scandinavians and Assyrian people procured this legendary drink as a vehicle for saturnalian revelry unmatched today. The Inca and Aztec Indians also brewed mead and held it in reverence.

Imbued with legendary intoxicating and aphrodisiacal qualities, mead heralded in and out many a fascinating orgy. Tales, stories and lies abound of the joy, happiness and tragedy mead has brought to its imbibers. Presently, most modern-day social gatherings are simply not of the unbounded caliber they once were. As for mead's aphrodisiacal character—well, the earth ro-

336

tates more slowly and perhaps we know a bit too much. . . .
You'll never know until you check it out.

WHAT IS MEAD?

In essence, mead is defined as yeast-fermented honey water.
Now if one should do an imaginative thing such as add fruit to
the honey water, the resulting fermentation is technically called
a melomel. With the addition of grapes, you have a melomel
called pyment. Becoming intrigued? Well, hold on, there's more.
A mead infused with herbs and/or spices is called a metheglin.
Honey and apple juice combine to ferment and make cyser.
Finally, a spiced pyment (melomel) is called hippocras.

Getting back to simple mead and present-day palates, one
is likely to find that haphazardly fermented honey water is not
to one's liking. Traditionally, mead has been and still is a fermented beverage brewed with the ratio of 1 gallon of water to
2½–4 pounds of honey, often resulting in a prolonged fermentation and an intoxicatingly sweet and very enjoyable honey
winelike beverage. As the amount of honey is increased, more
of the sugar content of the mead "wort" will not ferment due
to the fact that higher alcohol levels inhibit yeast fermentation.

If you can find commercially made mead, it's likely to be
sweet, old and stale, smelling like wet cardboard or old garbage.
Rare is the find of freshly made mead in good "health." But,
finding a commercially made mead in your neighborhood store
is improbable. To locate a commercially made "spiced" or "fruit"
mead was impossible up until the early 1990s, when meads began to catch the fancy of some small breweries and brewpubs.
Sometimes you may be fortunate enough to sample some at a
local small brewery. And what a treat it is.

It's another kind of "Relax. Don't worry."

Well, All right!

You say that you can brew beer? Well, then, if you can do
that, you are able to make some excellent mead, metheglin,
pyment, hippocras, cyser, spice, herbed, fruited or whatever
you'd like to call it—EASILY!

BUT FIRST . . .

ABOUT HONEY

Honey is derived from the nectar of flowers, processed and ripened with the aid of enzymes secreted by the honeybee. Because the source of nectar can vary, so does the quality and flavor of the honey. There are hundreds of different kinds, but mostly they are comprised of glucose and fructose sugars with trace amounts of sucrose and maltose. The water content of honey is usually less than 15 percent. The color and flavor are the most significant and recognizable characteristics to the mead maker.

Lighter honeys such as clover, mesquite, orange blossom and alfalfa often are considered to be the best for mead making because of their minimal contribution of strong flavors. This view of "best" may be debatable, because traditional mead was most likely made with whatever honey was available, usually wild and mixed blossoms.

There are many qualities of honey that help it preserve itself. Honey will keep for decades without spoiling.

ABOUT BOILING HONEY

Mead makers often will debate whether or not honey should be boiled before it is fermented. Boiling drives off some of the delicate floral character of the honey. Yes, I'm sure something is lost in the boiling process, but what is gained is a sweet mead "wort" free of wild micro-organisms that may or may not contribute to strange flavors. Also, boiling coagulates protein and aids in the natural clarification of the mead after fermentation.

A good compromise is to boil the honey with some water for only 15 minutes.

FERMENTATION TEMPERATURE

Unlike beer, mead is best fermented above 70 degrees F (21 C) and below 78 degrees F (26 C). Undesirable by-products common with high-temperature beer fermentation are minimal with honey fermentations. Cooler fermentations are not detrimental to mead flavor. It just takes longer to ferment.

NUTRIENTS

Of most importance, one should realize that honey lacks nutrients that are necessary for healthy yeast fermentation. The mead maker often adds nutrients to the ferment to help yeast do its thing more quickly. Without the addition of nutrients, mead still can be made, but the fermentation may take 3 months to a year before completion, rather than less than 3 weeks.

Commercially prepared "yeast nutrients" are available at all home wine- and beermaking supply stores. When added to the mead "wort" before fermentation begins, they will provide some nutrients for the yeast.

An excellent and all-natural source of complete nutrients for yeast is a product derived from yeast itself, called "yeast extract." It is often used as a vitamin supplement in the food industry and as a yeast nutrient in the wine industry. Yeast extract is basically the "guts" of yeast cells. Yeast is cultured specifically for this purpose, and is centrifuged, leaving behind the cell wall "skeletons." What is extracted is high in all of the nutrients that yeasts need for healthy fermentation. Yeast extract is all-natural and not derived from man-made chemical compounds. You are not adding anything to your mead that isn't already there. One-quarter to ½ ounce of yeast extract per 5 gallons of mead will be adequate for healthy and quick fermentation.

Of course, yeast nutrients would have no place in traditionally made mead. Excellent mead can be made without the addition of nutrients of any kind. You just may have to wait a little longer, that's all.

ACIDITY

When making traditional mead, you can add a small quantity of "acid blend" (a combination of 25 percent citric, 30 percent malic and 45 percent tartaric acids) to the ferment to give it a subtle fruity character and lessen the "hotness" of the alcohol flavor. Honey alone lacks acidity. A small amount of acid blend in the traditional mead recipes is included as optional for those who may prefer this character.

STUCK FERMENTATION

It can happen to the most experienced mead maker. Yeast may simply poop out, without warning, in the middle or close to the end of fermentation. Activity stops and specific gravity indicates that surely there is much more sugar to ferment. The causes of stuck fermentation are numerous, but the most common may be lack of nutrients at the onset of fermentation or the inhibition of fermentation by the presence of alcohol.

There is a naturally derived product available to home-brewers and winemakers that has been found to help "unstick" stuck fermentations. Called "yeast hulls," "yeast ghosts" or "yeast skeletons," they are essentially the cell walls left behind during the extraction process discussed earlier in the nutrient section. How they work when added to a stuck fermentation is not fully understood, but it is believed that the cell wall material adsorbs yeast "poisons" produced by yeasts that inhibit fermentation.

Adding yeast hulls in the amount of ¼–½ ounce per 5 gallons along with fresh yeast often will unstick stuck fermentation.

TRADITIONAL MEAD

Making a basic unflavored mead is one of the most challenging and satisfying endeavors for the mead maker. Challenging, because you, your honey, water and yeast are out there all alone, without the support of the fascinating flavors of fruits and spices. Making a clean, smooth and gentle-tasting pure mead is to connect yourself to the roots of all alcoholic beverages. While gazing up at the stars some evening, mead in hand, imagine that this is what it might have been like 8,000 years ago.

Traditional mead is a treasure capturing the essence of

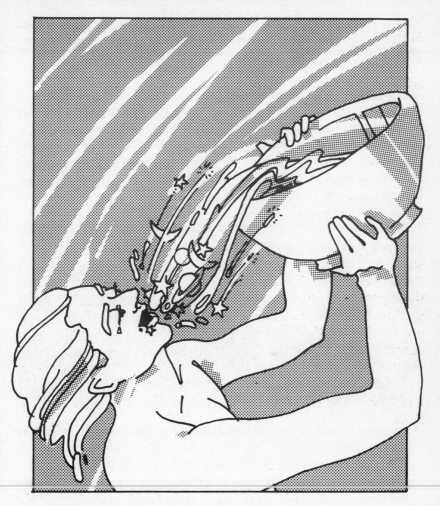

honey and the nectar of blossoms. It can be dry or sweet, but always 12–15 percent alcohol.

I owe a debt of gratitude to Leon and Gay Havill for introducing me to the experience of tasting fresh, pure and traditional mead. They run a small meadery in the south of New Zealand in Rangiora, a small town outside Christchurch, and make mead called Havill's Mazer Mead. The Havills always enjoy visitors should you be traveling in the area. And Havill's Mazer Mead is some of the best I've ever had.

I also owe much gratitude to Lieutenant Colonel Robert Gayre of Gayre and Nigg, a retired gentleman and the world's most knowledgeable person on the history and production of mead. He inspired in me an appreciation of mead's tradition and importance in world history. Lieutenant Colonel Gayre owned and operated a meadery in Cornwall, England, in the 1940s and in 1948 published a book, *Wassail in Mazers of Mead*, now reprinted by Brewers Publications, Boulder, Colorado, under the title *Brewing Mead: Wassail in Mazers of Mead*, with a how-to chapter written by myself. Lieutenant Colonel Gayre now resides at Minard Castle, Argyll, Scotland.

Mead, Honeymoons and Love

Who would have thought that the bees, the moon and the magical brews of man could combine to add to the bliss, luster and memories of weddings?

Mead is a beverage of love. The drinking of mead has been held responsible for fertility and the birth of sons. This is where the tradition of the honeymoon got its start. If mead were consumed for one month (one moon) after a wedding, then in nine months a son would be born and the mead maker congratulated. The custom of drinking mead at weddings and for one month after initiated our present-day custom of the honeymoon.

Interestingly, mead drinking developed quite a reputation for its ability to increase the chances of bearing sons. So much so that a special drinking cup, called the Mazer Cup, was handed down from generation to generation. The couple who drank from the cup would bear sons to carry on the family name and increase the male birth rate, important in the days of constant war.

Fact or folly? Scientists have been doing animal experiments and have found they can increase the chances of bearing males by altering the body's pH. It is known that the acidity or alkalinity of the female body during conception can influence the sex of the newborn. Blood sugar levels do alter pH.

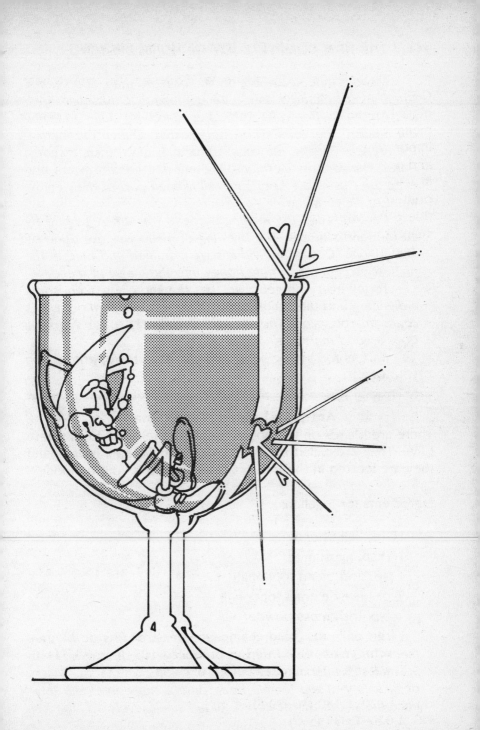

344 THE NEW COMPLETE JOY OF HOME BREWING

Mead is indeed a noble drink. For more than 5,000 years, Virgil, Plato, Plutarch, Zeus, Venus, Jupiter, Odysseus, Circe, the Argonaut, Beowulf, Aphrodite, Bacchus, Odin, Valhalla, the Sanskrit Rig-Veda, Thor, King Arthur, Queen Elizabeth I, the French, Greeks, Mayans, Africans, English, Irish, Swedes, Poles, Hungarians, Germans, present-day homebrewers and even the Australian Aborigines all likened part of their enjoyment of life to mead.

Centuries ago the making of mead was art, regulated by custom and statutes. The brewing of mead was not done by just anyone. Certain individuals were trained and held in the highest esteem for turning honey into the magic of mead.

Today every homebrewer has the know-how to become a dignitary and the maker of mead for those special occasions or for any occasion. The stronger versions keep for years, as does a good marriage.

And as for having sons, you will have to experiment on your own.

Antipodal Mead (Traditional)

There are islands on the opposite side of the world from where I live. They are called the Amsterdam and St. Paul Islands and they are located in the Indian Ocean. Where is your antipode?

Ingredients for 5 gallons:

15 lbs. light honey
1 Tbsp. gypsum
4 tsp. acid blend (optional)
½ oz. yeast extract (optional)
¼ tsp. Irish moss powder
14 gr. or ½ oz. dried champagne yeast or Pris de Mousse wine yeast rehydrated in preboiled 105-degree F (41 C) water for 10 minutes before pitching

O.G.: 1.120–1.130 (30–32.5)
F.G.:1.020–1.035 (5–9)

Add the honey, gypsum, acid blend and Irish moss to 1½ gallons of water and bring to a boil for 15 minutes. Skim the coagulated meringuelike foam off the surface (this is albumin-type protein). Be careful, honey worts will boil over just like beer worts. Leave the lid ajar and monitor the onset of boiling very carefully.

Transfer the hot mead "wort" to a closed fermenter system and cold water. Seal the carboy briefly and shake the contents to aerate the "wort." Glass carboys are ideal for mead fermentation. Rehydrate the yeast and pitch when temperature is below 80 degrees F (27 C). Ferment to completion, then carefully rack into a secondary (carboy) fermenter and let clear. Bottle when mead has cleared. It is ready to drink as soon as it has cleared.

Antipodal Mead may be flavored with fruit or herbs and spices to make melomels, pyments or metheglins. Use fruit in addition to all of the above ingredients but do not boil fruit, rather add it at the end of the boil and steep at pasteurizing temperatures at about 160 degrees F (71 C) for about 20–30 minutes before adding to the fermenter. After 1 week in an open fermenter siphon the fermenting mead off the fruit, which has either settled to the bottom or is floating on the surface. Proceed with closed system during secondary fermentation.

Chief Niwot's Mead

This traditional mead is not quite as sweet as Antipodal Mead. It is also carbonated to give the traditional flavor a bubbly disposition.

Ingredients for 5 gallons:

    13 lbs. light honey
    1 Tbsp. gypsum
    4 tsp. acid blend (optional)
    ⅓ oz. yeast extract (optional)
    ¼ tsp. Irish moss powder
    14 gr. or ½ oz. dried champagne yeast or Pris de Mousse

wine yeast rehydrated in preboiled 105-degree F (41 C) water for 10 minutes before pitching

⅓ c. corn sugar (for bottling)

O.G.: 1.110–1.120 (27.5–30)
F.G.: 1.015–1.025 (4–6)

Add the honey, gypsum, acid blend and Irish moss to 1½ gallons of water and bring to a boil for 15 minutes. Skim the coagulated meringuelike foam off the surface. Be careful, honey worts will boil over just like beer worts. Leave the lid ajar and monitor the onset of boiling very carefully.

Transfer the hot mead "wort" to a closed fermenter system and cold water. Seal the carboy briefly and shake the contents to aerate the "wort." Glass carboys are ideal for mead fermentation. Rehydrate the yeast and pitch when temperature is below 80 degrees F (27 C). Ferment to completion and bottle as you would beer with the addition of corn sugar. It is ready to drink as soon as it has cleared.

Barkshack Gingermead

A twentieth-century legend. Unlike traditional mead, Barkshack Gingermead and its variations are brewed with less honey per gallon, happily resulting in a dry effervescently clear beverage with a 9–12 percent alcoholic sparkle, reminiscent of white champagne, or more accurately like a dry (not sweet) alcoholic "ginger ale." Barkshack (Ginger) Honey Mead will take many brewers and friends by storm. In fact, 99 percent of the people who have tasted Barkshack Gingermead (or variations thereof) have pursued it as if it were a love affair. There are hundreds of brewers today who began their brewing endeavors because of the thrill of Barkshack Gingermead. It is wonderful. It is glorious. It is well worth waiting for. And wait you must.

Barkshack Gingermead is a brew that should be allowed to mature in a secondary fermenter for 1–1½ months before bottling. Then, depending on ingredients, it needs to mature for 3 months to 1 full year in order to reach its full taste potential and to allow immature flavors to disappear. Patience is indeed a virtue that, in this case, is well rewarded.

The recipe and procedures for brewing the basic Barkshack Gingermead are simple and should make sense to even the beginning homebrewer.

Points that are emphasized in the brewing of this recipe or variations are:

1) Honey should be boiled with water.

2) Champagne yeasts should be used for the more alcoholic versions of mead (percent alcohol in excess of 12 percent); otherwise, lager or ale yeast will suffice.

3) Slow primary fermentation is sometimes experienced with mead fermentation. Under no circumstances let the mead remain in an open primary fermenter for more than 7 days. Use a secondary fermenter with a fermentation lock.

4) Pasteurize all fruit that you may use. This can be done by adding fruit to the hot sparged or partially strained "wort." Do not boil the fruit as this may sometimes cause unsettling (pectin) haze.

5) When adding spice or herbs to the mead as flavoring, prepare a strong fresh "tea" and add it at bottling time. Flavors will be cleaner and fresher.

Ingredients for 5 gallons of Barkshack Gingermead:

7 lbs. light honey

1½ lbs. corn sugar

1–6 oz. freshly grated ginger root

1½ tsp. gypsum

1 tsp. citric acid

3 tsp. yeast nutrient (available at homebrew supply stores) OR ¼ oz. yeast extract

¼ tsp. Irish moss powder

1–6 lbs. crushed fruit (sour cherries, blackberries, raspberries [my favorite], blueberries, rhubarb, grapes, grape concentrate, cranberries, chokecherries, etc.)—all optional

3 oz. lemongrass (or other herb or spice flavorings—but go easy on the cloves, cinnamon, mint, hops; lemon or orange peel is also nice)—all optional

1–2 pkgs. champagne yeast

¾ cup corn sugar (for bottling)

O.G.: 1.055–1.060 (14–15)
F.G.: .992–.996 (!)

Hey now, relax, don't worry, have a homebrew.

Boil for 15 minutes 1½ gallons of water, the honey, corn sugar, ginger root, gypsum, citric acid, Irish moss and yeast nutrient. Turn the heat off. If you are going to add fruit, then take a small strainer and fish out as much of the ginger root shavings as you can, but don't worry. Then add your crushed fruit to the pot of hot wort and let it steep for 10–15 minutes.

Pour the entire contents of the "wort" (unsparged if fruit is added) into a plastic open primary fermenter and add about 3 gallons of cold water. When cooled to 70–78 degrees F (21–26 C) pitch the yeast.

After specific gravity has fallen to 1.020 (5) or within 7 days, whichever comes first, rack the brew into a secondary fermenter. If you use fruit, remove fermented fruit with a sanitized strainer, or carefully manipulate siphon hose so that no fruit (or very little) passes to the secondary fermenter.

Age 1–1½ months in the secondary fermenter.

Bottle with ¾ cup corn sugar. If herb, spice or tea flavoring is desired, add a strong strained tea to the finished mead at bottling time. In this manner, you may add the "tea" halfway through the bottling process, enabling you to bottle 2 flavors of mead!

The flavor of mead will change with age. Harsh and sharp flavors will mellow. A tasting after 6 months will give some indication of your results. But a sparkling cold Barkshack Gingermead of 1 year or more—now that's heaven.

Appendix 6
Sour Mash/Extract Beers and Belgian Lambic

Sour mash brewing is an unusual method resulting in beers that have varying degrees of sourness in their character. The sourness is a result of bacterial activity, but the end product is microbiologically stable. What this means for the brewer is that there is a method by which one can achieve any degree of sourness in any type of beer and the stabilizing effect that acidity imparts to the end product.

Why would anyone want to make sour beer? For some, a certain amount of sourness in beer is attractive. For certain beer styles such as Belgian Lambic, other Belgian ales, Berliner Weisse, Weizenbiers and even Guinness Stout, acidity is part of the character. Achieving sourness in beer without the introduction of wild micro-organisms to the fermentation has rarely been considered by the homebrewer. The problem here with homebrew is that we never pasteurize our beer, therefore our wild friends are not controllable and will usually run amok, producing unpredictable results.

My first sour mash beer was tasted in Kentucky in 1989. It offered much inspiration for experimentation and thoughts on how this technique could be applied to homebrewing to approximate some of the wilder and more sour beer styles of the world.

THE PRINCIPLES OF SOUR MASH BREWING

Bacteria that produce sourness and increase acidity of mashes and worts are ever-present on malted barley grain. By introducing crushed malted barley to sweet diluted malt extract or warm

349

mashes, the conditions are optimal for bacterial (especially lactobacillus) activity resulting in the souring of the mash. The degree of sourness can be controlled by temperature and time of activity.

After the souring activity is complete, the sweet and sour extract can be boiled with hops and the brewing process carried through to completion. The bacterial activity has been killed with boiling. The sourness remains, but further activity is stopped.

Cultured lager or ale yeast can be used to produce almost any style of beer with a "twang" of the sour mash. But even more interesting, homebrewers who have access to unique Belgian ale yeasts, such as *Brettanomyces lambicus* or *Brettanomyces bruxellensis*, can come pleasantly close to duplicating many of the characters that make Belgian ales and Lambics so unique.

BASIC PROCEDURES FOR PRODUCING SOUR EXTRACT FROM MASH OR MALT EXTRACT SYRUPS OR POWDERS

For 5 gallons—extract method:

5–6 lbs malt extract
½ lb. crushed pale malted barley

Dissolve the malt extract in 1½ gallons of hot water and stabilize the temperature at about 130 degrees F (54 C). Pour this hot, sweet malt extract into an odorless, sanitized, food-grade, 5-gallon bucket. Add the crushed malted barley. Stir to mix. Place a sheet of aluminum foil in contact with the surface of the liquid to form a complete barrier from the air. Fit lid snugly on the pail. Insulate the pail on all sides with a sleeping bag and/ or blankets to help maintain warm temperatures and promote lactic bacterial activity and souring. The lactobacillus will sour the extract very dramatically and will be noticeable after about 15 hours. Fifteen to 24 hours should be adequate for your first experiment with this process.

When you open the container, you may notice some mold growing on the surface. Don't worry. Skim off and discard the mold. The aluminum foil helped minimize this in the first place. You will definitely notice the absolutely abominable, putrid odor the bacteria has caused. Don't worry. It's supposed to smell awful. Almost awful enough to throw out. *But don't!*

Strain and transfer your sour extract to your brewpot, add any specialty grains and bring the sweet wort to a boil. Remove grains with a strainer and then add hops according to whatever recipe you are following. Most of the foul-smelling aroma will be driven off during boiling. Taste the wort. It will be sour, but fermentation and dilution with more water will lessen the sourness.

For 5 gallons—basic mash method:

> 6–8 lbs. pale malted barley
> specialty malts of your choice

Using an infusion, step-infusion or decoction method, mash all but ½ lb. of the pale malted barley. Transfer the full mash into an odorless, sanitized, food-grade, 5-gallon bucket. Let the mash cool to 130–135 degrees F (54–57 C) and add the ½ pound of crushed malted barley. My experimentation has taught me that mash temperatures, while not completely killing all lactobacillus, will kill enough to prevent a good start on the souring process, therefore cooling to 130–135 degrees F (54–57 C) is recommended.

Stir to mix. Place a sheet of aluminum foil in contact with the surface to form a complete barrier from the air. Fit lid snugly on the pail. Insulate the pail on all sides with a sleeping bag and/or blankets to help maintain warm temperatures and promote lactic bacterial activity and souring. The lactobacillus will sour the mash and will be noticeable after about 15 hours. Fifteen to 24 hours should be adequate for your first experiment with this process. More time will produce more sourness.

After the souring process, open the container (hold your nose), remove the aluminum foil and skim the scum from the surface and discard. Transfer the sour mash to a lauter-tun, drain and sparge with 180-degree F (82 C) water. Proceed as you would with an all-grain batch of beer, adding hops as called for in your recipe.

Vicarious Gueuze Lambic

Vicarious Gueuze Lambic achieves its sourness from bacterial contamination of diluted malt extract syrup or powder. Then ale yeast is added to the finished sour wort before or along with the specially cultured yeast strains of *Brettanomyces bruxellensis* and *Brettanomyces lambicus*. (These strains are difficult to handle and culture because they will kill themselves with the acidity they produce. They can be cultured on special mediums that neutralize their acidity—for a while). Fermentation by-product aromas and flavors will resemble the pungency of a Belgian Lambic.

Try a commercially available imported Gueuze from Belgium or go there yourself and try this style before you brew it. It is not a style for every beer enthusiast, but for those who are hooked, it is liquid gold.

Ingredients for 5 gallons:

6 lbs. light malt extract syrup
½ lb. crushed pale malted barley
½ lb. crystal malt
½ oz. stale old hops: 1–2 HBU
1–2 pkgs. ale yeast
Brettanomyces bruxellensis yeast culture
Brettanomyces lambicus yeast culture
¾ c. corn sugar (for bottling)

O.G.: 1.042–1.046 (10.5–11.5)
F.G.: 1.006–1.012 (1.5–3)

Add the crystal malt to 1½ gallons of water and bring to a boil. Immediately remove the crystal malt from the boiling liquid. Turn off heat and add malt extract. Dissolve and stabilize temperature between 120–130 degrees F (49–54 C). Gently pour this warm extract into a 5- or 4-gallon-size, food-grade, odor-free plastic pail fitted with a lid. Sour as described on page 350.

After you have soured your sweet wort, add the hops and boil for 1 hour. Sparge and transfer to your fermenter and cold water. Add ale yeast when temperature is below 75 degrees F (24 C). When primary fermentation is finished, add *B. lambicus* and *B. bruxellensis* yeasts. For a much more intensely sour beer you can add the *B. lambicus* and *B. bruxellensis* yeasts with the ale yeast.

With the yeast strains of Belgian origins you will notice that the surface of your fermentation will be covered with a white fuzzy skin. This is normal and a consequence of these wild yeasts. Belgian Lambics are traditionally aged for over a year before bottling. Don't worry, and go along the way your beer wishes to take you. Bottle when fermentation is complete and the mood strikes you as right. The intense acidity of some of these brews will mellow with age, somewhat.

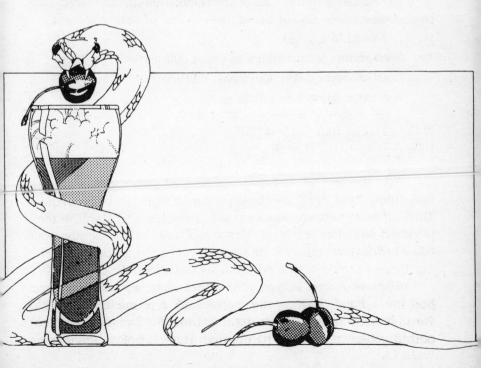

Loysenian Cherry Kriek

Belgian Kriek Lambic is a style of Lambic infused with strongly flavored and colored Belgian cherries during aging, which causes a secondary fermentation. The sourness of the sour mash/extract process produces sharp acidity. The lambicus and bruxellensis yeasts produce fruity, pungent and acidic aromatics and make some contribution to flavor. The cherries offer a ripe, refreshing fruitiness. All climax together, bringing the homebrewer closer to the real thing.

Ingredients for 5 gallons:

6 lbs. light malt extract syrup
½ lb. crushed pale malted barley
½ lb. crystal malt
½ oz. stale old hops: 1–2 HBU
10–12 lbs. sour cherries (if chokecherries can be found, substitute 3–4 lbs. of these for 3–4 lbs. of sour cherries)
1–2 pkgs. ale yeast
Brettanomyces bruxellensis yeast culture
Brettanomyces lambicus yeast culture
¾ c. corn sugar (for bottling)

O.G.: 1.042–1.046 (10.5–11.5)
F.G.: 1.006–1.012 (1.5–3)

Add the crystal malt to 1½ gallons of water and bring to a boil. Immediately remove the crystal malt from the boiling liquid. Turn off heat and add malt extract. Dissolve and stabilize temperature between 120–130 degrees F (49–54 C). Gently pour this warm extract into a 5- or 4-gallon-size, food-grade, odor-free plastic pail sealed with a lid. Sour as described on page 350.

After you have soured your sweet wort, add the hops and boil for 1 hour. Sparge and transfer to a fermenter and cold water to yield *only 4 gallons total volume.* Add ale and lambicus and bruxellensis yeasts when temperature is below 75 degrees F (24 C).

After 1–2 weeks, whenever vigorous primary fermentation has slowed down, siphon the 4 gallons of fermenting brew to a 6½-gallon glass carboy fermenter. Meanwhile, add the crushed cherries to 1 gallon of water and heat to 160 degrees F (71 C). Hold for 30 minutes to pasteurize the fruit. Immerse the covered brewpot (with cherries) in a cold water bath and cool to 70 degrees F (21 C). Then add fruit to secondary fermenter and encourage secondary fermentation for 1 month.

After 1 month siphon the beer to a third fermenter, leaving behind spent cherries, pits and yeast sediment. Bottle when fermentation is complete and the mood strikes you as right. Age well before serving.

Raspberries, peaches, blueberries and other fruits can be substituted for cherries.

I would like to have the men of Heaven
In my own house;
With vats of good cheer
Laid out for them.

I would like to have the three Marys
Their fame is so great.
I would like people
From every corner of Heaven.

I would like them to be cheerful
In their drinking.
I would like to have Jesus, too
Here amongst them.

I would like a great lake of beer
For the King of Kings.
I would like to be watching Heaven's family
Drinking it through all eternity.

—Gaelic poet   anon.

Appendix 7
Growing Your Own Hops

Hops can be grown with relative ease anywhere between the 40th and 50th parallels, both north and south of the equator. They have been grown with varying degrees of success in every state of the United States and probably will do well in your area with a reasonable amount of attention.

ESSENTIALS OF HOP GROWING

Hop plants will need plenty of sunshine and something to climb, as their vinelike growth will reach lengths of 20–35 feet in 4 months. It is not uncommon for well-tended plants to grow 1–2 feet in one day during the peak of the growing season.

Following harvest in August, the vines will completely die off and new shoots will rise the following spring from the ever-expanding root system.

SOIL

The soil in which hops are grown needs to be loamy, free of weeds, well drained, and fertilized with potash, phosphates and nitrogen. Manure compost and/or commercial fertilizer may be used for this purpose. During the growing season, the soil needs to be constantly moist for best results. It is important that the soil not be hard or claylike, as moisture will evaporate more readily from hard-packed soil.

Hops, relaxing in the sun.

PROPAGATION

Most hops in the United States are not propagated by seed but are cultivated from root cuttings. There are many varieties but only a few are commercially available. Grow what you can get, but it is desirable to obtain root cuttings 8–12 inches long from the female type of whatever variety you find. In the United States, females almost exclusively are cultivated without male plants; hence, the lack of viable seeds. On the other hand, wild hops, common in many mountain and rural areas, may be either male or female. Hops from these plants make a brew of variable quality. I have tried beer brewed with wild hops, some of which were poor and some of which were excellent. The bouquet that the hops exude gives you some indication of whether you want to brew with them. Experiment with small batches if in doubt and proceed from there.

I was fortunate to come across some female Cascade root stock from the Yakima Valley in Washington State. In their second year, there was a considerable mass of roots from which I dug, cut and further propagated. But it is best to wait until the third year before removing portions of the root and not risk diminishing the yield.

Hop roots are commercially available through many seed and nursery catalogs or sometimes through your local homebrew supply shop during the months of February and March only.

PLANTING AND CARE

Lay the roots 6 inches beneath the ground and at intervals of 2–3 feet. This should be done in early March or April along with your peas, radishes and other very early spring crops.

Wooden stakes need to be well driven into the ground close to the root. This should be done before any growth begins. Heavy string or cord should be tied to the stake and led to trellises, poles, fences, or your own unique network of macrame. Remember that hops grow extensively and need something on which to climb.

When the growing season begins, many shoots will present themselves. All but the strongest 2 or 3 should be thinned out. These shoots will quickly grow to 4–5-foot lengths in a matter of weeks. When they reach 2–3 feet it will be necessary to "train" the hops onto the string. Wind them clockwise around the cord that leads from the stake. Be sure it is clockwise so it will follow the sun across its southeast-to-southwest path (in the southern hemisphere train the hops counterclockwise).

As the hops race up the vine keep the soil moist at all times. Irrigation is best because the excessive wetting of leaves may promote mildew in some varieties. Continue to thin out new shoots as they appear.

PESTS AND PROBLEMS

At midseason in especially damp climates, leaves are removed from the ground level to the 5-foot level. This prevents the upward spread of leaf wilt, which can completely defoliate a hop vine.

Fungus and mildew are problems that may also arise if climatic conditions are favorable and precaution is not taken.

Aphids are pests that are attracted to hops. They can be controlled with lady bugs, nicotine, pyrethrum or other nonpersistent insecticides. Use caution when choosing insecticides even though the harvestable hop flowers do not begin to present themselves until late July and early August.

HARVEST

The green conelike hop flower is harvested toward the middle of August and into September, depending on the growing season. They should be harvested just before they begin to turn brown. Their ripeness is evident when flowers begin to fluff and an abundance of a fine, yellow, resinous powder called lupulin is present at the base of the flower petal. Ripe hops emit a pungent aroma when crushed between the fingers.

The lupulin is actually thousands of tiny sacks of fragrant, bitter oil. Exercise gentle care in harvesting and drying to preserve the best qualities of the hop. Hops should be air-dried until crisp. Sun drying is too harsh and is not recommended.

After drying it is important that the hops be stored in airtight bags and kept at freezing or near-freezing temperatures. Hops eventually will spoil when the bitter oils and resins are exposed to heat and oxygen.

With the first frost, the vines will die and can be removed to the ground.

You will find that with proper care, every year will produce an astounding amount of root crop for your fellow brewers. A more abundant crop will ensue with every harvest.

Appendix 8
Troubleshooting—Problem Solving and Bad Beer

- *This may be the most important section of this book for the homebrewer who continues to make beer. It isn't long, but the hints, tips, observations and advice given here can make the difference between perfect beer and disappointment. Read this after you've made your first 3 or 4 batches. You won't regret it.*

It's easy to blame bad beer on products, recipes and the personality of your Aunty Minna—but to try to find a reason and a workable solution to your problem may become one frustration after another. To begin with, don't worry. Worrying is likely to spoil the taste of beer more than anything else you've done wrong. It certainly isn't a solution. My first recommendation is to become concerned. My second suggestion is to try to understand why your beer tastes or appears the way it does and third, don't avoid the problem—do something about it. Your tiny efforts will surely pay off with a vast improvement in your beer.

I'd like to assume that, if you have been using the procedures in this book, this appendix is unnecessary, but maybe, just maybe, I better not assume anything . . . so just in case, here is a list of the most common problems that homebrewers have:

- cidery flavors
- sour flavors
- moldy beer
- cloudy or murky beer
- flat beer
- overcarbonated beer
- strange aftertastes
- apparent prematurely stuck fermentation
- poor or no foam retention

Let's address each of these problems and consider what may cause them.

Cidery flavors—Whether you mash or use malt extracts, cidery flavors are avoidable. Anyone who tells you differently has not addressed this problem appropriately. To my knowledge there are no known 100 percent malt extracts that should be faulted for cidery beers. The number-one reason why homebrewers may brew a cidery-flavored beer is that an excessive amount of corn sugar and especially cane (or beet) sugar is used. A homebrew kit that instructs the homebrewer to add sugar in the amount equaling 50 percent of the fermentable sugar is one to be wary of. Some kits are well designed so that the combination of specialty malts and yeast provided will not produce a cidery flavor. But in general, if you have problems with cidery-flavored beer, substitute the sugar called for in the recipe with malt extract. Read the list of ingredients on the package. If there is no malt extract, start wondering, because there should be.

By all means, if you have problems, avoid cane sugar. That "Prohibition" flavor is the result of corn sugar or cane sugar—not the result of malt extract. I won't even let you blame "cheap supermarket malt" because I have brewed with it and made an excellent beer.

Sour flavors—Don't blame the products. Face up to the fact that your procedures are not sanitary enough. Bacterial infection often enhanced by warm brewery temperatures and sluggish fermentations is to blame for sour beer. More on combating infections later. You might note that it is possible to brew beer that won't sour even in hot climates as long as bacterial infection hasn't taken hold.

Moldy beer—"Egad! There's something growing in my beer!" Because of beer's acidity and alcohol content, there are no known pathogens that can survive in beer; therefore, you aren't going to die. There are all kinds of molds that can contaminate your beer because of lax sanitation procedures. Sometimes infections do not perceptibly alter the flavor of your beer; other times they can be devastating. Your taste buds will tell you. Moldy beer is the result of inadequate cleaning of equipment and undue exposure to micro-organisms. Mold also is more likely to develop with inappropriate lagering (aging) at temperatures above 60 degrees F (16 C).

Cloudy beer—Perhaps your brew never did clear or perhaps it was clear when it went into the bottle, but then—whammo!—3 weeks later a permanent haze developed. The problem is, again, another kind of bacterial infection. It isn't the fault of the malt or the sugars, and unless you are using very old or contaminated yeast, it isn't the yeast's fault either.

Flat beer—You've done everything right. Followed instructions just like you've always done. One week, 2 weeks, 1 month . . . flat beer! I don't know of a reason unless you've left an excessive amount of sterilant in your bottles or you are storing your beer at excessively cool temperatures. If so, try storing the bottles at room temperature. If that doesn't work, uncap the beer and drop in a few grains of new dried beer yeast and recap. If that doesn't work, open the bottles again and add ¼ tsp. corn sugar to each 12-ounce bottle. If that fails, your final resort is to blend your flat beer with carbonated beer just before serving. It works every time.

Overcarbonated beer—The simple explanation is that you've added too much priming sugar. An adequate amount is ½–¾ cup of corn sugar to 5 gallons. When kegging your beer for draft, ⅓–½ cup corn sugar per 5 gallons is adequate. Sometimes, though, a seasoned homebrewer will experience a batch of aged homebrew that suddenly kicks into a mysteriously late fermentation in the bottle. This is usually the result of a bacterial infection that either ferments or allows the yeast to ferment otherwise unfermentable components in the finished beer. Almost all gushers are a result of bacterial contaminated beer. Again, keep it clean.

Strange aftertastes—If you've got 'em, either leave those baby diapers out of the brew or keep the risk of bacterial infections to a minimum.

Apparent prematurely stuck fermentation—More often than not you're worrying. Many malt extracts are designed and produced to have a dextrin (unfermentable) content. This gives body to the beer. Some very fine all-malt extract beers will begin a fermentation at 1.038 and finish as high as 1.013. Other high-gravity recipes will begin at 1.055 and be ready to bottle at 1.028. Aeration of the wort and choice of yeasts will make some difference, but usually minimal. Roll with the punches and bottle when fermentation has stopped or is negligible.

Poor or no foam retention—More often than not poor head retention is the result of a dirty glass, with residual grease, wax, soap or detergent left unrinsed. Wash your glassware with hot soapy water, but rinse well with lots of hot water. Households with hard water will have a more difficult time rinsing residuals from glassware. Sanitize your bottles and fermenters with bleach and cold water soaks and rinse well with hot water.

When you are sure the problem isn't your glassware, one likely solution is to take a look at your recipe and recall how fresh your hops were. Old and stale hops will detract from the head retention. Good-quality, fresh hops will definitely enhance head retention, especially with flavor and aroma hopping. Use the best hops, and freshest hops, in all your recipes. Hop oils enhance head retention.

BACTERIAL INFECTIONS

What are they? What do they look like? How do they taste? Where do they come from and what kinds of situations do they like?

Bacteria are micro-organisms that can be beneficial (and necessary) to many types of food processes (e.g., yogurt, pickles, soy sauce, sauerkraut, etc.). In the case of beer and homebrewing there are a few types that are more troublesome. That's because they are common and they will "pickle" your beer in 24 hours, if given the opportunity.

Lactobacillus is probably the most common bacteria encountered by homebrewers. It sours beer by producing lactic acid. Pediococcus is another very common bacteria that loves wort and produces nasty flavors and aromas. Acetobacter is a less common problem with beermaking, but it is responsible for making vinegar out of your beer by producing acetic acid. Bacteria will form hazes, promote gushing, form molds, alter flavors and produce strange, bizarre and undesirable aftertastes.

One of the best and simplest ways to recognize whether or not your beer is contaminated with bacteria is to take a look at your bottles of beer. Look at the surface of the beer where it contacts the sides of the bottle. Is there a deposit ringing the neck? Every gusher, hazy beer, sour-smelling and sour-tasting beer I've had the pleasure of judging invariably has a "ring around the neck"—a sure sign that there is bacterial or wild yeast contamination. Sometimes a bottle will have two or three ring deposits, all from different fill levels of different batches of beer; the contamination is perpetuated in the bottles until they are properly cleaned and sanitized. And if the bottles aren't properly sanitized then it is likely your siphon hoses and fermenters aren't either. Don't despair. It is no big deal to do it right.

The sources of bacterial infections in homebrew are usually easy to track down because bacteria are everywhere. Hands, countertops, porous surfaces, scratched surfaces, grain and grain dust (don't grind your grain in the brewhouse!). So if you have problems, it is likely that something not sterile came in contact with the unfermented wort.

Bacteria love malt. As a matter of fact they probably prefer your wort over anything else in your home. Research labs at hospitals use malt extract and gelatin as a culture medium for bacteriological studies. And bacteria love warm temperatures. You are asking for problems if you don't take care when brewing a batch of unprotected beer in the heat of the summer. Protect it and you'll be fine.

SOLVING THE PROBLEM

Here are a few simple, effective tips that will ensure excellent beer.

- Inspect your bottles for stains and bacterial deposits in the neck. Soak bottles and fermenters overnight in a solution made of 2 ounces of household (chlorine) bleach to 5 gallons of cold water. This will remove all stains and kill the bacterial infection. Forget the proprietary special sanitizing formulas you may find in the store. Use common household (chlorine) bleach to assure a thorough job. Rinse well with hot tap water.

- Siphon hoses should never appear stained or discolored. Sanitize them in a bleach-and-water solution. If the stains cannot be removed, retire the hose from beer siphoning purposes.
- Maintain sanitation throughout the brewing process, especially when wort temperature falls below 160 degrees F (71 C).
- Scratched surfaces on plastic brewing equipment harbor bacteria. Discard worn, stained and scratched primary fermenters and siphon hoses.
- Do not immerse anything in the cooled wort. Wooden spoons or hands can be a disaster.
- Do not suck on siphon hoses; rather fill the hose with water in order to begin siphoning. If you're a traditionalist, then gargle with brandy before sucking.
- Clean secondary fermenters immediately after each use.
- Remove stains with a bottle brush and with an overnight bleach-and-water solution.
- Use a fermentation lock correctly; keep it filled with 1 inch of water.
- Avoid undue lagering at temperatures above 60 degrees F (16 C). Two to 4 weeks is usually adequate for secondary fermentation at room temperature.
- Rinse bottles after each use—immediately.
- Boil priming sugar with water.
- Boil bottlecaps.
- Cool your wort and pitch yeast as soon as possible.
- Aerate your cooled wort in order to enhance fermentation.
- Siphon quietly. DO NOT AERATE OR SPLASH YOUR BEER ONCE FERMENTATION HAS BEGUN.
- Do not add ice to your wort in order to cool it.
- Avoid using low-grade plastic ("cubitainers") for secondary fermentations. They are difficult to sanitize and oxygen will pass through the plastic into the beer.

SOME FINAL COMMENTS

If you are brewing great beer already, you're doing fine. I've found that most beginners do not have drastic infection problems because malt-loving bacteria have had no reason to "hangout." But eventually sloppiness will catch up with you. The preceding outline of problems and solutions is presented especially for those who have experienced frustration in brewing good beer and for new brewers to use as a future resource. Remember, it's easy to make good beer.

An excellent resource for further reading on this subject is the 1987 Special Troubleshooting Issue of *Zymurgy* magazine, available from the American Homebrewers' Association, P.O. Box 1679, Boulder, CO 80306, USA.

Appendix 9
Beer Appreciation:
Tasting Beer—Perceiving Flavor

If the only kind of beer you've ever tasted has been light American pilsener, you haven't had much experience. However, as a homebrewer or as a beer drinker in pursuit of a variety of beers, you have undoubtedly tasted an overwhelming complexity of beer flavors.

There are different reasons why individuals drink beer. The most significant reason is enjoyment. Our perception of enjoyment will vary with the mood we are in, the food we are eating and the environment in which we drink. The beer that we remember enjoying on a hot summer day at the ballpark may not be as pleasing as an after-dinner beer. Likewise, that sweet stout that so wonderfully complements the finish of a meal or that warmingly full-bodied doppelbock just may not make it after a long drive home from work (or maybe it does?).

The more you know about beer, the more you will appreciate beer flavors and discover what it is you prefer; choosing the right kind of beer for that special mood and situation lends more enjoyment to your life.

It is not really justifiable for anyone to say, "I don't like beer." There are so many different kinds of beer that surely there must be a style of beer for everyone. I do allow someone to say, "I don't like *this* beer" or "I don't like to drink beer," but to generalize and say, "I don't like beer" is like saying "I don't like food."

Through experience and our perception of flavor we discover what we enjoy in a beer (no one, NO ONE, can tell you what you like, even though they may try). By summarizing all the things that we experience when we taste beer, we can form an opinion of the beer's overall enjoyability.

As already suggested, enjoyability is influenced by many things, one of which is the perception of flavor. Beer flavor is a complex science for some. For our purposes of enjoyment, the complexity and perception of beer flavor can be simplified so that you may cultivate your own appreciation of beer. What follows is an outline that will assist in determining the character and flavor of any beer.

BEER FLAVOR PROFILE

There are four major categories that you should consider when fully appreciating the taste of beer.

1) Appearance
2) Aroma/Bouquet
3) Taste
4) Overall impression

In this section we are not judging beer; therefore, numerical values have not been assigned. The purpose here is to help you more fully appreciate the flavor of beer.

1) Appearance

A. *Head retention and appearance*—A certain amount of head retention is desirable in most beers but is largely a matter of preference. Generally speaking, no head or an excessive amount of head (that interferes with drinking) are equally undesirable.

Head retention is influenced by the ingredients used in brewing. Generally, the more dextrinous the beer the better the head retention. All barley malt beers and those that use a lot of hops and the freshest of hops tend to have creamier heads.

Head retention suffers greatly in the presence of oils and waxes or when beer is served in a dirty glass.

B. *Clarity*—Some beers are not meant to be clear. More often than not, the clarity has little effect on the flavor of the beer. Beer that is normally clear at room temperature may develop a haze due to protein in the beer. This haze, called a chill haze, has very little influence on flavor. However, some hazes that may develop in beer are due to bacterial or wild yeast contamination and will not go away at room temperature. If bottle-conditioned beer is being considered for its clarity, a careful pouring is important so that the natural yeast sediment is not disturbed.

2. Aroma/Bouquet

The careful perception of aroma and bouquet of beer must be made within the first three or four sniffs; after that perception is dulled and not as acute, even though the aromatic presence may still be there.

A. *Aroma*—The aroma of beer can be defined as the smell of beer relative to the malt, grain and fermentation by-products. Malt contributes directly to many aromatics that we can perceive. The most common aromas are those of malty sweetness, caramel, toffee, roasted, toasted or chocolate. Malt contributes indirectly to many other aromas that are the result of fermentation. The most significant and noticeable aromas are those contributed by esters. Esters may give beer a fruity aroma reminiscent of apples, raspberries, strawberries, bananas, pears, grapefruit and others. Esters are often desirable to some degree and are particularly noticeable in ales and stronger beers. Butterscotch (from diacetyl) aromas are also a by-product of yeast metabolism and can be detectable in many beers.

B. *Bouquet*—The bouquet of beer can be defined as the aromatics that hops contribute to beer. The bouquet of beer will vary to a great degree. When it is present it can be described as flowery, spicy, pungent, etc.

C. *Odors*—Odors may be attributed to defects in the beer. Defective beer can be the result of mishandling (extreme temperature changes or agitation), bacterial contamination, oxidation or being "light-struck." Some of the more common odors associated with defective beers can be described as acidic, skunky (light-struck), garbagy, wet cardboard, winey and sherrylike.

3. Taste

The actual flavor of beer is quite complex. Everyone has his or her own way of describing flavors and their importance in the overall perception. I will explain some things about the perception of flavor, things that are known and not arguable. Then I will present an outline that can serve as a means of helping you summarize the taste of beer.

Your tongue perceives four different tastes. They are the perceptions of *bitter*, *sour*, *salt* and *sweet*.

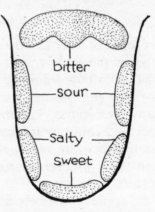

Bitterness is perceived on the back of the tongue. Sourness is perceived on the sides of the tongue. Sweetness is perceived on the tip of the tongue and saltiness is perceived just to the rear and on either side of the tip of the tongue.

When tasting, the beer should be moved to all parts of the tongue in order to experience maximum flavor. The tongue sends all of its messages to the brain and it is there that we combine the taste experiences into an overall flavor.

Beer contributes a variety of taste sensations to the tongue. The degree to which the four main sensations contribute to the flavor of beer is influenced by different ingredients and by-products of fermentation. The following outline summarizes how beer can affect the sensations of taste:

Bitterness—The degree of bitterness can be influenced by:

Hops—The most assertive influence on bitterness in beer. A dry bitterness.

Tannins—Tannins from husks and grains can contribute an astringent bitterness to beer.

Malt—Roasted malts can contribute to bitterness.

Minerals—Mineral salts can influence the extraction of bitterness from hops and malt, influencing flavor.

Sweetness—The degree of sweetness can be influenced by:

Malt—Malt has the most influence on the perception of sweetness. It can contribute unfermented sugars and unfermentable dextrins. The dextrins give beer a fuller body that can help perception of sweetness.

Hops—The flowery and floral nature of hops can sometimes be interpreted as a sweetness.

Esters—Esters are by-products of fermentation, are fruity in nature and can lend to the perception of sweetness.

Diacetyl—Diacetyl, a by-product of fermentation, is butterscotch flavored in nature and can lend to the perception of sweetness.

Sourness—The degree of sourness is proportional to the acidity of the beer and can be influenced by:

Carbonation—Carbon dioxide when dissolved in beer takes the form of carbonic acid. An excessive amount of carbonation will contribute an acidic flavor to the beer.

Contamination—Bacterial and wild yeasts can produce acids such as acetic acid (vinegar) and lactic acid.

Saltiness—The degree of saltiness is influenced by:

Minerals—An excessive amount of certain minerals can contribute to a salt flavor in beer. Calcium, magnesium and sodium are usually the culprits in the case of beer.

SUMMARIZING YOUR IMPRESSIONS

Distilling your impressions into a meaningful summary can become an involved and attentive process. What follows is a useful simplification that does not detract from the essential enjoyment that you should be experiencing.

Taste

A. Bitter/Sweet—Malt/Hop/Fermentation BALANCE

Generally speaking, most beers are made in a way so that fuller-bodied and sweeter beers are balanced with more bitterness. Likewise, a light-bodied delicate beer will not be as highly hopped (bitterness). A light-bodied beer that is excessively bitter is not in balance. A full-bodied sweeter beer that lacks hop bitterness (except in the special case of sweet stouts and the like) is usually not in balance.

B. Mouth-feel

This taste sensation describes how the beer feels (literally) in your mouth. It can be described as being full-bodied or light-bodied. A particular style of beer will determine the appropriate fullness or lightness of body. The unfermented sugars and dextrins contribute to the degree of fullness. A diet light beer would be classified as light-bodied. An Irish stout would be classified as full-bodied.

C. Aftertaste

This sensation is experienced after the beer has been swallowed. (Beer drinkers don't spit it out!) Sometimes an otherwise good-tasting beer will leave an unpleasant aftertaste (bitter, sweet, sour, astringent, fuzzy). The aftertaste of a good beer should be clean and not cloying. It should by all means encourage you to have another.

D. Carbonation

The tactile feel of bubbles in the mouth perceptibly determines the degree of carbonation. The feel of the bubbles can also vary with the ingredient used. A big and explosive bubble feeling in the mouth is due to the use of fermentable ingredients other than barley malt. A beer made with all barley malt will tend to have a smaller (almost a creamy sensation) bubble feeling in the mouth. This phenomenon can be explained in terms of physics, surface tension and bubbles, but need not be gone into here.

Over- or under-carbonation can also influence flavor. A highly carbonated beer will tend to be more acidic. As it goes flat, so does the flavor.

E. Overall Impression—Drinkability

This is the final "category" that you might consider when determining how you appreciate this beer. It is the most personal and subjective of the categories, but if you are taking notes it is probably the most important to consider.

The best way to use this category of perception is to determine whether or not you really enjoy the beer for what it is meant to be. Even if you don't particularly like a stout or a diet lite pilsener, you can still appreciate it for what it is meant to be for others. Keep this in mind.

MAXIMIZING YOUR PERCEPTION OF BEER FLAVOR

The following hints will help in perceiving the most flavor from your tastings.

- When tasting a variety of beers, begin with the lighter styles and finish with the darker, more full-bodied beers.
- Don't smoke or be in a smoke-filled room when you are tasting.

- Do not partake of salty or greasy food (greasy lips will devastate head retention) while tasting.
- Eat french bread or saltless crackers in order to cleanse the palate between beers.
- Do not wear lipstick or Chap Stick (the waxes will destroy head retention).
- Use clean, spotless glassware that has been thoroughly rinsed of soap or detergent residues.
- Relax. Don't worry. Have a homebrew.

YOU, THE CONNOISSEUR

With a little knowledge of beer styles and the use of meaningful guidelines for tasting you will be surprised at how much more you will come to enjoy beer.

Beer quality can be surprisingly determined and agreed upon by many; whether or not you prefer or like a particular beer will depend on the circumstances that you are in or just plain unexplainable preference.

Beer is what you personally perceive it to be. Use all your senses. Look at it, smell it, taste it, feel it and, above all, listen to it.

Listen to your beer! Listening to your beer can help you not worry and relax. When you've heard all there is to hear, well then . . . Have a homebrew!

Appendix 10
Judging Beer

Judging beer is the process of assigning a numerical value to the variable qualities of beer. There are a number of reasons why one would desire to go through a process of judging beer. Three of them are:

1) Judging beer to help the brewer improve the quality of beer being brewed.
2) Judging beer to determine a winner in a competition.
3) Judging beer just for fun.

Your reason for judging beer may determine the degree of sophistication used in judging. For the purpose of amateur brewers, two scoring systems are presented. The 50-point scale is useful for focusing in on the finer points of beer character. It is also useful for determining winners in large competitions. The 20-point system is essentially the same system but is more useful at informal beer tastings. The numbers are easier to add and the finer points of beer character are not so important to determine.

THE 50-POINT SCALE

BOUQUET/AROMA (as appropriate for style)   1–10 points _____

Malt (3)
Hops (3)
Other Fermentation Characteristics (4)

APPEARANCE (as appropriate for style)   1–6 points _____

Color (2)
Clarity (2)
Head Retention (2)

FLAVOR (as appropriate for style)   1–19 points _____

Malt (4)
Hops (4)
Balance (5)
Conditioning/Carbonation (3)
Aftertaste (3)

BODY (as appropriate for style)   1–5 points _____

DRINKABILITY & OVERALL IMPRESSION   1–10 points _____

                                        TOTAL POINTS _____

Scoring Guide: Excellent 40–50; Very Good 30–39; Good 25–29; Drinkable 20–24; Problem < 20.

THE 20-POINT SCALE

APPEARANCE (15%)   0–3 points _____

AROMA BOUQUET (20%)   0–4 points _____

TASTE (50%)   0–10 points _____
Hop/malt balance (4)
Aftertaste (3)
Mouth-feel (3)

OVERALL IMPRESSION (15%)   1–3 points _____

                                        TOTAL POINTS _____

Scoring Guide: Excellent 18–20; Very Good 15–17; Good 12–14.

Appendix 11
Formulating Your Own Recipes—
Adjusting Your Specific Gravity

FORMULATING RECIPES

The following information will be helpful in determining the influence various brewing ingredients have on the specific gravity of wort.

One pound of the following ingredients and water to make 1 gallon will (approximately) yield the specific gravity indicated:

Ingredient	Spec. Grav.	(Balling)
Corn Sugar	1.035–1.038	(9–9.5)
Malt Extract (syrup)	1.033–1.038	(8–9.5)
Malt Extract (dry)	1.038–1.042	(9.5–10.5)
Malted Barley	1.025–1.030	(6–7.5)
Munich Malt	1.020–1.025	(5–6)
Dextrine Malt	1.015–1.020	(4–5)
Crystal Malt	1.015–1.020	(4–5)
Grain Adjuncts	1.020–1.035	(5–9)

ADJUSTING SPECIFIC GRAVITY

Whenever a recipe is followed or a new recipe is formulated, it is usually the intention to come as close as possible to an intended specific gravity. Sometimes we miss our mark. The easiest way to compensate for discrepancies is to add more or less *the next time* and ferment whatever you have this time. But if you want to adjust the specific gravity of the wort, there are two options:

1) Add more sugars (malt or corn sugar) to the wort.
2) Add more water to the wort.

INCREASING THE SPECIFIC GRAVITY OF THE WORT

The addition of 1 pound of malt extract or corn sugar to 5 gallons of wort will increase the specific gravity approximately .004–.006 (1–1.5).

DECREASING THE SPECIFIC GRAVITY OF THE WORT

Sometimes you may find that you've put too much fermentable sugar in the wort and the resulting specific gravity is too high. You can dilute the wort and lower the specific gravity by adding water. The rate of dilution and the change in specific gravity are not the same at various densities. For example: Adding 1 gallon of water to 5 gallons of wort that is 1.045 will decrease the specific gravity by about .006. But adding 1 gallon of water to 5 gallons of wort that is 1.060 will decrease the specific gravity by about .010. The following tables will help you make approximate adjustments within the ranges used by most homebrewers.

FOR SPECIFIC GRAVITIES 1.035–1.048

5% (.25)	more water decreases the specific gravity by .001
15% (.75)	more water decreases the specific gravity by .005
30% (1.5)	more water decreases the specific gravity by .010
50% (2.5)	more water decreases the specific gravity by .016

FOR SPECIFIC GRAVITIES 1.048–1.053

5% (.25)	more water decreases the specific gravity by .002
10% (.50)	more water decreases the specific gravity by .003–4
25% (1.25)	more water decreases the specific gravity by .010
30% (1.5)	more water decreases the specific gravity by .011
50% (2.5)	more water decreases the specific gravity by .017

FOR SPECIFIC GRAVITIES 1.055–1.060

5% (.25)	more water decreases the specific gravity by .002
10% (.50)	more water decreases the specific gravity by .005
25% (1.25)	more water decreases the specific gravity by .012
30% (1.5)	more water decreases the specific gravity by .014
50% (2.5)	more water decreases the specific gravity by .018

NOTE: The numerical value in parentheses represents gallons of water added to (specifically) 5 gallons of wort.

Appendix 12
Treatise on Siphoning
by Professor Surfeit

Dedicated to Bernoulli, who, alas, never surmised that his thoughts would be passed on to the homebrewer.

The science of siphoning—the art of siphoning. What is the difference? One, you get it to work; the other, you get it to work for you.

The ancient problem of the homebrewer presents itself: How does one get the beer from one container to another without disturbing the sedimentary deposit? Only the marvel of the siphon evinces itself to this accomplishment.

The siphon is a gravitational "pump" which avails itself to the homebrewer as a means of passing beer from one container to another without disturbing bottom sedimentary deposits.

Drop an apple and see what happens. It falls down. But if we place this apple at its own level on a table, it remains until the skin rots and is no longer able to gather itself.

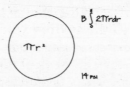

Place a bucket of brew on a table. Surprisingly enough it remains there. Now take a cherry bomb and tape it to the base of the beer bucket. Light the fuse and run into the next room (you may snicker and chuckle if you wish, but be sneaky and enjoy yourself). When the explosion has occurred, run back into the room and observe the stream of beer. It flows out and down. Peculiarly enough, if we had taped the bomb to the bucket above the level of the beer—no fluid flow would have occurred. Why? The question may seem trivial, but with the answer the universe opens up before us (and after us). Once again, may I ask you, why?—because there exists no force which would bring the beer up to the hole and enable it to escape.

Thus, we are able to surmise that there must exist some force which "pushes" the beer through the bottom hole. "Gravity?" you say. Well, not quite true, for gravity is not force. Force in this case is: gravitational acceleration times mass ($F = mg$). Gravity is always constant at the point of departure. But the mass of the beer in the bucket decreases as it empties; thus, the force decreases. To prove this, watch the stream of beer empty itself from the bucket onto the floor. At first, the beer gushes out quickly, then gradually the flow decreases to a slow trickle. So we see that the rate of flow is directly proportional to the height of beer above the hole and nothing more (to prove this, do the same experiment on a higher table).

Ten gallons of beer is heavy. Five gallons of beer is half as heavy. Refill your one-holed bucket to the 10-gallon mark and quickly place another cherry bomb halfway up and blow out another hole. Observe. The beer flows faster out of the bottom hole than the middle-of-the-bucket hole. Why? Well, of course, there is more pressure (pressure = force per area; pounds per square inch) exerted by 10 gallons of beer than by 5 gallons of beer. If you hesitate to accept this, do the following: Empty a 10-foot-deep swimming pool of its water and then refill the pool with beer. Immerse yourself in the pool of beer and swim to the bottom. As you swim to the bottom you will feel the weight (pressure) of the beer increase upon your eardrums. The pressure is greater at the bottom of the pool than it is at the halfway point. A simpler experiment can be conducted. Drive up to the top of a mountain. Now drive quickly down the mountain. Your ears pop. Why? Because on the top of the mountain there is less atmosphere above you, and as you come toward sea level there is more atmosphere above you. The weight of this air above you presses against your eardrum until the air pressure inside your ear is the same as that on the outside.

Now where does that leave us? It leaves us standing in a puddle of beer with the knowledge that the greater the height of beer above the hole, the faster the beer will flow out.

Now, my dear friends, let us proceed. You have a hole in

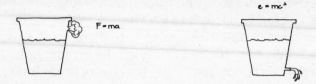

your bucket. Let us stuff 2 feet out of 6 (sextipus) of clear plastic hose through the hole in the bottom of the bucket so that the only way the beer can come out is via the hose.

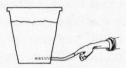

Place your finger tightly over the end of the hose. Fill the bucket with ale. Remove your finger from the end of the tube and watch the ale flow out. Lower and raise the tube and observe the various rates of flow. Guess what? Believe it or not (you better believe it), the end of that tube is a "movable hole" in the bucket. The more ale above the "end" of the hole, the faster your kitchen floor will get wet. If you raise the end of the tube above the level of the ale, you won't get any flow (like the hole in the bucket above the level of the beer).

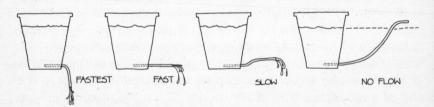

You can bend and twist your hose into any shape, but the only thing that matters is where the hole (end of tube) is with respect to the top level of the ale. Amazing, eh?

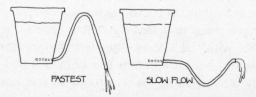

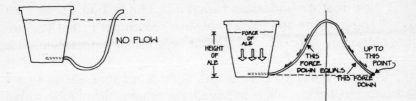

Let us go one giant step further—let's reposition the tube and patch up our hole with sanitized chewing gum. Eureka!

We have the exact same situation as before. Once begun, ale flows out because of the distance between the end of the tube and the surface of the ale.

Aha! Now here comes a really amazing revelation. Let's bring the end of the tube, which is immersed in the ale, close to the surface.

So we see that it doesn't matter a goat's foot where the "X" end of the tube is in the ale. The flow remains simply a function of the distance between the surface of the ale and the "Y" end of the tube. So when siphoning beer, just concern yourself with not sucking the pasty sediment off the bottom.

If you want faster flow, have a greater distance between the "Y" end of the tube and the surface of ale.

Now here's a little trick. Let's say you want to pause in your siphoning to answer the telephone (there's always someone who is going to call you in the middle of siphoning, because it's just one of those kinds of things). Get a load of this next diagram.

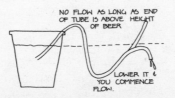

Now that we ~~understand wh~~at a siphon is, how do we start one? The number-one thing to always remember is that you are not siphoning gasoline out of your neighbor's automobile. This is beer. Don't be afraid of it.

The only way you can start a siphon (for that matter to get a siphon to work at all) is to have a continuous flow of ale within the tube. Any large air spaces in your hose will halt the flow of ale or beer. As an air bubble travels through the tube to the end we have a situation which will reverse itself. Fill your hose completely full of water. Immerse one end into the beer and lower the other end at least to a level below the surface of the beer. Voilà, it's working.

Here's a final trick: You have one full bucket and one empty bucket. Siphon one into the other, and flow stops when each has the exact same height of beer.

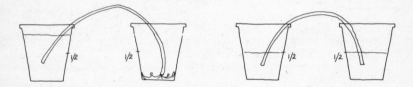

So remember: 1) It doesn't matter where the immersed end of the tube is in the beer. It's the distance between the surface of the beer (in the bucket) and the end of the tube that counts. 2) The lower the "hole" or end of the tube is, the faster the flow (you can slow it down by pinching the tube, too). 3) Avoid air spaces.

Whatever happens, remember that you have mastered this art only when you are able to drink and enjoy your own home-brew—for only then does everything come into perspective.

Appendix 13
Conversions and Measurements

TEMPERATURE

To convert degrees Centigrade to Fahrenheit:

(degrees C $\times$ $\frac{9}{5}$) + 32 = degrees F

To convert degrees Fahrenheit to Centigrade:

(degrees F $-$ 32) $\times$ $\frac{5}{9}$ = degrees C

VOLUMES

1 U.S. barrel = 31 gallons = 1.17 hectoliters
1 U.S. gallon = 4 quarts = 8 pints = 16 cups = 3.79 liters
1 U.S. quart = 2 pints = 32 ounces = .95 liter
1 U.S. cup = 8 ounces = 16 tablespoons = 48 teaspoons

1 British gallon = 1.2 U.S. gallons
1 U.S. gallon = .833 British gallons
1 liter = .26 U.S. gallons = 1.06 U.S. quarts
1 hectoliter = 100 liters = 26.4 U.S. gallons = .85 U.S. barrels

DRY WEIGHTS

1 pound = 16 ounces = .454 kilograms = 454 grams
1 ounce = 28.35 grams
1 gram = 0.035 ounces
1 kilogram = 2.2 pounds

MISCELLANEOUS

1 part per million (ppm) = 1 milligram per liter (mg/l) = 1 milliliter per liter (ml/l)

Appendix 14
Bibliography of Resources

Books

Brewers Publications. *Beer and Brewing Series*. Vols. 1–5 and 6–10. Boulder, Colo.: 1986–90.

Briggs, Hough, Stevens and Young. *Malting and Brewing Science*. Vols. 1–2. New York: Chapman and Hall, 1971.

Eckhardt, Fred. *The Essentials of Beer Style*. Portland, Oreg.: Fred Eckhardt Associates, 1989.

East West Journal. *Shoppers Guide to Natural Foods*. Cambridge, Mass.: 1983.

Fix, George. *Principles of Brewing Science*. Boulder, Colo.: Brewers Publications, 1989.

Food Learning Center. *Co-op Food Facts*. Winona, Minn.: 1980.

Forget, Carl. *Dictionary of Beer and Brewing*. Boulder, Colo.: Brewers Publications, 1988.

Foster, Terry. *Pale Ale*. Boulder, Colo.: Brewers Publications, 1990.

Gayre, Lt. Col. Robert. *Brewing Mead: Wassail in Mazers of Mead*. Boulder, Colo.: Brewers Publications, 1986.

Guinard, Jean-Xavier. *Lambic*. Boulder, Colo.: Brewers Publications, 1990.

Institute for Brewing Studies. *Brewers Resource Directory, 1990–91*. Boulder, Colo.: Brewers Publications.

Jackson, Michael. *The Pocket Guide to Beer*. New York: G. P. Putnam Sons, 1982.

———. *The Simon & Schuster Pocket Guide to Beer*, 2nd ed. New York: Simon & Schuster, Inc., 1988.

———. *The New World Guide to Beer*. Philadelphia, Penn.: Running Press, 1988.

———. *The World Guide to Beer*. New York: Exeter Books, 1977.

Master Brewers Association of the Americas. *The Practical Brewer*. Madison, Wisc.: 1946.

———. *The Practical Brewer*, 2nd ed. Madison, Wisc.: 1977.

Morse, Roger A. *Making Mead (Honey Wine)*. Ithaca, N.Y.: Wicwas Press, 1980.

Proceedings of the National Homebrewers Conference. Al Andrews (1982), Roger Briess (1982), Professor Dr. Helmut Kieninger (1983), Ron Siebel (1983). Boulder, Colo.: American Homebrewers' Association, 1982, 1983.

Periodicals

The Amateur Brewer. Fred Eckhardt. Portland, Oreg.: Amateur Brewer Publications.

The Journal of the American Society of Brewing Chemists. St. Paul, Minn.

The Journal of the Institute of Brewing. London, England.

The New Brewer Magazine. Boulder, Colo.: Institute for Brewing Studies.

Zymurgy. Boulder, Colo.: American Homebrewers' Association.

Individuals, associations, institutes and businesses that provided technical assistance and information for this book

The Adolph Coors Company, Golden, Colorado
  Darwin Davidson, *Manager, Brewing Research*
  Michael Mefford, *Manager, Engineering*
  Gil Ortega, *Supervisor, Pilot Brewery*
  Dave Schisler, *Microbiologist, Research and Development*
Briess Malting Company, New York, New York
  Roger Briess, *President*
Edme Ltd., Mistley, Manningtree, England
  Richard Holt, *Director*
  Dr. E. East, *Group Research Chemist*
  A. R. Lansdown, *Production Manager*
Lieutenant Colonel Robert E. Gayre of Gayre & Nigg, Argyll, Scotland
Havill's Mazer Mead, Rangiora, New Zealand
  Leon and Gay Havill, *Owners and Meadmakers*
Hopunion USA Inc., Yakima, Washington
  Gregory K. Lewis, *Vice President and Technical Director*
Itona Products Ltd., Wigan, England
  Jeffrey Hampson, *Director*
Lallemand, Montreal, Quebec, Canada
  Clayton Cone, *Technical Consultant*
  Jim McLaren, *Production Manager*
Master Brewers Association of the Americas, St. Louis, Missouri
Munton & Fison, P.L.C., Stowmarket, England
  Michael Chaplin, *North American Sales Representative*

Gregory Noonan, Burlington, Vermont
Paines, P.L.C., St. Neots, England
  Lance Middleton, *Director*
Premier Malt Products, Grosse Pointe, Michigan
  Susan Hamburger, *Sales Director*
S.S. Steiner, Inc., Yakima, Washington
  Herbert Grant, *Technical Consultant*
Siebel Institute of Technology, Chicago, Illinois
  Ron Siebel, *Director*
Ray Spangler, Erlanger, Kentucky
University of California at Davis
  Professor Michael Lewis, *Food Science and Technology Department*
  Jean-Xavier Guinard, *Graduate Student*
University of Saskatchewan, Saskatoon, Canada
  Professor W. Michael Ingledew, *Department of Applied Microbiology and Food Science*
Wander, Ltd., Kings Langley, England
  William Thorburn, *Industrial Sales and Marketing Manager*
Western Water Specialists, Boulder, Colorado
  John Martin

Special thanks to the following friends for the dedication and personal contributions they have made to teaching me and improving the quality of beer and beermaking in the United States:

  Al Andrews, Riverside, California
  David Bruce, Hungerford, England
  Byron Burch, Santa Rosa, California
  Fred Eckhardt, Portland, Oregon
  George Fix, Arlington, Texas
  Terry Foster, Milford, Connecticut
  Paul Freedman, Washington, D.C.
  Michael Jackson, London, England
  Bill Litzinger, Boulder, Colorado
  David Miller, St. Louis, Missouri
  Greg Noonan, Burlington, Vermont

Additional Readings and Resources for the Homebrewer

Books

American Homebrewers' Association. *Winners Circle: Ten Years of Award-Winning Homebrew Recipes.* Boulder, Colo.: Brewers Publications, 1989.

Anderson, Stanley F., with Hull, Raymond. *The Art of Making Wine.* New York: Hawthorne Books, Inc., 1970.

Beach, David R. *Homegrown Hops—An Illustrated How-to-Do-It Manual.* Junction City, Oreg.: David R. Beach, Publisher, 1988.

Brewery Operations Series. Boulder, Colo.: Brewers Publications, 1986 to present.

Brown, Sanborn. *Wines and Beers of Old New England.* Hanover, N.H.: University Press of New England, 1978.

Burch, Byron. *Brewing Quality Beers.* Santa Rosa, Calif.: Joby Press, 1986.

De Raysor, Roberto. *Alcohol Distillers Manual, For Gasohol and Spirits.* San Antonio, Tex.: Dona Carolina Distillers, 1980.

Leistad, Roger. *Yeast Culturing for the Homebrewer.* Ann Arbor, Mich.: G. W. Kent, Inc., 1983.

Miller, David. *The Complete Handbook of Home Brewing.* Pownal, Vt.: Garden Way Publishing, 1988.

———. *Continental Pilsener.* Boulder, Colo.: Brewers Publications, 1990.

Noonan, Gregory. *Brewing Lager Beer.* Boulder, Colo.: Brewers Publications, 1986.

Orton, Vrest. *The American Cider Book.* New York: Farrar, Straus and Giroux, 1973.

———. *The Homemade Beer Book.* Rutland, Vt.: Charles E. Tuttle Co., 1973.

Proulx and Nichols. *Sweet and Hard Cider.* Pownal, Vt.: Garden Way Publishing, 1980.

Van Doorn, Joyce. *Making Your Own Liqueurs.* Dorchester, England: Prism Press, 1977.

See main Bibliography (page 388) for additional books not listed above.

Periodicals

All About Beer Magazine. Bosak Publishing Co., 4764 Galicia Way, Oceanside, CA 92056.

World Beer Review. WBR Publications, Box 71, Clemson, SC 29633.

Zymurgy. American Homebrewers' Association, P.O. Box 1679, Boulder, CO 80306-1679.

Of *Special Interest*:
    1985 Special All-Grain Brewing Issue
    1986 Special Malt Extract and Recipe Issue
    1987 Special Troubleshooting Issue
    1988 Special Brewers and Their Gadgets Issue
    1989 Special Yeast and Beer Issue
    1990 Special Hops and Beer Issue
    1991 Special Beer Styles Issue
    1992 + Forthcoming

Associations

The American Homebrewers' Association, Box 1679, Boulder, Colorado
    80306-1679.
    Activities include:
    Annual National Homebrewers' Conference
    Annual National Homebrew Competition
    Annual Great American Beer Festival
    Annual National Microbrewers' Conference
    National Beer Judge Certification Program
    Publications include:
    zymurgy (Magazine and Index)
    The New Brewer (for the Professional Microbrewer)
    Annual Transcriptions of Conference Proceedings
    Brewers Resource Directory

Acknowledgments

An illustration by Joe Boddy appears on page 42.

Illustrations by Jamie Elliot appear on pages 9, 10, 25, 43, 79, 115, 132, 157, 201, 249 and 362.

Illustrations by Steve Lawing appear on pages 6, 12, 38, 48, 83, 91, 100, 159, 175, 180, 184, 187, 194, 202, 207, 211, 214, 216, 218, 220, 224, 231, 237, 240, 242, 253, 288, 334, 336, 341, 343, 353 and 356.

Illustrations by Peggy Markel appear on pages 13, 14, 61, 67, 71, 139, 257 and 372.

Illustrations by Brent Warren appear on pages 4, 119, 146 and 363.

Illustrations for the "Treatise on Siphoning" (pages 384–386) provided courtesy of Zymurgy magazine.

Photos by Michael Lichter appear on the following pages: 16, 18, 19, 21, 24, 27, 28, 29, 30, 32, 34, 35, 36, 37, 41, 52, 55, 56, 57, 59, 62, 69, 71, 130, 134, 277, 278, 284, 285, 287, 290, 294, 303, 305, 327, 358 and 377.

The photo on page 109 appears courtesy of the Adolph Coors Company, Golden, Colorado.

Photos on pages 293 and 328 appear courtesy of Andrews Homebrewing Accessories, Riverside, California.

Index

Thirsty for an Exotic Home Brew?

Anxious to Get Started on Your Own Home Brewery?

Let Brewing Expert
CHARLIE PAPAZIAN
Show You How With:

THE NEW COMPLETE JOY OF HOME BREWING
76366-4/$12.00 US/$16.00 Can
Learn first-hand about the history of beer;
discover the secrets of brewing world class styles of beer;
and find out how to add "spice" to your favorite blend

THE HOME BREWER'S COMPANION
77287-6/$12.00 US/$16.00 Can
Special advice on fermenting, yeast-culturing and
stovetop boiling; helpful trouble-shooting tips;
and answers to the most often asked questions

—And Don't Miss—
BEER:
A History of Suds and Civilization
from Mesopotamia to Microbreweries
by Gregg Smith
78051-8/$11.00 US/$15.00 Can